CRUELTY AND COMPANIONSHIP

CRUELTY AND COMPANIONSHIP

Conflict in nineteenth-century married life

A. James Hammerton

London and New York

To
Liz, Marisia and David

First published 1992
by Routledge
11 New Fetter Lane, London EC4P 4EE

Simultaneously published in the USA and Canada
by Routledge
a division of Routledge, Chapman and Hall, Inc.
29 West 35th Street, New York, NY 10001

Typeset in 10 on 12 point Palatino by
Computerset, Harmondsworth, Middlesex
Printed in Great Britain by
T J Press (Padstow) Ltd, Padstow, Cornwall

British Library Cataloguing in Publication Data
Hammerton, A. James
Cruelty and companionship: conflict in nineteenth
century married life.
I. Title
305.48906550942

Library of Congress Cataloging in Publication Data
Hammerton, A. James.
Cruelty and companionship: conflict in nineteenth century married life /
A. James Hammerton.
p.   cm.
Includes bibliographical references and index.
1. Marriage—England—History—19th century. 2. Domestic
relations—England—History—19th century. 3. Conjugal violence—
England—History—19th century. 4. Divorce—England—History—
19th century. I. Title.
HQ615.H357   1992
362.82'92'094209034—dc20   91-45648

ISBN 0-415-03622-4

CONTENTS

ACKNOWLEDGEMENTS

It would be impossible to do justice to the many debts I have accumulated since I began work on this book. They span a dozen years and three continents, and have contributed in various and invaluable ways to my evolving views on the history of family life. It is a pleasure, though, to acknowledge the help of those few I can list here.

Writing English social history in Australia can be a solitary enterprise, but Australia, and La Trobe University's History Department, has been a good place to practise history. At La Trobe especially I benefited from the warm engagement of a supportive department, which has given me encouraging and critical hearings in a succession of seminars. I owe much to Rhys Isaac, Lotte Mulligan, June Philipp and John Hirst for their comments, and to John Cashmere and Tony Barta for their interest and encouragement at crucial moments. Feminist historians in Australia have created a stimulating atmosphere in which to write about the family, and I have learned much from them, especially Marilyn Lake, Diane Kirkby, Marian Aveling, Judith Allen and Esther Faye. Years ago Barry Smith encouraged me to pursue the early stages of this study on domestic violence, and has offered ready assistance ever since. David Philips, Pat Jalland and Ian Britain shared helpful advice and discussion. My students in the honours seminar on marriage and the family at La Trobe have been a critical sounding-board for my ideas, and I owe them a great deal. I am also grateful to La Trobe University for the generous periods of leave which enabled me to undertake research in England, and to the School of Humanities for periodic travel assistance.

During extended visits to England I have enjoyed the help of innumerable historians, whose enthusiasm served as a reliable boost to morale. Happily, the supportive advice has often merged into valued friendship. Leonore Davidoff's model criticism was combined with salutary encouragement when I most needed it, and on two occasions her Social History seminars at Essex University have ensured a lively and critical forum for my offerings. Anna Davin always offered a sympathetic ear, astute advice and warm hospitality. Discussions with Jane Lewis, Pat Thane, Elizabeth

Roberts, Logie Barrow, Catherine Hall, Keith McClelland and Raphael Samuel were stimulating and fruitful. Jane Rendall, Jim Walvin, and others at York University, provided hospitality and helpful discussion at their departmental seminar. Other visiting historians in London, notably Peter Bailey and Philippa Levine, shared their ideas, valued company, and, perhaps more important, the anomie of the peripatetic scholar. My initial debt to Felicity Ashbee was for allowing me to consult her family papers, particularly H. S. Ashbee's diaries, but since then I have to thank her too for her warm friendship and for sharing her intricate knowledge of her family with me; her own work on her mother, Janet Ashbee, deserves to be better known and widely published. Bill Southwood, Margaret Kenny-Levick and Ruth Richardson offered priceless accommodation and hospitality in London at various times, and for two extended stays I owe thanks to the William Goodenough House Trust.

Frequent visits to seminars and conferences in Canada and the United States have also provided a welcome audience of critics and friends. Receptive and critical listeners at McGill, Carleton, Toronto, Guelph, Wilfrid Laurier, Manitoba, British Columbia and in 1989 the CHA conference at Québec City and the AHA at San Francisco all helped to shape my thinking. I am also grateful to Gail Savage, Doug and Joyce Lorimer, Andrée Levesque, Deborah Gorham, Rod Phillips, Ellen Ross and George Behlmer. Jim Winter at U. B. C., who was my thesis supervisor more than a quarter of a century ago, has remained an astute critic and precious friend, and helps to make the long journeys to Canada a welcome prospect.

For access to valued collections and facilities I gratefully acknowledge the help of King's College Library, Cambridge, Cambridge University Library, the Fawcett Library, the Bodleian, University College Library, London, Elizabeth Roberts's oral history collection at Lancaster University and the National Register of Archives. Staff at the British Library, the Institute of Historical Research, the University of London Library and the Public Record Office in Chancery Lane were invariably helpful and patient with my relentless inquiries. Closer to home, La Trobe University Library has been a never-failing and essential resource, not least because of their helpful staff, and here I owe special thanks to Margot Hyslop.

An earlier version of material in chapter 1 has appeared in *Gender and History*, 1991, vol. 3 no. 1; similarly, some of the material in chapter 4 appeared in *Victorian Studies*, 1990, vol. 33, no. 2. I am grateful to the editors of these journals for permission to reproduce this material.

A. James Hammerton
October, 1991

A CHRONOLOGY OF KEY EVENTS AND PUBLICATIONS

The following chart lists some of the more significant events and publications, mentioned in the text, which might be understood better when viewed in their chronological relationship. For complete references consult the bibliography.

	Legislative		Case law		Literary & autobiographical
1790			*Evans* v. *Evans* (Stowell definition of legal cruelty.)		
1839	Infants Custody Act allows separated wives custody of children under seven.				
1843					S. S. Ellis, *The Wives of England.*
1853	Aggravated Assaults upon Women and Children punishable by up to six months' prison.				
1857	Divorce Act and new Divorce Court.				
1858			*Bostock* v. *Bostock* and *Curtis* v. *Curtis* (Cresswell allows verbal threats to cancel 'condonation' of earlier violence.)		
1868–9					A. Trollope, *He Knew He was Right.*
1869					J. S. Mill, *The Subjection of Women.*
1869–70			*Kelly* v. *Kelly* (Penzance accepts non-violent abuse as legal cruelty.)		
1870	Married Women's Property Act allows wives control over their earnings.				

1871–2 G. Eliot, *Middlemarch*.
1878 F. Cobbe, 'Wife-Torture in England', *Contemporary Review*.

1883 W. Landels, *The Marriage Ring*.

1888 M. Caird, 'Marriage', *Westminster Review*. *Daily Telegraph* marriage debate. H. Quilter, *Is Marriage a Failure?*

1878 Matrimonial Causes Act – provision for maintenance and separation allowances for abused wives.

1882 Married Women's Property Act extends wives' control over own property.

1886 Provision for maintenance and separation allowances for deserted wives.

1895 Summary Jurisdiction Act, extends separation and maintenance allowances for 'persistent cruelty' of husband.

1895 *Russell v. Russell* (Court of Appeal rejects legal validity of 'mental cruelty'.)

1910–12 Royal Commission on Divorce and Matrimonial Causes.

1923 Matrimonial Causes Act abolishes double standard in divorce.

1937 Matrimonial Causes Act extends grounds for divorce.

GENERAL INTRODUCTION

In the late twentieth century divorce and family breakdown have become commonplace issues, routinely handled by public administrative bodies. We take for granted not only a high divorce rate, but also a highly public means of regulating conflict in marriage. A large bureaucracy of family lawyers, police and social workers, counsellors and therapists is charged with intervention and management of marital breakdown, and occasionally with reconciliation. But while the attendant procedures are firmly located in the public domain, they mostly take place behind closed doors and excite little interest or comment. Only the outrage of intransigent moralists, chilling stories of violent abuse and failing royal marriages provide good copy for today's newspapers. The routine dramas of sexual antagonism in marriage, though still the stuff of modern novels, are no longer regarded as vehicles for moral lessons or social titillation.

All this is of very recent origin. Historians of divorce now stress the rapid development of the modern, western 'divorcing society', especially since the Second World War, hastened by the transition of divorce from a judicial to an administrative procedure. They have also noted the historically distinct processes of divorce and marital breakdown. While frequent divorce is relatively new, marital dissension and breakdown have a much longer history. If relationships were not simply terminated unilaterally, economic imperatives forced most couples to live with their unhappiness, persecution and combat until the recent past, so that marriage was far more likely to be ended by death rather than, in our own time, voluntary divorce. Marital discord mostly remained private and secluded from the public eye, except when some sensational litigation or shaming communal ritual exposed private misconduct to wider scrutiny.[1]

The rapidity of this transition in recent times tends to obscure its basic origins and progress in the nineteenth century, which is the main subject of this book. In the second half of the nineteenth century, marriage, and especially middle-class marriage, just as it became established as a bastion of privacy and domesticity, supposedly secure from outside

1

interference, was subjected increasingly to unprecedented public scrutiny and regulation. The public gaze could not help but expose common patterns of marital misconduct and stimulate demands for ever more intrusive degrees of matrimonial legislation. It focused increasingly on the darker side of conjugal life, on behaviour, from both sexes and in all social classes, which was inconsistent with the middle-class domestic idyll and with heightened emotional expectations of marriage. Demands for regulation came from a wide ideological spectrum, from feminists to conservative moralists. But even by Edwardian years, despite a general awareness of the greater disadvantages in marriage suffered by women, only a few reformers aimed at any vision beyond companionate harmony within a framework of patriarchal dominance and separate spheres.

Our understanding of this process has been clouded until recently by anecdotal histories of divorce obsessed with the sensational adulteries of the well-to-do.[2] More serious studies of the history of marriage have provided some challenging hypotheses of long-term trends in marriage patterns. But they have been scarcely more helpful in their reliance on modernization models of marriage drawn from narrow class experience, and too often make easy associations between cultural ideals and actual behaviour. Much-discussed theories postulating a modern sexual revolution, a rise in sentiment and fluctuating transitions from patriarchal to companionate family forms do point to some genuine long-term changes in the ways ideals of the family evolved from viewing it as an economic institution to a private relationship. But these have done little to illuminate the process of change in the more recent past, and give no impression of the extent to which gender may have worked to differentiate sharply the experience of men and women as marital ideals were modified. The confusion is particularly marked for the nineteenth century, since much of the research which has led to the grand theorizing originates from earlier periods, but this has not prevented some writers, like Lawrence Stone, from advancing sweeping concepts, such as the Victorian 'revival of patriarchy' as a short-term interruption to the more fundamental companionate transition.[3] Perhaps the most important contribution of this book to the debate is evidence that patriarchal and companionate marriage were never stark opposites. Theoretical questions of husbands' authority, and women's practical challenges to it, continued to operate within a framework which re-emphasized the value of patriarchal structures. The very terms of the debate thus need to be re-examined.

In an attempt to find a way through the confusion this book focuses on the rich and varied evidence of marital conflict in Victorian and Edwardian England.[4] It examines both the experience of conflict for men and women and the wider discourse which drew on it and attempted to regulate conjugal behaviour. At some risk, it casts a wide social net in seeking to understand experience and trends in both working-class and middle-class marriage. But since contemporary understandings of marital behaviour were so deeply rooted in wider class perceptions, some degree of cross-class understanding is essential to the exercise. Most Victorian commentators clung to rigid notions about the way conflict was expressed differently in the marriages of different classes. They associated the stigma of domestic assault almost exclusively with the degraded lives of the very poor, assuming smugly that the middle classes subjected each other mostly to more genteel forms of mental torture. Only a few reformers adjusted these views to the vast accumulation of more complex evidence by Edwardian years. But despite this rigidity, by the end of the nineteenth century the exposure of marital misconduct among men of all social classes had brought an unprecedented amount of attention to proper ideals of male behaviour in marriage, so that one result of the long marriage debate was a challenge to prevailing concepts of masculinity. The 'manliness' of husbands was tested increasingly by their marital conduct, and not only their breadwinning capacities, which could not help but encourage more intense questioning of their family authority.

The sources for this study are necessarily wide-ranging, but the core of the analysis is based on records of marital litigation, partly from local magistrates' courts, and more extensively from the Divorce Court after 1857. Historians have already recognized the value of such records for the study of marriage and divorce, but so far mostly through the ecclesiastical courts before 1857, and particularly for the seventeenth and eighteenth centuries.[5] The records of the later Divorce Court have been drawn upon mainly as a basis for studies of divorce as a unique phenomenon, rather than as a vehicle for illumination of patterns of marriage.[6] But there can be no doubt of their special value in this respect. It is rare for other sources, however private, to reveal a similar degree of intimate conflict, often carried on over years, between contending couples. The fact that so much of this dissension was of a relatively mundane type, focusing on disputes over routine measures of persecution, over finances and differing views of authority, rather than sensational adulteries and criminal assaults, enhances their value. Here these records bring us as close as we may come to opening a small window onto the routine domestic politics of Victorian married life.[7]

Some will no doubt regard all this as an exercise in futility. An examination of marriage through its 'hard cases', especially at a time when marital litigation involved such a tiny proportion of all marriages, runs obvious risks of judging the mainstream from the experience of the exceptional. To some extent all social history which draws on legal case histories encounters similar problems. Not only were the divorcing minority often unique for their relatively prosperity, which gave them the financial ability to take their marriages to court (though with some

3

important exceptions discussed in chapter 4), but their willingness to expose their differences to public scrutiny also set them apart at a time when the stigma of divorce ran so deeply.

The methodological difficulties posed by these objections are real ones, and dictate great care in handling court records, especially in distinguishing genuine allegations from those which were legally inspired. But they cannot possibly justify the neglect of such unique texts, which, like all sources, need to be located in their wider context. The analysis in this book is based on the hypothesis that common themes in the hard cases before the courts were echoed in a much wider discourse, crossing ideological boundaries, which focused on marital conflict and sought varying measures of reform and regulation of married life. The analysis therefore moves from court records to prescriptive texts, autobiography, fiction and political and reformist commentary. There are undoubted advantages in bringing these diverse sources together. They may not support the sort of sweeping statements about long-term change we have come to associate with family history, but they do illuminate the complex relationship between prescription and behaviour.

In a sense the interplay between experiences exposed in court and the more general discourse on marriage provides an important cross-check on the social relevance of each set of sources. Complaints aired in court, which signified heightened expectations of conjugal behaviour, provided evidence for those advocating higher standards and more intrusive intervention into domestic life. Judges, for example, responded directly to wives' complaints of their husbands' non-violent persecution by liberalizing the law of matrimonial cruelty.[8] The empirical evidence which brought them to this provides a vivid example of the way in which sexual politics were a product of negotiation at both experiential and theoretical levels. All this points to a more general social process, in which the sexual antagonism dissected in the courts played a vital role.

There is a broader objection to this kind of inquiry. As I have discovered in countless seminars around the world, any attempt to use marital dissension as a basis for wider analysis usually meets with scepticism. Tolstoy's much quoted dictum in *Anna Karenina* that 'All happy families are like one another; each unhappy family is unhappy in its own way', inspires a conviction that conjugal intimacy is so private, so unique and so variable as to defy any attempt at generalization, although this does not seem to have prevented substantial generalizing about the widely assumed companionate harmony which supposedly prevailed in most Victorian marriages.[9] The charge reflects a defeatist sense that the individual operates at a level free from the kind of broader social processes, mediated by the general community, mentioned above. It is also belied by much of the evidence in this book illustrating ways in which the forms of sexual antagonism were conditioned by contexts of

4

class and gender. Middle-class wives, for example, like judges, were acutely conscious of their husbands' role as responsible providers, and were often spurred to class insults by men's failure or refusal to provide as expected. Similarly, middle-class husbands, obsessed by their increasingly contested family authority, could be driven to the borders of mental illness by defiance, and could themselves resort to an armoury of class humiliations to punish their wives. Such common themes point to the intricate ways in which class and gender assumptions conditioned the unique individuality of marital quarrels, and should prompt us to think again about Tolstoy's famous aphorism.

None of this, it should be obvious, implies that all Victorian marriages were afflicted by the same antagonisms detailed throughout this book. The profound tributes paid by so many Victorian men and women to their happy marriages may well have captured the essence of their relationships as they experienced them, and historians are right to take such evidence seriously in their elaboration of the dimensions of companionate harmony. But it should, at least, prompt us to scrutinize surface pronouncements of love and companionship, like surface evidence of conflict, with care, and where possible to seek to explicate more complex patterns in past relationships, where antagonism and companionship coexisted over the long years of a marriage. Despite all the changes in the forms and expression of marital authority over the past century, our own experience should teach us that such complexity and diversity in relationships is likely to be the rule rather than the exception.

The content of this book travels far, through disparate and seemingly unrelated territory. There is a long distance, for example, between the literature on charivaris and outrage against General Haynau's 'woman flogging', in the first chapter, and clergymen and other professionals treating their middle-aged wives like unruly children, discussed in chapters 3 and 4. Similarly, the wife-beaters who drove their wives to seek separations in magistrates' courts seem far removed from the late-Victorian and Edwardian husbands, in chapter 5, who sought to maintain their authority by subtler means. But there is an intricate link between all these themes. The tenuous shift from violent wives to violent husbands as targets of charivaris, noted in chapter 1, reflected a wider perception that more humane standards of conjugal conduct were coming to prevail by the early nineteenth century, and this perception, though only a half truth, framed much of the subsequent discourse on marriage into Edwardian years. The controversy over the marital behaviour of respectable workmen triggered off by the Haynau incident, together with routine expressions of outrage over continued high levels of wife-abuse, did provide important hints that domestic violence was more than simply an historical survival confined to the marriages of the casual poor. Yet throughout all the resulting debates the contradictory assumption persisted, even among some feminist reformers, that wife-beating was the exclusive product of a culture of poverty. These contradictions persisted in discussion of both working-class and middle-class marriage, and are central to an understanding of the ways in which particular aspects of marital experience, once exposed to public scrutiny, were given emphasis over others.

Much of this book documents a clear pattern of women's resistance against husbands' power, which was ultimately translated into public recognition and discourse. In that sense it shares a preoccupation of much recent women's history with aspects of female agency.[10] But an important distinction needs to be drawn here between private and public dimensions of women's resistance, and between law and experience. We know a good deal about the resistance of feminist reformers to women's legal inequality in marriage. The doctrine of *couverture*, which, as Sir William Blackstone had pronounced in the eighteenth century, suspended a wife's legal existence in marriage and incorporated it into that of her husband, was the persistent target of feminists.[11] By the early twentieth century they had achieved encouraging victories in the direction of marital equality. Yet much of the resistance charted here often had little direct bearing on the main legal targets. A wife might, for example, retain property and income in her own hands which, legally, could be claimed by her husband, and still succeed in a divorce petition against a partner who had attempted, unsuccessfully, to enforce his rights with physical abuse. Much of the conflict which wives complained of by-passed the major legal preoccupations of reformers, but their private protests, once exposed to persistent public gaze, became central to the formulation of larger feminist visions of change. The process raises basic questions about the way feminism was shaped by the ordinary experience of women's 'private' lives, which are usually seen as separate from the more 'public' political campaigns. Boundaries between private and public spheres, again, appear to be shifting and indistinct, rather than fixed and immutable.

The structure of the book, divided into separate Parts discussing working-class and middle-class marriage, reflects sharply distinguished features in contemporary discourse. Working-class publicity focused overwhelmingly on the issue of violent abuse, whereas debates on middle-class marriage dealt with a wider range of discord and contests over power, and lent themselves more readily to discussions of feminist ideals of marital friendship. Each Part, though, concludes with a discussion of feminist and other reactions to the diverse range of publicity and legislation. It is here that the common themes become most apparent. For while there was continuous criticism of wives for their failure to live up to ideals of companionate behaviour and duty, the most dramatic development was the progressive construction of men's conjugal behaviour, and patriarchy in marriage generally, as a problem to be regulated. Moreover, this perception was common to both feminist and conservative critics, all of whom contributed to the same discourse. This common thread of disillusion with patriarchal marriage, stemming from men's apparent failure to live up to companionate ideals, marked a fundamental turning point in thinking about conjugal relationships, with implications for the history of feminism as well as marriage.[12] But it will perhaps come as no surprise to discover that efforts to reconstruct men's behaviour, and marital relationships generally, failed to match the heightened criticism. The intense questioning of men's authority in marriage, leading to a more egalitarian ideal of companionship, continued to be conditioned by a reassertion of the structure and values of the patriarchal system itself.

Despite recent convincing criticisms of the generic concept of patriarchy as a means of understanding gender relationships, it will be obvious that I have not entirely abandoned the term. The concept has mostly been criticized for its lack of cultural specificity, its failure, for example, to account for the structure of social relations in a system where the 'classic patriarchal structure' has broken down.[13] But a narrower construction of the term, mostly limited to the idea of the 'patriarchal family' as understood by Victorians, remains useful to this analysis. In late-Victorian England the legal underpinnings of patriarchal power in the family were being eroded, and it was continuing abuses of that power, often of no more than its vestigial elements, which so aroused contemporary critics. In this sense the Victorian understanding of patriarchal marriage, its contradictory reification as a companionate relationship, and the refusal of many critics to sacrifice it entirely despite progressive legal restrictions, sustains the value of the term for understanding ways in which power was modified without being abandoned. Throughout this book there is persuasive evidence of the progressive weakening of the old paradigm of religiously sanctioned patriarchal authority. But there is equally persuasive evidence that elements of the old paradigm persisted in the newer ideal of egalitarian and companionate partnership.

The sources of marital conflict allow little direct analysis of its relationship to broader, demographic developments, but the demographic context is of key importance, and needs to be kept in mind throughout much of the discussion. Aspects of mortality, family size, kinship and the birth-rate, while all enormously variable according to location, gender, class and occupation, underwent important changes in the later nineteenth century, although we know that the more rapid changes took place in the twentieth century. Thus, while life expectancy in England gradually improved, from about 36 in the late eighteenth century to about 40 in the mid-nineteenth century, and then to 52 (male) and 55 (female) in 1911–12, much Victorian family experience continued to be dominated by early death, especially in working-class groups. Some 19 per cent of marriages contracted in the 1850s, for example, lasted less than 10 years, and 47 per cent less than 25. Widowed, single-parent families were common, the population was youthful and grandparenthood mostly of short duration. Hence the opportunity for marital relationships to undergo significant changes over the life-cycle were diminished among those groups with the higher mortality, although, as we shall see, women's opportunities to contest men's authority could increase with age if the marriage lasted long enough. More crucially, improvements in life-expectancy coincided with the most portentous demographic change from the 1870s, the decline in the birth-rate, starting with the middle classes. We cannot prove direct links between the deliberate limitation of family size and more exacting expectations of the marriage relationship evident in the following chapters, but the coincidence clearly warrants further scrutiny.[14]

The research for this project began over a decade ago, initially as a much more limited study of domestic violence. Since that time it has accumulated a number of historiographical debts as new publications have opened up exciting areas of research and more challenging ways of thinking about gender relations in the past. These have helped to shape the direction of the analysis and have built up a wide research base that would be impossible to undertake independently. Foremost among these debts is Leonore Davidoff and Catherine Hall's *Family Fortunes*.[15] Their elaboration of the gendered dimensions of middle-class domesticity in the early nineteenth century, and particularly of men's deep commitment to the soothing virtues of domestic harmony, forms an essential foundation for understanding the later critique of middle-class marriage and masculinity. In a sense this study takes up where *Family Fortunes* ended, at a point where the domestic idyll based on separate spheres had been constructed as a fortress of privacy. The fortress, though, was never immune from public intrusion, whether from the state, the courts or the press, and this is highlighted here by examination of the darker side of domesticity in the later nineteenth century, through sources that were not available to Davidoff and Hall.

A further debt is to some of the recent large-scale studies of marriage and divorce, which have raised fundamental questions about presumptions of marital fulfilment in the past. Foremost among these is John Gillis's *For Better For Worse*, for its pioneering exploration of the ways in which in England the private conjugal relationship alone never provided the range of satisfactions so often prescribed for it.[16] In the first chapter I note specific differences of interpretation with Gillis, and despite the focus here on marital breakdown, I would argue that Gillis's unrelieved pessimistic view of working-class marriage since the mid-nineteenth century needs to be qualified by the wide diversity of marital experience dictated by subtle gradations of class and region. But these are minor differences which should not obscure the relevance of Gillis's analysis of the ways in which conjugal privacy has always been mediated by the wider community, and his challenge to views which see marriage historically determined by forces of modernization.

Similarly, Roderick Phillips's study of divorce in the West, *Putting Asunder*, traverses, more generally, territory which is central to the analysis here.[17] His elaboration of the ways in which heightened expectations of marriage developed in a context of complex socio-economic change illuminates the process which enabled the frustrations of Victorian wives to break free from old constraints and enter the public arena to seek relief. Thus the much misunderstood 'stigma' of divorce, which is salient to almost every chapter in this book, and still deserves further research, was shown by Phillips to have been less than the often-assumed monolithic deterrent to legal action by discontented spouses. Instead it was conditioned by class difference, and more crucially by the steady growth of the incidence of divorce and the more intense entry of issues of marriage into public discourse.

Finally, without half a generation of feminist scholarship on domestic violence and marriage, the research and direction of this book would have been substantially different. Nancy Tomes's 1978 discussion still provides an essential prerequisite to the historical understanding of domestic violence.[18] Ellen Ross's rich evocation of women's experience of family life in East End London gives unsurpassed contextual detail of the kind of sexual antagonisms that appear so often here.[19] Elizabeth Roberts's oral histories offer perspectives of working-class marriage that emerge only rarely in the written sources.[20] And Iris Minor's analysis of the limited benefits of matrimonial law reform for working-class women from the later nineteenth century remains a valuable corrective to the whiggish impression of uninterrupted progress which this book questions.[21] More recently, Mary Shanley's work offers new insights into a broad range of historical issues touching feminism, marriage and legal change.[22]

The bulk of this scholarship focuses on working-class marriage, which is one reason why the second Part of the book, dealing with middle-class marriage, where our knowledge of conflict is so much less, is longer than the first. Phyllis Rose's fascinating dissection of literary marriages is one of the few recent texts to take conflict seriously in her analysis of individual relationships among elites; her contentious view that marital equality consists 'in perpetual resistance, perpetual rebellion', stimulated my thinking about these themes.[23] Similarly, while it will be apparent that I do not share Peter Gay's explicit Freudian slant, I have gained much from his scholarly, meticulously documented and always readable discussions of nineteenth-century marriages.[24] Still, despite a constant stream of autobiographies and biographies of the middle and upper class, our understanding of their marriages has remained limited, and the rich documentation which has survived on working-class marriage continues to invite the more extensive analyses. This book offers a different perspective on these complex matters, and hopefully will augment the valuable scholarship which has done so much to inspire it.

Part I

WORKING-CLASS MARRIAGE

INTRODUCTION

The dramatic effects upon the structure of the working-class family resulting from the pressures of industrialization and urbanization are well known. Rather less well known until recently have been the tensions making for conflict between family members which were intensified by the changes. The breakdown of village culture, the replacement of seasonal work-disciplines by those of the factory or workshop, the rise of wage-labour and the ideal of the male breadwinner's 'family wage' capable of supporting a dependent family, together with new religious and secular controls over behaviour, all placed enormous stress on family relationships in a domestic setting that was, relatively, more isolated. From the beginning the male breadwinning ideal was threatened by the cheaper, unskilled labour of women and children, which provoked persistent fears of the undermining of men's natural family authority.[1] But achievement of the ideal family form of male breadwinner and dependent, home-making wife, partly modelled upon the increasingly pervasive middle-class prescription, was no guarantee of domestic felicity. Economic marginality, pressures from large numbers of children (and larger numbers of births) and separate, homosocial cultures of husbands and wives provided fertile ground for sexual antagonism. The familiar burdens for women of household budgeting on inadequate income, which so often resulted in self-deprivation, was very likely to stimulate resentment, whether or not it was expressed overtly. Less familiar conflict could arise from uneven access to vital skills like literacy, which until later in the nineteenth century was rarely achieved by more than one family member, and, in those districts where this was more likely to be the wife, resentments stemming from implied threats to male authority might be aggravated.[2] Only at the end of our period did some evidence of the decline in the birth-rate begin to emerge among the working class,[3] but it is likely that issues arising from contested control of sexuality and reproduction had provided an additional domestic battleground for much longer, which may well have been deepened by pressures of urban crowding and poverty.

13

Conflict arising from such issues could be expressed in a variety of forms, but for the working class the most visible form, and the one most likely to leave surviving records, was domestic violence. The violence, of course, was most often men's violence, which was often only the concluding act following other events, grievances and arguments. But the public visibility of the resulting violence offers the best way of understanding working-class marital conflict and the way it affected both family experience and the wider perception of the idea of the family. It is probably no accident that the increasing criticism of family violence charted in this section coincided with a general decline in recorded levels of violent crime. We cannot be certain whether or to what extent English society was becoming less violent during the nineteenth century, but there is no doubt that critical scrutiny of violence was intensified, and that the family, seen increasingly as a locus of conflict, received a large share of the scrutiny. The next two chapters are concerned as much with the direction and evolution of this discourse of criticism as with the effects of violence on women and their various responses to it, ranging from dogged submission to overt resistance and appeals to the law. Criticism of male behaviour was at odds with an idealized model of manliness focusing on the respectable ethic of self-improvement, which was expected to flourish in a domestic setting. The contradictions and doubts are apparent in the debate which followed the Haynau incident and other reflections of working-class men on the problems of domesticity. By the end of the nineteenth century the criticism had turned to regulation, as both feminists and conservatives attempted to reform men's behaviour to conform more faithfully with middle-class ideals. For feminists the critique was an essential element in their wider thinking about the ideology of the family and gender equality; for the state the critique contributed to a more general approach to welfare in which surveillance and regulation were integral to social policy.

1

THE TARGETS OF 'ROUGH MUSIC': RESPECTABILITY AND DOMESTIC VIOLENCE

On Midsummer's day, 1883, in the Yorkshire village of Welburn, a villager, who 'had become notorious as a wife-beater', was treated to 'the almost obsolete practice' of stang-riding, the traditional northern version of 'rough music', a noisy custom of popular protest intended to demonstrate collective disapproval of local offences against communal norms. According to the *Folklore Journal*'s correspondent, 'five young men' mounted a masked effigy of the offender in a cart, yoked 'a lot of juveniles' to the shafts and paraded through the village chanting an old doggerel rhyme and beating the effigy, which was later burnt in the fields. At various spots on the road a speech was recited, and a police constable reported that about two hundred spectators gathered. The men called at the offender's house and asked him 'to pay for it'. When the case was brought to the Malton Sessions on 14 July the magistrates insisted that the demonstration was a 'silly old custom which ought to be put a stop to' and had constituted an illegal obstruction of the highway. Despite that they dismissed the case, agreeing that the men 'thought they were not creating an obstruction'. They also recommended that the case should be recorded in the *Folklore Journal*.[1]

On the basis of many accounts such as these historians have constructed an interpretation of the nature of English rough music rituals in the nineteenth century which has evolved to the point of uncritical repetition. According to this view late eighteenth-century England witnessed a shift in the targets of local popular justice through rough music rituals from nagging or violent wives and adulterers to wife-beaters.[2] Whatever its origins, the change is often seen as part of a wider growth of community intolerance towards violence generally and domestic violence in particular. At the general level, evidence of an absolute decline in violent crime during the nineteenth century, while problematic in its origin, reflected the change.[3] A more critical climate of opinion also opposed and abolished ritualized violence associated with aristocratic privilege and male codes of honour, such as duelling.[4] This process is usually associated with a hardened attitude to domestic violence and more rigorous legal control, and some historians have claimed that the new attitude did act as an effective discipline. One recent study of violence between working-class men and women in London argued that some real changes in behaviour were evident by mid-Victorian times, that domestic assaults genuinely declined and that wives traded their new-found security for relative loss of power in the family, increased isolation and conformity to standards of respectability influenced by middle-class values.[5]

The evidence of growing intolerance in the nineteenth century to violence generally, and violence to women in particular, is undeniable, apparent in legislation as well as judicial and public attitudes. At the same time the case for a uniquely intolerant attitude to wife-beating in England can be overstated, and this section will explore different aspects of overstatement. More particularly, evidence of changing attitudes does not establish corresponding changes in men's behaviour to women, and the link between the two remains, at best, tenuous. Even much of the evidence usually cited to support the shift in attitude does not suggest dramatic change so much as inconsistency and ambiguity, which was marked by the coexistence of tolerance and condemnation of domestic violence. The inconsistencies were evident at least as early as the seventeenth century, and continued well into the Victorian period. A reassessment of the targets of rough music rituals should shed some light on this process, but the inherent unreliability of so many accounts of these incidents suggests the need to consider them alongside other evidence of changing values. Respectable working-class men were often deeply implicated, in contradictory ways, in changing attitudes to domestic violence, and what follows will highlight their attitudes and conduct.

The Welburn 'stang-riding', cited above, amply demonstrates the tenuous nature of many reports of rough music rituals against wife-beaters, especially by the later nineteenth century. Significantly, the 'five young men' chose the evening of 21 June, or Midsummer's day, a traditional date for community celebration and carousing, for their action, suggesting that the urge for a good time weighed at least as strongly as outrage against the offending husband. The actors in the ritual were all men and boys, and while we know nothing of the composition and attitudes of the crowd of two hundred who gathered, a crowd would not be difficult to attract at 8 p.m. on Midsummer's day, whether for a street football game – with which the magistrates equated the event – or a stang-riding. The magistrates' response, both in airily dismissing the case and in referring it to the *Folklore Journal*, suggests that by the 1880s such events, while regarded as a public nuisance from adolescents out for a lark, were coming to be seen as quaint anachronisms. Any dissension provoked by the event seems to have been between two

16

generations of men. The targeting of a violent husband for the riding remains significant, but in most respects the event fell far short of the popular enforcement of community moral standards stressed in the literature on charivaris.

By the 1880s, perhaps, when rough music was at best a lingering relic of an earlier tradition, such ambiguity was to be expected. But E. P. Thompson, who first advanced the thesis of a shift in the targets of rough music in 1972, himself stressed the tenuous nature of the change. His article in *Annales*, '"Rough Music": Le Charivari Anglais', pioneered what has come to be the conventional wisdom about these rituals in England, but his argument was marked by caution. Thompson suggested, guardedly, that the rising concern to protect wives from the violence of their husbands may have been an early indication of the advanced breakdown of a previously secure patriarchal structure and set of values, so that the brutal husband, rather than, for example, the virago, became the most common focus of collective righteous indignation. He was careful to add that the evidence for such a shift actually signifying patriarchal decline was tenuous, its meaning uncertain. The shift in targets was clear enough, but it was expressed in rituals that were dominated, though not monopolized, by men and boys, whose motives may have been caught up with patriarchal gallantry and civility at a time when some of the social protection traditionally offered to women by the law, the church or customary opinion had largely evaporated.[6] His caution was underlined in a 1981 article from a French conference on charivaris where he stressed the need for a long-term research programme to decode the 'symbolic vocabularies' of charivaris.[7]

If Thompson was cautious in his conclusions the same cannot be said for some of his successors who have drawn on his work. Edward Shorter, in his *The Making of the Modern Family*, intent on showing that charivaris were the key instrument by which traditional communities imposed patriarchal norms on individuals with what he called a 'steely force', concluded from Thompson's evidence that the shift in English targets represented 'the early modernization of domestic relationships'. For him the increase in rough music rituals against wife-beaters simply reflected the wider diffusion of more egalitarian relationships in England, so that earlier vestiges of patriarchal authority, like wife-assault, became intolerable to the community and the rebuke of violent husbands became more common. By contrast, when a similar degree of egalitarianism developed in France, the charivari had already died out as an active custom before it could be turned against violent husbands.[8] More recently, John Gillis, in *For Better For Worse: British Marriages, 1600 to the Present*, drawing particularly on some Welsh evidence, simultaneously expanded on Thompson's argument and turned it on its head. He argued that during the early nineteenth century the sexual balance of power shifted, that

17

women became more independent with the beginnings of mining and industry and that this was reflected in changes in the communal politics of courtship and marriage.[9] While he followed Thompson's view of the shift in rough music targets, he attributed the change more to women's growing independence than their vulnerability.

It takes little scrutiny of nineteenth-century rough music rituals to suggest that some of these interpretations might be exaggerated, and, to go further, that the general claim that attitudes hardened towards violent husbands during the nineteenth century has been overstated. First, it's useful to recall that if, indeed, there was an upsurge in popular rituals against wife-beating, other traditional targets continued to be charivaried throughout the nineteenth century – notably violent or nagging wives, adulterers and other notorious deviants like homosexuals. Some dramatic evidence of widespread misogyny in late eighteenth- and early nineteenth-century popular culture emerges in Anna Clark's recent study of rape, which found that rough music could be used against rape victims who prosecuted their attackers, but rarely against rapists themselves.[10] Moreover, while there is little indication of rough music against violent husbands in the seventeenth century, there is evidence of even late Elizabethan writers like Thomas Lupton favouring harsh popular retribution against them.[11] Martin Ingram's study of seventeenth-century charivaris reminds us that the balance of authority between husbands and wives in early-modern England varied considerably, that assertive and active wives were appreciated and that there was much uncertainty as to which version of the old proverb was preferable: 'better to marry a sheep than a shrew', or 'better to marry a shrew than a sheep'.[12] It's a reasonable surmise that there was similar ambivalence towards violent husbands well before the late eighteenth century. This is confirmed in work on seventeenth-century charivaris outside England. Natalie Zemon Davis, drawing on English as well as French evidence, argues persuasively that the frequent resort to the ambiguous notion of 'woman on top' in the world of play made the option of 'unruliness' for women a more conceivable one in family life.[13] By the end of the eighteenth century, then, rough music episodes betrayed as much continuity with the past as change.

Furthermore, if all these rituals, as most writers suggest, were directed, willy-nilly, at any signs of instability in the patriarchal system, which was perceived to be threatened by excessively violent husbands as much as by the inversion of husbandly authority represented by nagging or violent wives, it is also evident, as Thompson noted, that the individual targets were selected very carefully, usually in terms of their known personal history within the community. Hence, while not all wife-beaters might be punished, those who had already committed other aggravating acts, or who had antagonized influential neighbours, would be the most likely victims.[14] It's clear both from folklore evidence and more recent social history of the later nineteenth century that marital conflict, frequently including violence, was mostly taken for granted in many working-class communities; in itself it was rarely sufficient to warrant communal censure. A traditional ceremony in Essex awarded the rare prize of the 'Dunmow Flitch' – a large side of bacon – to couples who could swear a traditional oath that their married life had been free from 'household brawls or contentious strife'. The applicants for the flitch were rare and renowned, but its persistence in folk memory is more significant than its practical use. One lord of the manor reputedly offered the flitch to Queen Victoria after she had been married a year and a day, but she declined, for what reason we aren't told.[15] As late as 1859, J. T. Staton, a Lancashire dialect writer, represented an archetypal nag sarcastically taunting her husband, 'We'st not be dooin eawr duty if we dunnot put up for that flitch o' bacon uz theaw wur readin abeawt th' other day, which they gien at Dumshow to th' couple ut have lived together th' happiest.'[16] The durability of so many proverbs and puppet shows depicting the 'battle of the sexes', especially the popularity of the physical contests between Punch and Judy among adults, until the show's sanitization for children in the later nineteenth century, all testify to a stoical tolerance of conflict.[17] With such ingrained assumptions of sexual antagonism in marriage it pays to be circumspect about the real meaning of the shift of targets to wife-beaters by the late eighteenth century.

A richly described Welsh episode of the 1830s, which is recounted at length in Gillis's book, underlines the need for care in explicating the complex layers of meaning represented in some accounts of rough music. Charles Redwood's account of a 'Coolstrin' – one of the Welsh versions of rough music – dealt with a wife in Glamorgan accused of beating and nagging her husband, a woman well known for humiliating Rissin, a timid tailor, by publicly hauling him away from his friends in the tavern. After an assault, which drew blood, the local men solemnly set up a formal 'Coolstrin court', complete with mock magistrate, and proceeded to pass sentence on the wife, Nest, by instituting an elaborate Coolstrin riding. The resulting noisy procession marched, as was the custom, through three villages, with two actors impersonating Nest and Rissin, and two standard bearers, one carrying a petticoat atop a pole, the other flying a pair of breeches, which had been reversed to signify the inversion of domestic authority. Throughout its travels the procession excited 'no small commotion in the little villages', with enthusiastic shouts and bell-ringing from the men. But, as Gillis noticed, the occasion also provoked hostility from local women; in the outer villages they 'kept within doors and only mocked at them through the windows', but upon return to their own village the women had collected to scoff, and even drowned out the clatter of kitchen-music, while, in the grand climax, the two standards were fixed outside the tailor's cottage, and the petticoat pelted with mud until it dropped, leaving the breeches to fly un-challenged on the roof 'as the standard of masculine government'.[18]

If this was the extent of our knowledge of the event, there would be little reason to doubt Gillis's view that the riding was distinguished from 'a very old-fashioned charivari' by the women's hostility, a response 'very different from that of the traditional peasant or artisan com-munity'.[19] But a striking feature of Redwood's account is the persistent reference by the Glamorgan men to the customary nature of the threat represented by their wives' fractiousness, a tension by no means of recent origin, but recognized by the 'Welshmen of old times, who gave us this custom of Coolstrin to guard our liberties from the WOMEN.'[20] 'Old Gronow Punter', the mock magistrate, couched his warnings of the 'danger' represented by Glamorgan women in terms of a pattern of conflict dating from time immemorial. It was a 'more perilous thing', he pronounced,

> keeping ourselves free from them, than from the *Saison* or *Franks*, or any other outlandish folks, I warrant you: and as for the Lord of the Manor, who would not do him suit and service when called for, than be slaves to our wives for everlasting?[21]

Redwood himself recounted the local belief that the Coolstrin had been 'profoundly instituted by the old Welsh Lawgivers as a corrective for that virulence in women which is so much exacerbated by the air of our mountains'.[22] Sexual antagonism, whether expressed individually or collectively, had no need to wait upon the 'independence' of women stemming from mining and industry, which, in any case, had hardly touched the predominantly rural Vale of Glamorgan. In Wales and England women continued to be treated to doses of rough music in the nineteenth century and continued to express their antipathy to the proceedings. Any evidence of a shift to popular preoccupations with wife-beaters needs to be viewed in that context. Increased concerns to provide protection to some abused women did not signify the end of sexual antagonism, nor the collective preoccupation with it among men and women in Welsh and English communities.

Rough music rituals, then, provide a frail and uncertain vehicle for reading changes in attitudes to gender relations and domestic conflict. The evidence of most of them is drawn from isolated descriptions by antiquarian folklorists, who, as Thompson noted elsewhere, were mostly parsons and 'genteel antiquarians negotiating themselves across a gulf of class condescension'.[23] Many of the folk customs they described with such relish, as we have seen, had, by the later nineteenth century, come to be regarded as quaint. The very rediscovery of folk culture as an objective study, noted recently by Davidoff and Hall, served as a distancing mechanism for a middle class acutely conscious of its gentility, just as other elements of rural and traditional culture – fairy tale, the supernatural and elements of carnival – were reserved for children and 'childlike inferiors'.[24] The texts which represent charivaris to us clearly involve interpretive hazards which cannot easily be argued away by customary warnings about the need for sensitivity of reading. This is not a gesture of despair, nor a plea to ignore these fascinating rituals, which the anthropologically minded would be loath to do. But it does suggest that they need to be read alongside other evidence of popular attitudes to gender relations and changes in private behaviour.

Popular retribution against violent men could, indeed, be swift and spontaneous without necessarily sharing the characteristics of traditional rituals in settled communities. The possibilities are illustrated by a murder case in Leeds in 1846, in which a popular, but ill-fated, protest was conducted entirely by women in an unpremeditated fashion. A 29-year-old itinerant pedlar of hardware, William Walshaw, known as 'Sheffield Bill', returned to his lodgings intoxicated one night, began quarrelling and fighting with his *de facto* wife and beat one of their children. After arousing some neighbours with her shouts, the woman fled, and a neighbour rescued the child.

> Walshaw then went away, hooted by a large body of women who had assembled in the yard. . . . In the mean time his wife got all the women around her, and began to expose his cruel treatment. The women resolved to mob him, and on his return two of them entered his lodging, while others outside were calling for him to be turned out.[25]

The two women who entered the building were confronted by Walshaw, who, with an open clasp-knife in each hand, attacked them, wounding each fatally. His attempted escape was then foiled by a passing policeman. Significantly, both victims were themselves wives of pedlars and the incident took place in the Old Post-Office-yard, Kirkgate, 'the resort of the lower class of itinerant Irish, English pedlars, and low travellers'. Until the policeman arrived, only four men had been involved, one of whom assisted in his detention after a woman had thrown him to the ground, and four others who said he should be released because he had done nothing wrong.[26] The women's prompt response and sense of outrage here contrasts sharply with the more carefully orchestrated rituals and sense of frivolity so often associated with charivaris. Moreover, its occurrence among itinerant pedlars, a traditional group less directly affected by the impact of industrialization and urbanization, marks the long-standing nature of women's readiness to vilify brutal men without necessarily drawing on the strategies and patriarchal norms of the wider community.[27]

A well-reported demonstration by London workers in 1850, which involved the Austrian military leader, General Haynau, provides a rather different opportunity to evaluate attitudes to violence against women and to the widespread presumption of a more humane attitude of restraint in English married life. The incident was not a typical charivari, nor a charivari at all, although newspapers like the *Illustrated London News* and the *Morning Chronicle* did describe it that way,[28] but it does highlight some of the problems inherent in interpreting evidence of outrage against the physical abuse of women. The incident was, apparently, a spontaneous one, far removed from the carefully orchestrated communal disapproval displayed in charivaris, which were reported only infrequently in London. It was one of a long series of traditional popular demonstrations, reminiscent of the Gordon riots and Queen Caroline protests, where protestors defended popular liberties against corrupt usurpers, and celebrated specifically English virtues and freedoms, so that xenophobia was combined with the rights of the free-born Englishman. But both the incident and its subsequent history drew on popular assumptions similar to those in charivaris castigating violence against women, which have been interpreted as evidence of more civilized, or modernized, standards in gender relations in England.

The simple story of the Haynau incident is most often recounted in studies of international relations and biographies of the foreign secretary, Lord Palmerston.[29] During the suppression of the Hungarian and Italian rebellions against the Austrian empire in 1849 and 1850, General Haynau had earned a notorious reputation in England for ordering brutal reprisals against local populations, summary hangings, floggings and other atrocities, which were described at length in lurid detail in the English press. In England the best-known of these acts was the public flogging in 1849 of an upper-class Hungarian woman, Madame Madersbach, by Austrian officers under Haynau's command. Soon after the event a letter from Madame Madersbach detailing the outrage reached the British press, noting that her husband had shot himself and her son had been conscripted as a soldier into the Austrian army in Italy.[30] Press reports later commented that even if English labourers could not read, they 'must have seen in every small stationer's window [Haynau's] picture representing him in the humane and gallant act of flogging women'.[31] The radical press, in particular, had concentrated their criticism of the ruthless suppression on Haynau, who had become known as 'General Hyena', so when he made a private visit to London in September, 1850, the ground had been well prepared for a demonstration of popular revenge.

Nevertheless, Haynau's visit to London was not at first widely publicized. When he turned up at Barclay and Perkins' brewery at Bankside
(on the south side of the Thames) on 4 September, with a letter of
introduction from the wealthy MP for the City of London, Baron
Rothschild, he was not recognized at first and it seemed he would have a
peaceful and unremarked tour of a well-known English brewery. But
within minutes of signing the guest book, according to the press reports,
his identity had been communicated throughout the brewery. The draymen, or beer-carters, and labourers quickly turned out in force, and by
the time Haynau was viewing the stables he was knocked down by a bale
of straw descending from the loft, and on regaining his feet was struck in
the face by a shower of the most offensive missiles that one might find in a
stable. With his companions, a nephew and an interpreter, Haynau then
fled from the brewery, only to be met in the street by a larger crowd,
which, the reports claimed, soon swelled to over 500. This consisted of
carters, coalheavers, men from the Borough market and an unstated
number of women. Many were armed with long whips and brooms,
which they used on Haynau's back, while the coalheavers belaboured
him with their fantail hats. As he reached Bankside, his coat was torn and
his hat was tossed in the air, and an attempt was made to throw him in the
Thames. Most humiliating of all, one man with a large knife attempted,
though unsuccessfully, to cut off his long and notorious 'moustachios'.
Chased down Bankside, Haynau raced into the 'George' public house
and hid, followed by the crowd who threatened to tear the building
down. He was found hiding in a back-room dustbin, and escaped again
to one of the upstairs rooms where he hid until the police arrived and
conveyed him outside and across the river to Somerset House in a police
galley.[32]

Insofar as this episode has attracted historians' attention, their interest
has been confined to the international incident which resulted. On one
side the Foreign Secretary, Lord Palmerston, a stalwart foe of Austria,
supported the crowd action, maintained that Haynau ought never to
have come to England and refused to apologize to the enraged Austrians
without making his own views known. He told the Home Secretary that
the visit was a 'wanton insult' to England and that instead of striking
Haynau the draymen should have 'tossed him in a blanket, rolled him in
the kennel, and then sent him home in a cab (fare paid)'.[33] On the other
side Queen Victoria, supported by Lord John Russell, the Prime Minister, furiously condemned the mob and engaged in a heated
correspondence with Palmerston until Russell forced him to send a more
fulsome apology. The Austrians, the queen and press critics of the so-
called 'rioters' all insisted, without evidence, that the assault had been
'got up' by refugees of the Hungarian rebellion resident in London, while

23

radicals saw Haynau's humiliation as just retribution against a brutal tyrant.[34]

For social historians, though, the episode is significant for rather different reasons, particularly the preoccupation of Haynau's attackers, and their press supporters, with his flogging of Madame Madersbach and the idolization of 'Barclay and Perkins' Draymen' as popular and chivalrous heroes and defenders of female honour. Both of these themes were played out in subsequent press debate and in the radical meetings of congratulation which followed. They testify to the traditional nature of the demonstration, in the mould of earlier protests like the Queen Caroline riots, which castigated the unmanliness of upper-class rulers and defended the virtue of English workers.[35] Radical responses drew on the strong elements of internationalism in Chartism, while simultaneously anticipating the later xenophobia of jingoism.[36]

The first theme, the obsession with Haynau the woman-flogger, followed naturally from the kind of publicity that had greeted his atrocities in England in 1849, and especially the widespread visual representation of Haynau, with his easily recognizable 'moustachios', in the act of flogging Madame Madersbach (although Haynau himself did not administer the flogging and had not been present at the time). It is tempting to relate the preoccupation with this act to the much more potent and sustained sexual symbolism in France, where 'Liberty' and the 'Republic' were represented by female figures.[37] Images of the flogging of Madame Madersbach translated easily to the scourging of European liberty. Certainly it testifies to the continuing greater impact of visual representations over the written word. The newspaper accounts of the incident stressed the shouts from the crowed as they pursued Haynau, such as 'Oh, this is the fellow that flogged the women is it?' 'We won't have him here, the Austrian butcher; we'll teach him to flog women'.[38] Moreover, the large section of the press which supported the action – extending well beyond the most radical journals like *Reynolds's*, the *Red Republican* and *Lloyds* – saw the main justification for Haynau's treatment to be the notorious 'un-English' flogging. *Reynolds's* attempted to elaborate on the chivalrous, indeed patriarchal, mental process that produced such a fierce reaction: 'What husband', it wrote,

> as he gazes upon his wife – what brother as he contemplates his sister – what father as he caresses a beloved daughter, can feel otherwise than irritated almost to a pitch of frenzy at the thought of the hideous indignity that was offered to a lady who was herself a wife and mother?[39]

In Harney's *Red Republican*, the fictional 'Howard Morton', suspected by Harney's biographer, Schoyen, to be the socialist-feminist, Helen

24

Macfarlane,[40] took the reasoning, with a note of gender-conscious irony, to its most threatening conclusion:

> Of what terrible, revolting crime had these unhappy women been guilty? They had aided their husbands, their fathers, their brothers, in the Hungarian and Italian insurrections. They had aided those to whom they were bound by every natural and *legal* tie. They had committed the horrible crime of taking for granted, that those whom they had been taught from their infancy to respect, whom they had been sedulously instructed to *reverence* and *obey*, on whose judgement they had been accustomed to rely, – were better judges than they, as to the propriety of shaking off the Austrian despot's yoke. For this horrible crime against 'family property' and 'order', – these women were stripped naked and flogged, by order of the infamous, unmanly coward, – his excellency the Herr Baron Von Haynau.[41]

The more moderate *Illustrated London News* commented on 'the brave woman-flogger in the full enjoyment of the *charivari* which the stout 'sons of freedom' so cleverly improvised for his reception'.[42] And *Punch*, tongue in cheek and satirically, as always, ruminated that, since Mrs Benfield, the landlady at the 'George', had given him shelter, and if Haynau 'were indeed the Haynau of the journals how delicious to behold the brave General that whipped the fair sex taking shelter from chastisement beneath a woman's petticoat!'[43]

Such chivalrous indignation was not unfamiliar in English journalism, but it was made doubly potent in combination with a celebration of Barclay and Perkins' draymen as noble avengers, although, as already noted, the draymen had been accompanied by various labourers, porters, coalheavers and some unidentified women, and apart from the draymen only the women attracted press and popular attention. Two popular ballads were very quickly printed and sold in the London streets, both of which praised the brewery's workers, and the draymen in particular.[44] Each was in tune with praise in various journals like the *Standard*, the *Illustrated London News* and *Punch*, as well as the radical press and later Chartist meetings which cheered the draymen. They coupled radical outrage with a celebration of the brewery's workers, and, like much of the popular comment on the episode, apparent also in street illustrations, praised women's part in avenging Madame Madersbach. The London correspondent for the *Sydney Morning Herald* reported that the 'mass of the people' applauded the draymen; at busy street corners there were popular 'balladmongers with stentorian lungs shouting doggrel praises of the men, who always come in as the burthen of every verse as "'Twas Barclay and Perkins's draymen.'" A mock trial, advertised as the 'case of

"Butcher versus Brewer'", was held in Bow Street and a public dinner was planned to thank the draymen.[45]

Domestic class tension, evident in one ballad's association of Haynau with the 'great Tories and high-titled dames' of the West End, was the theme most played up at the radical meetings which followed (one of them at the 'George' pub in Bankside and one addressed by Frederick Engels), where Julian Harney saw the brewers' action as a herald of a coming class war throughout Europe between the oppressed and their royal and aristocratic tyrants.[46] Notably, the attack on Haynau, approved by such unlikely allies as Palmerston and sections of the middle-class press, failed to arouse any of the old Chartist tensions between moral and physical force tactics. Unity of hatred against foreign tyranny overshadowed the old animosities and 'excitements', which were fading rapidly.[47]

The obsession with domestic class conflict provides an important reminder that the Haynau protest had never been related directly to the issue of wife-beating. The 'unmanliness' of upper-class oppression was marked by the savage treatment of women in public, by men with no ties of blood or marriage, and thus with no legitimate rights over them. Haynau's offence as a 'woman-flogger' merely compounded the evil of his ruthless oppression of the Hungarians and Italians, but was never to be confused with the English workman's relationship with his own wife. In working-class communities the legitimate prerogative of a husband to maltreat his wife had long been distinguished from assaults on women of no relation, which were generally regarded with disapproval by men and women.[48] From the draymen's point of view there was never any reason why the two issues should have been confused. But critics of the attack soon determined to confuse the issues in a way which was bound to become uncomfortable for the self-declared defenders of female honour.

Critical opposition to adulation of the chivalrous and radical draymen was quick to make the connection between private and public abuse of women. Foremost among press critics were *The Times* and the *Morning Chronicle*, both singled out by Chartist speakers for vilification. Haynau, now an old man, they insisted, had only been doing his duty as a soldier, and the draymen's cowardly treatment violated every principle of English neutrality, hospitality and protection invariably extended to foreigners, from Napoleon to the current rabble of European refugees. Furthermore, there was nothing so unique about military executions or the flogging of women in wartime. The British had done it during the Irish rebellion and under Wellington in Spain. Also large crowds had cheered the flogging of the first female Quakers in Boston, and, to crown the hypocrisy, the Hungarian rebels themselves had committed atrocities and executed women for their loyalty.[49] But the attack soon shifted to the qualities of the brewery workers in particular and London labourers in general. *The Times* spoke for a number of correspondents questioning the chivalry of Haynau's attackers when it asked:

> If one of Messrs Barclay and Perkins' brewers discovered his wife with a paramour, or found that by her drunkenness she had caused the death of a child, would he appeal to the laws – would he in the former case sue for damages in Doctors' Commons, or petition Parliament for a divorce? No. He would give his wife a sound thrashing, and all the world would think it a very natural act, considering his condition and circumstances. But we are sorry to say that the labourers of the metropolis occasionally beat their wives for a much less reason. Nay, if the first stone was to be thrown by him that was without blame, we would very much suspect that the Austrian 'woman-flogger' would have got out of the brewery scot free.[50]

The accusation was reinforced by letters to the editor deploring daily press reports of 'the perpetration of every imaginable brutality, often ending in death, by operatives in London on their wretched wives'. Another accused 'the class to which these excitable gentlemen belong' of boastfully favouring the terms 'thrashing' and 'walloping' to describe their favourite pastime with their wives.[51]

Criticism of the domestic brutality of working-class men by the conservative press had implicit political overtones. Although Chartist agitation for manhood suffrage had subsided since 1848, the meetings which followed the attack warned that the issue remained very much alive.[52] *The Times*'s execration of 'five hundred infuriated savages' and their supporters was no doubt intended to discredit the continuing political claims.[53] As late as 1853 it continued to mix its outrage against wife-beaters with references to the hypocritical draymen.[54] Ironically, during debate on legislation to permit summary conviction of aggravated assaults on women and children, it called for corporal punishment, insisting that such brutes, unlike soldiers, could not be further brutalized by a degrading flogging.[55] More intriguing, though, is its coupling of condemnation of London workers with justifications of violence against wives whose moral or domestic duty fell short of respectable standards, where husbands had no legal recourse against them. Middle-class outrage against wife assault, in this sense, continued to be qualified by acceptance that it could still be men's ultimate legitimate sanction against recalcitrant wives. Such pronouncements reflect a wider intention to cultivate images of respectable working-class manhood, where gender and family relations, as well as political behaviour, were central. But even here some violence was not altogether inconsistent with respectability. As many later commentators implied, 'understanding' of working-class domestic violence could come very close to condonation.

But whatever *The Times*'s hidden agenda its charge against London workers generally was a weighty one. It was only too true that such reports from magistrates' courts appeared daily in the London press. Within a week of the Haynau attack a journeyman furrier was brought before the magistrate in Southwark, where Barclay and Perkins were located, charged with causing his wife's death by 'knocking her down and kicking her in the abdomen while far advanced in pregnancy'. Neighbours had heard the husband demanding money from his wife and the surgeon later found her body covered with bruises.[56] Similar reports are very easy to find in both the national and local press, which is perhaps why the radical journals preferred not to reply to the charge. Even their own pages were occasionally testimony to the savage treatment some British husbands gave their wives. But it is less easy to find hard evidence to establish that such behaviour was common among the celebrated draymen of Barclay and Perkins.

We know very little about either the draymen or brewery workers generally, but the draymen's general image was one of sturdy, respectable yeomen, conservative or uncommitted in their politics and devoted to wife and family. *Punch* noted that they had been quick to enrol as special constables on 10 April, 1848 to protect the city against the large Chartist demonstration,[57] and reports of their presence at meetings of Chartist and 'Fraternal Democrats' congratulating them on the attack all acknowledged that they were unaccustomed to attending such meetings or to hearing such radical rhetoric.[58] But whether they shared the propensity to domestic violence with so many London labourers is more difficult to discover. The *Sydney Morning Herald* correspondent, who reflected on the nature of the whole press debate, suspected that they did, but thought no less of them for it:

> In the first place, although I would much rather that a huge drayman, or any other man, would not commit the dastardly act of beating a poor weak woman, I yet think that it is possible that a drayman may do this, and still, not be altogether destitute of sound and manly feelings, or as the common phrase goes, that he may be a good hearted sort of fellow nevertheless. Some women are very trying to the temper even of a philosopher, as even some of the philosophers of *The Times* would admit; how much more trying then to brewers' draymen, who do not set up for philosophers at all. Uncultivated men, little accustomed to restrain the natural language of their feelings, may, and often do commit acts which in calmer moments they condemn whether in themselves or others. . . . If a lecturer were publicly to inculcate the propriety of regular, periodical, wife floggings, he would be hunted out of the room even by wife floggers themselves; and the *Times*, I suppose would say as in the present case, 'inconsistent men, in denouncing a doctrine which

you yourselves occasionally practice.' Such accomplished writers as are on the *Times* cannot but know that *all* men (themselves included) are more virtuous in contemplation than in action. Hence I recognize a virtuous impulse at the bottom of this apparent excess of these now celebrated draymen.[59]

Such middle-class male rationalizations of wife-beating render the little we know of its incidence among respectable workmen less surprising. For although there was a strong ethos of respectable family values and protective fatherhood among skilled artisans, as there was in the lower middle class and related groups of occupations, none of them are notable for their absence among reported cases of wife abuse. In 1878 Frances Power Cobbe found a substantial grouping of these occupations, alongside unskilled labourers, among cases of what she called 'wife torture' – including murder – reported from around the country.[60] We will examine these claims more fully in the next chapter, but there is no hard evidence which proves that London draymen's behaviour exceeded or fell short of the norm in these respects; their reputed respectability, at least, was no certain guarantee of their domestic pacifism.

But such uncertainty as exists for the draymen hardly applies to the other London workers reported to have joined in the Haynau affray. Some of the coalheavers, for example, had been characterized by Henry Mayhew as a 'rude class', heavy drinkers and brutal to their wives, and he quoted a long statement from a wife of one of them who, with her children, had suffered twenty years of abuse and near starvation.[61] Some of his evidence also suggested that many of the coalheavers' wives were themselves substantial drinkers, often drinking in company with their husbands and arriving at the beer-shop at night to demand their wages.[62] Ross's model of the physically stout and combative East End London wife at the end of the nineteenth century may well have been appropriate to some of these women, as also to the wives of market-porters and other casual labourers.[63] Family life among London's unskilled labourers was characterized as a domestic battleground governed by sexual antagonism which was deeply rooted in conflicting economic and social priorities.[64]

So for the skilled or the unskilled, the rough or respectable, there is an apparent paradox as to why Haynau's flogging of an upper-class Hungarian woman inspired such protective fury. Was it, as *The Times* implied, simply a matter of hypocrisy, of radical proletarian politics and insular xenophobia against an easy target eclipsing a more basic misogyny in male popular culture? Did Haynau just happen to present a fortuitous target to make a class point about those 'great Tories and high-titled dames' of the ballad? On one level the simple distinction made by working-class communities between husbands' abuse of their wives and more general violence against unrelated women provides an explanation for the apparent paradox. But the press's charges against the male demonstrators touched a raw nerve, highlighting the problematical nature of marital conflict for many men from the respectable working class. Domestic violence sat uneasily with the upwardly aspiring values of self-improving and respectable male workers. By the mid-nineteenth century the issue was coming to be recognized as a problem by some working-class writers, resulting in a degree of agonizing which warrants some scrutiny.

In his autobiography, Eric Bligh, the grandson of one of Barclay and Perkins' managers, speculated that Haynau's woman-flogging may have incensed the draymen so much because they were 'tired of upper-class jokes about wife-beating'.[65] Such jokes aren't so easy to find in print as one may imagine, although a note of patronizing drollery often lurks behind much of the press reporting. *Punch's* later satire at the time of Frances Power Cobbe's wife-torture campaign in the 1870s was directed as much against legal misrepresentation and government inaction as it was against working-class brutes.[66] But Bligh's suggestion does at least acknowledge that the assumption of ubiquitous husbandly brutality was a sensitive one for the respectable working class, that it could simultaneously embody both a sense of guilt or unease about their own behaviour and resentment of upper-class hypocrisy about theirs. The periodic mirth in court which accompanied some cases of wife assault, and their patronizing treatment in the press, may have been particularly galling.[67] Similar upper-class behaviour had, after all, been exposed not so long since, in the Caroline Norton case, and much of the criticism of working-class men, which surfaced intermittently in the press from the late 1840s, conveniently deflected the focus back on to them.[68] Domestic violence was, indeed, anathema to many respectable working men, and, as we have seen, the radical press's castigation of Haynau for his woman-flogging drew on an idealized patriarchal model of marital roles and relations.

The literate working class were exposed to most of the themes in middle-class prescriptive literature which preached the virtues of conjugal harmony through both separate spheres and companionate marriage. Catherine Hall has examined the early-nineteenth-century process by which those themes came to constitute a distinct working-class discourse, evident in such texts as William Cobbett's *Cottage Economy* and *Advice to Young Men*, where he celebrated women's domestic accomplishments, condemned those without them, and advised husbands to stay at home with their wives and be kind and considerate to them.[69] For working-class men, like their middle-class counterparts, conjugal harmony required sympathetic understanding of their wives' hardships together with disciplined forbearance in times of crisis. The fact that so many working men were aware of these prescriptions, but too often failed to live up to them, may have promoted a disturbing sense of guilt and some confusion over the nature of their masculinity.

Companionate prescriptions coexisted uneasily with an earlier but still surviving tradition of verbally and physically combative marriage, and, as most reformers stressed, the ever-present temptation of drink meant that conjugal harmony was often on a knife edge, with violence never far beneath the surface. The well-known illustrator, George Cruikshank, in his series, *The Bottle*, which became his own famous personal passage to teetotalism, highlighted, melodramatically, the vulnerability of many respectable working-class homes to those risks, with the murder of a wife, the corruption of the children and the guilt-ridden madness of a husband.[70]

To explore the complexities of men's attitudes we need to turn to other, less direct sources. Surprisingly, regional working-class dialect poetry perhaps came closest to encapsulating the sense of guilt felt by men over their own propensity for violent behaviour. It reminds us, again, that violence was an ever-present possibility in many homes of the respectable working class, contemplated, at least, if not indulged. In her study of working-class literature Martha Vicinus noted correctly that such poetry in Lancashire reflected a sentimental preoccupation with middle-class idealizations of family life in a working-class setting – the ultimate embourgeoisement of the labour aristocracy.[71] This poetry is striking testimony to the continuing popularity of the discourse of domestic harmony among working-class readers, although it would be wrong to represent it as a simple parroting of middle-class ideals. One of the most famous of this genre, written during the Lancashire cotton famine of 1861–5 and frequently recited in public, was Samuel Laycock's 'Welcome, Bonny Brid', which celebrated affectionate fatherhood in hard times.[72]

But there was another side to the proud and sentimental celebrations of domestic commitment and harmony, and this, too, was a regular theme in dialect poetry. In their preoccupation with the material hardships of married life on limited incomes, with domestic conflict, mutual frustrations and violence, dialect poets also reflected the sense of guilt felt by many of their male readers about their own behaviour, as well as confusion over their masculine identity. 'Manliness', as middle-class men had been learning, was now to be tested not only among male peers but in the domestic sphere by more civilized behaviour towards women. In the 1860s, for example, Samuel Laycock's 'Uncle Dick's Advoice to Wed Men' saw Uncle Dick berating and sermonizing young married men for their 'kicks and their blows' and knocking their wives about after a few drinks. It's likely, though, that for Laycock all Uncle Dick's urging to be good, 'honest, monly an true' was not very hopeful counsel. If, as he admitted, the mentor himself was guilty of the same domestic failings as

31

his younger peers, the outlook for reform was bleak ('aw'm guilty no deawt;/We'n o bits o failin's – we're noan on us beawt').[73]

The resigned tone with which dialect poetry continued to treat domestic conflict well into the twentieth century reinforces this impression. Some poets approached the subject more cautiously, preferring to reflect on married women's domestic hardships or on familiar stereotypes of feckless husbands and nagging wives.[74] Dialect prose dwelt on similar themes, nowhere more explicit than in J. T. Staton's 'Missis Caustic's Hearthstone Lectures', a thinly disguised Lancashire version of Douglas Jerrold's 'Mrs Caudle's Curtain Lectures' in *Punch* fifteen years earlier. Job Caustic, returning too late at night from his lodge, would be greeted by an aggrieved wife well prepared with a catalogue of his failings, and those of men in general: 'yoa men have aw lost yoar conshunces; un there's no eend o yoar expectations'.[75] The resignation hinted at the sense of guilt which could be felt by men conscious of their apparent inability to reform. It is possible, too, that feelings of guilt over treatment of their wives may have been bound up with sentimentality in memories of their mothers. We know far too little about mother–son relationships among the working class, apart from a general tendency for mothers to favour their sons compared to more conflict-laden relationships with their daughters.[76] Nostalgia about memories of mothers does seem to be more pronounced among men.[77]

Such reflections on domestic life were precisely the kind of material which, David Vincent recently noted, were conspicuously absent from the autobiographies of working-class men, who seem to have felt that revelations of marital conflict, as well as sexual experience, were undignified and inconsistent with their desire to improve and instruct their readership.[78] Significantly, most self-improving autobiographers studiously excluded their wives from their quest for self-fulfilment and saw family life as an obstacle rather than an aid to personal development; William Lovett blamed such men for not tutoring their wives, feeling that many domestic 'bickerings and dissensions' stemmed from the wife's failure to appreciate her husband's literary and political interests.[79]

These sources, originating from working-class men themselves, though far from conclusive, do bring us somewhat closer to their own perceptions than do the politically inspired attacks of the conservative press. The note of self-doubt and confusion recalls David Morgan's suggestion that the most fruitful way to investigate masculinity in history might be to focus on a period or issue which rendered gender identity problematic by calling its norms into question.[80] His advice is pertinent to the anxiety evident here stemming from men's private behaviour. There were clear contradictions embodied between the discourse of domestic harmony and the more private lived experience of working-class men imbued with notions of self-improvement and respectability during an important transitional period.

Morgan's notion is directly relevant to the clash of widespread companionate marriage prescriptions, which challenged earlier concepts of 'manliness', and the continued incidence of domestic violence. The conduct of working men in the privacy of their homes could be manifestly at odds with popular notions of working-class respectability, which, Peter Bailey has shown, might be no more than partial, the product of a 'single role-performance', often designed to impress middle-class observers.[81] Gender relationships, far more even than men's behaviour at leisure, could illustrate the limited relevance of idealizations of the respectable, self-improving, working man.

None of this conclusively refutes Thompson's argument that increasing nineteenth-century communal disapproval of wife-beating represented a significant trend. The growing disapproval is clear enough. But it does reinforce the need to go beyond the uncertain records of rough music rituals. It also points to the centrality of the distinction between public ideology, collective rituals and private behaviour, which were rarely consistent. Like the labourers who roughed up Haynau, many of the men who charivaried wife-beaters may themselves not have had such a spotless domestic record. So we should not infer too much about private and communal behaviour from ideological prescription. In the famous Jackson case in 1891, a woman who had been kidnapped and incarcerated by her husband was finally released by the court of appeal, only to be charivaried by locals for defying her husband when she returned to her home town of Clitheroe in Lancashire.[82]

The contradictions between public ideals, communal responses and private conduct took many forms. But by the later nineteenth century public exposure had succeeded in making the issue of domestic violence part of a larger public discourse about conjugal behaviour. Violent husbands increasingly came before the courts, were vilified or defended in public, entered the popular press and were managed, counselled and legislated against. Paradoxically, though, the solutions offered to cure their patriarchal excesses invariably required a more thorough commitment to respectable family values, where the worlds of men and women were more rigidly separate, where women's economic dependence and marginality were entrenched, and where women were thus more vulnerable to male abuse.[83] The 'solution' to domestic violence thus re-emphasized the very structures and values of inequality from which it sprung. But if, in the public sphere, there was growing evidence of a sentiment that patriarchal marriage needed to be tempered with larger doses of companionate assumptions and humane treatment, that proves little about marital behaviour, and claims that domestic violence declined correspondingly need to be scrutinized carefully. In the next chapter we will examine reported cases of assaults to assess the relationship between experience and prescription.

2

'ROUGH USAGE'

THE INCIDENCE OF VIOLENCE

On the morning of 21 November, 1888, according to a local newspaper, the town of Preston was 'startled' by the rumour that 'a butcher had kicked his wife to death' the previous night. While the tragedy conveyed nothing of the sensation of the recent 'Jack the Ripper' murders, 'those appalling incidents or horrible tactics which have so significantly characterized the brutal, blood curdling butcheries in the South of England', and lacked the extreme violence which engaged the 'morbid minded', it still conveyed an important lesson. The affair provided another example 'of the infernal, inhuman fatal use the clog has ever had in Preston, and brings to justice, no doubt, a man who, perhaps naturally, still most unfortunately, looked for persuasion and correction in his foot instead of his head'.[1]

At the inquest Robert Knowles, the butcher, 35 years old, was characterized as a 'hard working, affectionate husband', deeply remorseful for his action. By contrast his wife, Alice, 31, until recently a weaver in a Preston mill, was depicted as a provoking drunkard. The defence claimed that 'she might have lived a happy life had she left drink alone, as her husband often advised her'. Alice's sister testified to the unhappiness of the couple stemming from the wife's excessive drinking. Their 8-year-old daughter, an eye-witness, added that by the time of the crime her mother had been drinking for two days with a neighbour, Ellen Windle, also a butcher's wife. According to Windle, about 11 p.m. Alice said that she was afraid to go home, but soon afterwards her husband came to fetch her. When he asked her to come home she replied 'I will ——; I'll show you whether I will come home or not; I will come home when I think on it.' He responded by striking her on the side of her face with his hand, causing her to fall off her chair, and then kicked her once in the back of the head, at which his daughter called out to stop, or 'you'll kill her'. The kick, apparently, was enough to cause her death within a few minutes.[2]

Hearings at the magistrates' court, the inquest, and a week later at the Manchester Assizes, all stressed Alice's drinking and Robert's subsequent regret; immediately afterwards in the police station, as well as at the inquest, he 'manifested considerable sorrow and wept bitterly'. The Coroner, summing up, noted the lethal nature of the 'formidable weapons' worn by Robert, steel-tipped wooden clogs, but directed the jury to reduce the charge from murder to manslaughter because of 'the sufficient amount of provocation the prisoner had received'. The trial in Manchester again highlighted Robert, the industrious husband, and Alice, the drunkard, 'a scandal to her sex'. Even the prosecution did not think to stress Alice's fear of returning home to Robert before she was assaulted. The jury's 'guilty' verdict was accompanied by a recommendation to mercy, and after condemning 'the use of clogs in Lancashire' the judge sentenced Robert to one month's imprisonment with hard labour.[3]

This case is instructive as much for the attitudes it reveals of the press and courts as for insights into the nature of domestic violence in Lancashire. Magistrates and judges, acutely conscious of Lancashire's reputation as the 'kicking district' for wife-beaters, were preoccupied with men's misuse of their clogs at least as much as their more general propensity for violence at home. Periodically magistrates in the Preston Police Court announced their determination to 'put down kicking'.[4] As late as 1903 one declared:

> The great use of clogs in Lancashire was bringing the county into disrepute. He did not know another county where kicking with clogs was so much resorted to as in Lancashire, and one felt ashamed of the county in which one lived when charges of this kind were made.[5]

This focus on the most convenient, albeit lethal, weapon tended to deflect attention from the more general problem of domestic violence, but it also prompted a democratic sharing of condemnation between the poorest working-class men, often described as 'good for nothing' or 'worthless', and the more respectable, particularly skilled artisans and those in retail trade. Butchers like Robert Knowles, for example, appeared commonly enough in the Preston police court on charges of wife assault, but their behaviour could not easily be dismissed as a curiosity of the deviant, alien world of the casual poor.[6] So while the preoccupation with 'clogging' facilitated a reluctance to engage with the deeper causes of domestic violence, at the same time it acknowledged implicitly that the problem was more generally cultural, and not confined to a narrow section of the working class.

We should not be surprised to find butchers, and similar men well removed from the ranks of the labouring poor, charged with wife-assault. Poor, unskilled men, certainly, were most often vilified for abuse of their wives, but skilled workers, shopkeepers and men with a variety of occupations from the lower middle class appeared no less frequently in the Preston police court on wife-assault charges. This, at least, is the finding of a sample of Preston newspaper reports of cases of domestic violence reported between 1836 and 1913, an imperfect and arbitrary source, but the best available from these courts.[7] Table 2.1, in fact, shows that, where occupations were stated, more than half were from skilled, higher textile, lower-middle or middle-class occupations, with only 42.97 per cent identified as labourers, unskilled and unskilled unemployed. Even allowing for the possibility that court reporters might be more likely to specify skilled and middle-class occupations, and to ignore those of labourers, the representation of 'respectable' occupations is significant. Moreover, as table 2.2 reveals, from the 1870s, when the reporting of cases became more routine, the relative proportions of unskilled and others were roughly consistent.

The smallness of this sample, the large number of unidentified occupations, and unavoidable reliance on the vagaries of newspaper reporting, should warn against leaping to precipitate conclusions from such limited evidence. But it is significant that some contemporary middle-class observers made similar judgements about the class dimensions of domestic violence. In 1856 J. W. Kaye, though confident that most wife-beating cases in the London police courts came from the overcrowded 'fetid steamy atmosphere' of poor districts, still noted the 'deplorable fact that the best workmen are generally the worst men'. The skilled workman's easier command of high wages gave him more time and income to spend in 'rioting and drunkenness' with consequent dangers for his wife.[8] Frances Power Cobbe, promoting her campaign against 'wife-torture' in 1878, wrote of her long list of cases including 'shoemakers, stonemasons, butchers, smiths, tailors, a printer, a clerk, a bird-catcher, and a large number of labourers'. Her profile of cases was not unlike that in the Preston sample, but her analysis, which focused on 'lives of hard, ugly, mechanical toil in dark pits and hideous factories', shed little light on violence in the homes of better-off artisans and the lower middle class.[9]

Domestic violence, as we have seen, posed serious problems for the much-vaunted respectability of the self-improving artisan, but like Cobbe, most contemporary analysts and critics of wife-abuse focused on the poorest inhabitants of overcrowded urban slums. Henry Mayhew's portrait of rough costermonger men and their long-suffering women provided an early model for the intricate investigations of domestic life among the poor, and its violent dimensions, which proliferated after the middle of the nineteenth century.[10] The well-publicized proceedings of magistrates' courts, and, in 1910, the detailed evidence of the Royal Commission on Divorce, provided ample material for close scrutiny of proletarian marriage, whether the motive be middle-class titillation, enlightenment or more serious reform.[11] Cobbe's campaign for

Table 2.1 Class breakdown of husbands' occupations in police court reports of domestic violence, Preston, 1836–1913 (128 identifiable out of 283)

Unskilled	
Labourers	18 (14.06%)
Unskilled	20 (15.63%)
Unemployed	17 (13.28%)
Total unskilled	55 (42.97%)
Skilled	
Skilled textiles	12 (9.38%)
Other skilled	29 (22.66%)
Total skilled	41 (32.03%)
Shopkeepers, lower middle- and middle-class	32 (25%)
Total	128

Source: Police court reports, *Preston Chronicle, Preston Pilot, Preston Guardian, Preston Herald*, 1836–1913, one year in ten; see appendix 1.

Table 2.2 Decennial class breakdown of husbands' occupations in police court reports of domestic violence, Preston, 1836–1913 (128 identifiable out of 283)

	1836	1846	1856	1866	1878	1888	1893	1903	1913
Labourers	-	-	1	-	2	1	4	10	-
Unskilled	-	-	-	-	4	3	1	8	4
Unemployed	-	1	1	1	2	4	4	1	3
Total unskilled	-	1	2	1	8	8	9	19	7
			(22%)	(11%)	(40%)	(47%)	(56%)	(45%)	(58%)
Skilled textiles	-	-	2	-	4	-	1	4	1
Other skilled	-	1	3	3	3	3	4	11	1
Total skilled	-	1	5	3	7	3	5	15	2
			(56%)	(33%)	(35%)	(18%)	(31%)	(36%)	(17%)
Shopkeepers, lower middle- and middle-class	1	-	2	5	5	6	2	8	3
			(22%)	(56%)	(25%)	(35%)	(13%)	(19%)	(25%)
Total specified	1	2	9	9	20	17	16	42	12
Total unspecified	3	4	9	20	17	38	28	24	12
Combined total	4	6	18	29	37	55	44	66	24

Source: Police court reports, *Preston Chronicle, Preston Pilot, Preston Guardian, Preston Herald*, 1836–1913; see appendix 1.

separation and maintenance legislation for abused wives was preceded by several earlier demands, such as Kaye's article, 'Outrages on Women,' in the 1850s, periodic moves in Parliament, and a paper in 1876 at the Social Science Association by Mr Serjeant Pulling. Like most reformers, Pulling, who drew on the brutality of the 'kicking district' of Liverpool, assumed that the key 'incentive' to men's brutality was their 'gross ignorance', just as education was the key 'preventive'.[12]

It followed from this that the central explanation for domestic violence was environmental. According to Cobbe, only in the slums of manufacturing, mining or mercantile districts were men 'rude, coarse, and brutal in their manners and habits, and the women devoid, in an extraordinary degree, of all the higher natural attractions and influences of their sex'. Thus, while Cobbe insisted on the relevance of improvement in women's legal status, she mostly shared the pessimism of others that 'marital tyranny among the lower classes is beyond the reach of law, and can only be remedied by the slow elevation and civilization of both sexes'.[13] The elitism in such arguments undoubtedly owed something to the influential feminist work of Harriet Taylor and John Stuart Mill, who depicted the lowest male 'ferocious savages' persecuting their 'household slaves', the only beings in the pecking order they could dominate. This contrasted with Mill's marital ideal of two equals 'in rights and in cultivation'.[14]

But if environment created the conditions for domestic violence, its amelioration could offer the cure, and by the end of the nineteenth century there was a growing feeling that the spread of education and respectability among the working class had brought some significant improvement in men's treatment of their wives. The stigma attaching to wife-assault, it seems, like the stigma attaching to divorce, was spreading downwards. Elizabeth Wostenholme Elmy, best known for her feminist campaign against marital rape, reflected in 1901 that a generation had seen profound changes in community toleration of domestic brutality, at least in one Lancashire village:

> In 1866, when Mr Elmy went to Mobberly as manager of a great crape works, the first reform he introduced was to pay the married women's wages to *themselves*, – the husbands till then had come for the women's wages, as if they were their own. A few years later, wife-beating was still the regular Saturday afternoon and evening's amusement in the village. *Now*, the husband who struck his wife would lose caste forever. Every other man and all the women would treat him as a coward and a brute – so some progress has been made.[15]

It would not be difficult to cite conflicting anecdotes against Wostenholme Elmy's story, notably the communal scorn visited upon

Emily Jackson in 1891 when she returned to Clitheroe after defeating her husband's attempts to vindicate his legal right to lock her up.[16] The Royal Commission on Divorce from 1910 provided ample evidence that wife-abuse, far from being a lingering remnant of more barbaric times, continued to pose a profound social problem, and that changes in attitudes were far from consistent. But the view that increasing community intolerance of domestic violence had brought about significant changes in behaviour as well as law was a common one by the early twentieth century.[17]

Recent historical analysis has mostly endorsed this view. Nancy Tomes's work, the only attempt to investigate the actual level of aggravated assaults on women, based on convictions, concludes that the nineteenth century witnessed a genuine decline in marital violence as respectable values defined such conduct as unmanly.[18] With few exceptions, most historians since have followed this interpretation.[19] The decline in official convictions for aggravated assaults on women, including those between husband and wife, is undeniable, and is consistent with the more general decline in violent crime evident in the nineteenth century.[20] But the extent to which a decline in such convictions represented a genuine decline in domestic violence remains an unresolved, and probably unresolvable, question. Tomes herself speculates that the apparent decline may be explained in part by increasing privacy of working-class housing, a corresponding decrease in surveillance by neighbours, and greater reluctance of the victims, more economically dependent on their husbands, to report it, all strong possibilities in newer, less densely populated, suburbs.[21] Such possibilities raise serious questions about the relationship between recorded and actual domestic assaults.

A scrutiny of the legal process in magistrates' courts, where most of the convictions took place, gives some pointers to the difficulties involved in undue reliance on their records. Records of convictions, recording a genuine decline in violent assaults, still cannot be taken to reflect the true level of behaviour, for the simple reason that during the period of statistical decline these courts increasingly became courts of conciliation as well as summary conviction. With the Matrimonial Causes Act of 1878, which provided for separation and maintenance allowances for wives of husbands convicted of aggravated assaults,[22] local magistrates' courts increasingly took on a more paternalistic role, eager to intervene in an attempt to make the wife forgive, the husband reform and the family reunite, and thus avoid the fragile division of slender economic resources. Magistrates, together with a growing army of police court missionaries, probation officers and clerks of the court came to see themselves as marriage menders.[23]

While magistrates in courts of petty sessions had traditionally assumed a paternal role towards marital friction, the growing court bureaucracy now made it more effective in limiting prosecutions.[24] The result was that more and more cases ended, formally at least, in reconciliations rather than convictions and separation. A police court missionary from Middlesbrough, John Palin, described the process to the Royal Commission on Divorce this way:

> You would find in almost every case if some sensible tactful person intervened the man and wife would be reconciled. In our court at Middlesbrough we have an admirable plan. Almost every person who applies for a separation order is referred to myself. I go and visit them in their homes. We try and get to the root of the trouble, and in cases where immorality has not taken place, and sometimes in cases where immorality has taken place, one finds with a little talk – pointing out their folly and giving them some kind advice and encouragement – that they are reconciled again.[25]

Any study of reported cases of domestic assaults in the later nineteenth century soon reveals the extent of this process. One typical case in Preston, in which a husband was charged with striking his wife in the face, choking her and threatening to kill her with a carving knife, concluded, after the bench had recommended conciliation, in the clients retiring with their solicitors to discuss the case, and agreeing to live together again after the husband 'had undertaken to provide her with a comfortable home. The Bench expressed their satisfaction at this result, and dismissed the case.'[26] While these 'reconciliations' were rarely long-lived, and, indeed, the separation and maintenance provisions themselves were of dubious value for wives whose means of support remained more uncertain than ever once a meagre household income was divided,[27] the courts' increasing mission to conciliate could not help but give a misleading impression of the decline in reported convictions of marital violence.

Much the same is true of the notorious reluctance of many wives to prosecute their violent husbands, even after calling the police and taking out a summons to stop a severe beating. This could stem from wives' fear of further violence after a prosecution and conviction, from anxieties about jeopardizing an already marginal family income, or, as often stated, a genuine wish not to punish the husband, only to stop his violence, and magistrates were often seen as a legitimate channel of appeal simply to warn off brutal husbands.[28] But women could earn stern reproof from the Bench when cases were brought by neighbours or police and the victim herself contradicted their evidence. In a case headlined 'Brutal Assault and Perjury' in 1856, John Gregson was proved by three eyewitnesses to have severely injured his *de facto* wife, Jane Greenwood, by kicking her in the head. In court Greenwood denied the entire incident, prompting this warning against 'gross perjury' from the magistrates:

> Some steps should be taken to put a stop to such attempts as she had made to contravene the ends of justice. . . . It is a great pity to see what you have done out of devotion to that brute – that you have come here and deliberately sworn before heaven that he never laid a hand on you. I don't know whether the magistrates are doing right in allowing you to leave the court, but they will do so, recommending you to be more careful in the future.[29]

The official level of convictions was further reduced, following new legislation in 1886, by the willingness of magistrates to award separation and maintenance orders on the grounds of desertion rather than cruelty or assault.[30] Frequently the desertion had been caused by a husband violently throwing his wife out of the house after a series of assaults, often putting her in fear of her life. One woman, married for sixteen years with six children, was driven out by her husband when she said she wanted to fetch the 'cruelty man', a revealing hint of the meaning that the police court facility carried for some women.[31] Some couples appeared in court several times within the space of a year on mixed charges of assault and desertion, often because of the Bench's efforts at reconciliation.[32] But in all such cases the offence was entered as desertion, further diminishing the record of assaults.

After 1895, as well, the number of separation and maintenance orders made out for 'aggravated assaults' on wives bore even less relationship to total cases of domestic violence, since magistrates became free to give relief to abused wives for 'persistent cruelty' without recording a conviction against the husband. Much more systematic and comprehensive research is needed to be certain of aggregate trends, but the erratic information provided to the Royal Commission on Divorce gives no consistent impression of any decline in acts of violence. In some districts separation orders requested and granted, for all purposes, including drunkenness and neglect to maintain, showed a steady increase after 1895. In Leeds, for example, the orders granted jumped from 142 in 1896 to 344 in 1903, declining only to 288 by 1909.[33] In one district where the different grievances were broken down, the Staffordshire Potteries, the clear decline in orders following convictions for aggravated assaults was matched by a marginal increase in those for persistent cruelty.[34] All such figures tell us more about the willingness of women to approach the courts and seek relief, and the readiness of magistrates to grant orders, than about any changes in behaviour, but they cannot be used to show that domestic violence was on the wane.

Newspaper reports of wife-assault cases can shed little further light on the question of declining incidence, since the number of cases reported bore little relationship to cases heard. In the Preston survey, as table 2.2. illustrates, the cases reported fluctuated markedly, peaking in 1903 at 66, and declining, equally abruptly, to 24 in 1913. In that year the police court chairman, faced one day in September with a 'blank sheet', signifying no charges, donned the white gloves in ritual celebration and congratulated Preston on its improvement:

> He had always hoped it might be his fate to receive the white gloves. In his opinion . . . the absence of crime could be accounted for in that the education of people was beginning to tell on the general public. He believed the habits of the people had very much improved. As he looked back twenty years he remembered that every day in the year they had a 'kicking' or 'wife-beating' case, or something of that sort, and many of them were of the most vicious kind. He was glad things had changed, and the fact that . . . there should be no cases of crime in the town, as far as they could see, led them to assume that the community – or the Preston community at any rate – was better than it was twenty years ago.[35]

It is intriguing here to see wife-assault becoming a metaphor for the general level of crime. The chairman's fading memory certainly seems to have led him to exaggerate the frequency of cases twenty years earlier, just as he overlooked the persistence of severe 'kickings' still brought to the court in 1913.[36] But the impression that a real change in behaviour had taken place was significant, though its timing is rather later than Tomes's London figures, from 1840 to 1890, suggest.[37]

At the very least there are hints here of the widening public face of respectability in some working-class communities, where wife-abuse was judged to be inconsistent with changing definitions of manliness. But there was no corresponding decline in interest in the marital proceedings of the magistrates' courts. One London magistrate expressed his amazement at the continuing popularity of the police court reports in the local papers, despite what he thought was their relatively colourless style and concern for facts before readability.[38] The greater proportion of cases reported certainly seem to have been selected with an eye to their likely sensational impact. In 1888 in Preston, for example, when reports of domestic violence were increasing, the numbers fluctuated considerably from month to month, determined partly by the routine judgement that 'there were no cases of public interest' and other editorial considerations such as competing news items.[39] Impressions of the level of violence in working-class homes must have varied dramatically in time and space as publicity wavered between sensational and brutal cases and praise for the improving 'habits of the people', but the available evidence cannot sustain any conclusions that domestic violence was declining before 1914.

Observers who attempted to explain the intractability of domestic violence among the poor invariably confronted many of the same conditions that we have already seen acting as inhibitions on women's willingness to prosecute their husbands. Foremost among these was their sense of a level of community tolerance of marital violence, shared by both men and women, up to a certain threshold short of severe injury or murder.[40] Magistrates and other court workers frequently used the term 'rough usage' to describe what they felt women virtually took for granted in married life. 'There is a great deal of rough usage without being exactly gross cruelty', commented one London magistrate, John Rose.[41] Alfred Plowden insisted that the applications of women to the court were rarely impulsive; 'it is the last straw which makes the women come', he commented, usually after many years of a build-up of grievances.[42] Many stressed that rough usage didn't represent for poor women what it would for women of higher classes, and hence required different treatment, since it was bred in harsh conditions, a product of the extraordinary tolerance and 'long-suffering' nature of women without alternatives.[43] In this context non-violent husbands, like the straw-plait worker, Lucy Luck's Will, recommended highly to her by others because he would 'make you a good husband and will never beat you', might be seen as rare good fortune. But there is also a persistent theme of wives' defence of their violent husbands, particularly against outsiders, like the Ripon woman who resisted seeking a separation with the retort, 'he may be a brute but he is my husband'.[44]

The temptation to romanticize this seemingly dogged commitment to violent husbands was too strong for some middle-class observers to resist. Many witnesses at the Royal Commission, anxious to prove that there was no demand among the poor for easier access to divorce, stressed the importance, especially to women, of maintaining their 'marriage lines' at all costs, so that violence, unless it became life-threatening, was no cause for seeking legal redress; even after obtaining a separation, poor women readily took their husbands back for the same reasons. Such women, as a matter of course, showed the 'utmost forbearance', were a 'very forgiving set', and 'would put up with anything almost rather than come and see a missionary even'.[45] On the Commission Cosmo Lang, the Archbishop of York and chief author of the minority report, which opposed extension of grounds and facilities for divorce, directed his questioning carefully to elicit such views; prompting the magistrate from Middlesbrough, he suggested that 'there seems to be some affection, or force of custom, or some other strange cause that operates more strongly than even the remembrance of blows or words?'[46] The sentimentalization reached its height in music hall songs, where Gus Ellen, the cockney songwriter, depicted the scars of violence as virtual badges of affection:

We treads this part o' life as every married couple ought,
Me and 'er – 'er and me;
In fact we're looked on as the 'appiest couple down the court,
Me and 'er 'er and me.
I must acknowledge that she 'as a black eye now and then,
But she don't care a little bit, not she;
It's a token of affection – yuss, in fact that is love
Wiv me and 'er – 'er and me.[47]

Other close observers of living conditions among the poor gave more
prosaic explanations, focusing on material dependence, to account for
women's tolerance of rough usage. The London magistrate, Cecil
Chapman, stressed that it was simply their pecuniary dependence which
forced women to 'submit to atrocities' from their husbands. He found
that a woman's position improved dramatically when she became a
breadwinner or ran a shop. Her life became more tolerable as soon as 'the
woman has something of her own to depend upon. The man treats her
with greater respect, and she treats herself with greater respect.'
Chapman, incidentally, was among the few who concluded from this that
women should be given a legal right to wages from their husbands'
income.[48] Margaret Llewellyn Davies, speaking for the Women's Co-
operative Guild, explained how material dependence coloured women's
attitude to every aspect of their marriage, inhibiting any legal action
against violent husbands, sometimes for fear of losing their children. A
maintenance order, many knew, would barely feed a divided family, so
the wife 'covers up everything for the sake of the children'.[49] The district
nurse, Margaret Loane, who wrote a long series of books recounting her
experience among the poor in an effort to enlighten the middle class,
concluded that under conditions of such dependence women resented
many other offences more deeply than violence.

Comparatively few working-class women would break their hearts
over an amount of rough usage that, skilfully described, would
rouse the wrath of any jury in England, while their very soul is
embittered by insults that a man cannot be made to understand, or
they are driven to fury by acts that in the eyes of matrimonial law are
no offence against them. I have known a woman work hard to gain a
bare subsistence for her children, and the husband has literally
taken the food from their hands and given it to dogs. Another
woman walked miles to beg food from her aged parents living on
out-relief, and carried it home to her half-starved babies, with the
same result. Neither of these men beat their wives. To outsiders the
hopeless villain is the man who occasionally gives his wife a black
eye; to the woman herself it is the man who starves her, robs her of
her earnings, and ill-treats her children.[50]

These portrayals present a low standard of poor women's expectations of marriage. Loane agreed that they were not exacting standards, but added that wives still judged abusive behaviour harshly once it passed the threshold of rough usage. The characteristic comment, 'He never laid a finger on me acept when he was in drink', might conceal a grim picture of routine violence meekly tolerated, but it also hinted at the limits of tolerance. Loane found that 'the lightest blow given deliberately' was more deeply resented than lifelong injuries received from a drunken husband.[51] Most of this evidence provides powerful support for the depressing picture of working-class women's experience of marriage in the nineteenth and twentieth centuries recently drawn by John Gillis. The 'myth of conjugal love' was never translated into reality, and at best marriage might survive as a dogged companionship, with both sexes finding greater emotional support in homosocial groupings, for men in the worlds of the pub and sport, for women with the maternal family and female neighbours.[52]

If any relief is to be found from this pessimistic image in the literature on domestic violence it is in the early twentieth century, when some observers detected a rise in women's expectations. By 1911 Loane thought that the standard of 'wifely dignity' was rising steadily and the woman who submitted 'tamely' to violence was regarded as a 'traitor to her sex' or, at best '"a poor thing" whose weakness does almost as much to degrade manners as her husband's wickedness'.[53] Margaret Llewellyn Davies, too, told the Royal Commission of a 'strong and growing feeling' that the old notions of rough usage were wrong and should no longer be accepted; it was linked to a growing conviction that children should be 'born well, and . . . brought up in a good home'.[54] While, as we have seen, the record of actual assaults cannot confirm this sentiment, it was sufficiently widespread on the eve of the war to hint at a significant shift of opinion, where the public stigma attaching to domestic violence was socially more diffused.

In recent years feminist scholarship has produced a rich literature on the history of domestic violence, which has made enormous strides in advancing our understanding of the dynamics of violent conflict in working-class marriage.[55] These studies reflect much contemporary comment in highlighting tensions over the family economy as a primary cause of violent disputes. Inadequate family income; unequal distribution of the income within the family, often dictated by husbands' drinking and leisure activities; and a variety of women's survival strategies, from self-deprivation to surreptitious pawning of husbands' property, all sowed potential seeds of explosive conflict. Related to this, but not directly economic in origin, were sexual and territorial jealousies, persecution of wives during pregnancy, husbands' resentment of wives' friends and neighbourhood networks, and the much closer alliance of wives with their children, who often defended their mothers physically as they grew older.[56] Not surprisingly the most regular theme, seen as the root cause of violence in poor families by many contemporaries, was drink. Drunkenness and wife-beating were, undoubtedly, common partners, but the cause and effect relationship between the two was far from simple.[57] Jan Lambertz, for example, noted one contemporary's observation that even the most drunken man chose his victims with care and calculation, rarely attacking his children, which would have brought more serious consequences, but reserving his attacks for his wife.[58] The drunkenness was not nearly so blind as was commonly believed, nor was it unique to poor families, so its explanation as the distinguishing feature of working-class sexual antagonism is limited. But for contemporaries intent on uncovering the dynamics of domestic discord among the poor, it was a crucial dimension of a culture of poverty in which violence was taken for granted.

The survey of cases in Preston reflects all these themes. It also reflects one of the most common distinctions made by contemporaries and noted by historians, that between wives as helpless victims or as combative, provoking viragos. Frances Power Cobbe detected two kinds of wife-beating, distinguished mainly by wives' responses. The first, 'wife-beating by combat', she described as largely equally matched, although 'the woman generally gets much the worst of it . . . simply because cats are weaker than dogs'. Invariably here both parties drank to excess, and it was only in such drunken quarrels that 'the hateful virago gets beaten at all'. Even Cobbe could muster little sympathy for such a woman:

> Such a termagant is often the tyrant of her husband, nay of the whole court or lane in which she lives; and the sentiments she excites are the reverse of those which brings down the fist and the clogs of the ruffian husband on the timid and meek-faced woman who tries, too often unsuccessfully, the supposed magic of a soft answer to turn away the wrath of such a wild beast as he.[59]

The 'timid and meek-faced woman' characterized Cobbe's second type of wife-beating, and her main preoccupation, the passive, long-suffering victim, invariably brutalized by a drunken husband. Usually such attacks were unprovoked, or arose over financial tensions and the husband's squandering of housekeeping money on drink. Cobbe described several typical cases where the husband came home drunk, dragged his wife out of bed while asleep, often during or just after a pregnancy, and administered a savage beating that often advanced to what she called 'wife-torture' or murder. She also considered, but quickly dismissed, a third stereotype, characterized by 'that ideal Wife-beater of whom we hear so much, the sober, industrious man goaded to frenzy by his wife's temper or drunkenness'.[60] Cobbe was right to identify this as a commonly reported image, often used in defence or mitigation of wife-beaters, but in neglecting to investigate it she inevitably restricted her inquiry to the poorer sections of the working class.

The provoked husband certainly figured prominently in the police court reports, especially where occupation and background implied a degree of respectability. In the Knowles murder case, which opened this chapter, the sustained criticism of Alice Knowles's character, which resulted in no more than a nominal sentence, affords some insight into the compliant, respectable behaviour expected of working-class women, which was evident in both the courts and the press. Victim-blaming of this order was commonplace, especially where wives were given to excessive drinking. If their drinking led them to assault or threaten their husbands, the weight of the law could exact disproportionate retribution compared to similar offences committed by men. In 1866 Elizabeth Anyon, described as a 'respectable looking woman', the wife of a yarn-agent, was summoned with threatening to assault her husband. He alleged she had contracted 'intemperate habits', had told him she had a pistol with which she would shoot him, and had hidden his razor until he bought her a gill of beer. Elizabeth claimed that her husband 'had acted like a tyrant towards her for the last three years'. But, while the threat had not progressed to action, this did not deter the magistrates from sending her to prison for three months, a sentence well above the average for routine wife-assaults, which often earned no more than seven or fourteen days in the 1860s.[61]

Even without the aggravation of drinking, wives who resisted their husbands or fought back physically could receive short shrift from the police court. In 1888 Jane Cook charged her husband, James, a canal boatman, with kicking and striking her when he came home drunk after a fortnight's steady drinking. But, despite several previous convictions for assaulting his wife, the case was dismissed when James's witnesses denied the assault and alleged that Jane had bitten his finger.[62] Wives' defiance of violent husbands and mutual combat between spouses were clearly common occurrences in working-class marriage, being explicitly mentioned in 11.3 per cent of the reports in the Preston survey of domestic violence.[63] But its exposure in court was unlikely to work in women's own interest.

Cobbe's brutalized, long-suffering victims, who rarely raised a finger in their own defence, also appeared routinely in the court reports. The headline 'Brutal Wife-assault' invariably signified such one-sided per-secution, where, if any physical defence was offered, it came from children or neighbours.[64] In court magistrates usually castigated such men severely, and in extreme cases would resist their habitual propensity to encourage reconciliation and willingly grant the wife's request for separation and maintenance. After hearing evidence of a dock labourer's savage kicking of his wife, threatening to 'Blackpool murder her' (a reference to a Blackpool husband who stabbed his wife to death only a week earlier), and smashing up the house, the magistrates dismissed his promises to behave better, insisted it would be unfair to ask her to return to him, and granted a separation order with weekly maintenance of 8 shillings.[65]

What most distinguished magistrates' responses to such cases, though, was less their revulsion against the extreme violence than their stern disapproval of husbands who failed to live up to their proper role as providers and family protectors. This was particularly evident after separation and maintenance legislation from 1878 prompted the courts to delve more deeply into domestic affairs and to become more familiar with the working-class family economy. Men who preyed on their wives' wages came in for special criticism, especially in a textile town like Preston where women's factory employment was common. John Holland, for example, received three months in prison after he beat and kicked his wife when she refused to give him money for drink out of her wages on the way home from the mill; the bench noted that 'it was simply disgraceful for a man, who would not work himself, to waylay his wife and so cowardly assault her.'[66] 'Monstrous . . . unmanly and cruel' were the epithets commonly reserved for husbands who combined their assaults with failure to maintain their wives adequately.[67] In 1903, sentencing an unemployed husband for assault, the mayor added that 'defendant had taken his wife's earnings to spend in drink, and he hoped that the magistrates would put down such things.'[68] On trial here was husbands' manliness, measured as much by their attitude to work and capacity as breadwinners as by acts of physical assault.

The problem was compounded by temptations of leisure, since many women reported their assaults during weekends and holidays when the opportunities for drinking and quarrelling were greater.[69] In 1903 several women dated their husbands' abuse from the time of the Preston Guild of 1902, a major festival held once every twenty years, which engaged the town and county in extended festivities. John Wignall, a joiner who earned 35 shillings a week, for example, had given up work at the time of the Guild, and when summoned in 1903 was still being maintained by his wife, a weaver. The mayor, granting a 10-shilling maintenance order, gave some 'good advice' to Wignall on his conjugal responsibilities.[70] There may, indeed, be a stronger relationship of domestic violence to patterns of leisure than to cycles of employment and unemployment. The evidence examined here casts little light on the influence of economic trends, although most contemporaries invariably made the predictable cause-and-effect link between violence and poverty, usually in a static rather than a cyclic sense.[71] But recreation, which was more accessible to the better-paid, defied these simple economic explanations, and inevitably directed attention away from the poorest families.

On the few occasions when contemporaries departed from their preoccupation with sub-cultures of poverty as the sole explanation for domestic violence, they were drawn to the recreational habits of respectable working-class men outside the family, which militated against the fulfilment of companionate ideals. The otherwise civilizing tendencies of working-men's clubs, for example, could be seen as disruptive to family harmony. Thomas Harris, the Chief Constable of Wakefield, with thirty-seven years' police experience (and a member himself of two clubs), told the Royal Commission of their divisive effect in alienating husbands from their homes and wives. In spite of their often successful efforts to encourage moderate drinking and respectable entertainment, Harris saw their segregating effect as dangerous.

> My experience is that any club, or any society of men that has an attraction for young married men after a certain time of being married, has a tendency to cause trouble at home; that is my experience; because it takes him away from home especially in the evenings, which as you know the ordinary working man spends at home or taking his wife out for a walk, or helping in the garden or something of that kind. Now, immediately he gets home he scarcely has time to get his tea and wash before he is off for his own amusement.

Harris admitted that drinking habits had become more moderate among respectable workers in the clubs, but saw a larger problem in the separate cultures of man and wife, and thus urged that the clubs should become sites of family entertainment.[72] His suggestion was unlikely to find much favour among the clubs, which took pride in their moderation and respectability, and, as Peter Bailey has noted, were popular among many members as a refuge from the 'wife and family'.[73]

Whether the wives of respectable workers resented the structured absence of their husbands, as Harris maintained, or preferred their own quiet sanctuary at home, there were other voices prepared to draw attention to their marital plight. At the Royal Commission, representatives of the Women's Co-operative Guild claimed to speak expressly for wives of respectable artisans and trade unionists, as opposed to the very poor, and insisted that their needs, if not their marriages, were unique. Margaret Llewellyn Davies, the general secretary, claimed that these women mostly suffered marital cruelty in silence because of the lack of any appropriate means of seeking redress. The Divorce Court was largely financially inaccessible and operated on restricted grounds, and police courts were widely regarded as being courts of the poor, their dealings irrevocably staining the reputation of respectable women. The very poor,

Davies argued, 'are so very much used to being interfered with, that they would not resent mediation in a way that a better working-class woman would'. Hence the intervention of courts through police court missionaries eager to effect reconciliations was seen by many as impertinent and 'almost dangerous'.[74]

At about the same time Anna Martin, who had lived with working-class women in a Rotherhithe settlement, noted a similar phenomenon, in which respectability worked as a deterrent to exposure. The higher a family's social standing, she claimed,

> the less willing is the woman to confess that her husband ill-treats her, partly from a desire to uphold the reputation of her home in the eyes of the world, and, partly, from that curious group-consciousness which often makes people feel more disgraced by the bad behaviour of a near relative than if they were themselves guilty. Shame, too, often holds the women back from speech. 'It's not because they distrust you,' explained Mrs H., who has risen from the ranks and speaks with knowledge, 'but they feel so much of their lives with their husbands to be a degradation that they conceal the truth as long as they can.'[75]

The reluctance of these better-off women to reveal their experience, Martin argued, made it virtually impossible to make reliable assessments of the real extent of marital cruelty.

The Guild had canvassed their members' opinions on the divorce question widely, and were most explicit on the hidden cruelty that these women would not recount to a magistrate, and for which there was no redress, that is sexual cruelty, including marital rape, infection with venereal disease, and infliction of unwanted pregnancies followed by violent attempts to cause a miscarriage.[76] In a long appendix of specific cases from representatives, one spoke of the impossibility of outsiders, including neighbours, knowing the 'inner life' of abused women; a woman had told her that no one would believe her about her husband's cruelty and neglect:

> He was so soft-spoken in front of other people, and they always said he only wanted a little managing. 'Good heavens!' she said, 'I wish they could have him to manage for one month. I have been married to him for eighteen years and these last three nights I have slept on the floor rather than in the same bed.' Yet I don't think enquirers would learn any reason for a divorce unless they took the woman's single word for it. Even her own children do not know.[77]

The substantial proportion of wives of skilled workers and the lower middle class in the Preston survey might suggest that not all such women were as reluctant to approach the police courts as the Guild speakers claimed. Regional variations undoubtedly accounted for some inconsistencies. But other witnesses testified to ways in which the police court's reputation in some towns as a 'poor man's' or 'poor woman's' court of justice could operate as a powerful deterrent to others.[78] A Yorkshire rescue worker for the Church of England described a Sheffield case which divided the neighbourhood, 'and they all went down wearing different coloured ribbons, according to whether they decided with the man or the woman. . . . That kind of thing is dreaded.'[79] The need for anonymity and the fear of publicity powerfully conditioned many women's willingness to seek relief from their marriages. If the increasing publicity given to wife-beating by the end of the century constituted a 'tip of the iceberg' in any way, the iceberg must certainly have been concentrated among the better-off working class and lower middle class represented by the Guild. Their situation alone makes it impossible to speak of any steady decline in domestic violence by Edwardian years.

The respectable working-class wife's tragedy was that the stigma that deterred her from seeking redress in public left her more vulnerable to continuing abuse than both her poorer and wealthier sisters. Ironically this became apparent just when an unprecedented amount of time and resources was being devoted to working-class family breakdown, and especially to domestic violence. One result was the construction of men's behaviour as a problem, to be investigated, regulated, punished and rehabilitated. The preoccupation with men's marital conduct paralleled and overlapped with similar attention directed at middle-class men, which we will explore in Part II. But significantly the focus on violent husbands mostly developed within a discourse of social investigation of the poor and of cultures of poverty, where strategies of surveillance and intervention became most highly developed.[80] Dedicated researchers, from Booth and Rowntree to Pember Reeves, Lady Bell, Mary Higgs, Helen Bosanquet and Margaret Loane, constructed intimate portraits of working-class life, and were followed by enthusiastic social and moral reformers.[81] We know that, while women could welcome some of the information provided, the reformers' efforts were frequently resented by the very poor they attempted to reform, and there is evidence that this applied equally to some police court missionaries in their zealous efforts to remake the family life of the poor in a middle-class image.[82] But it is hardly surprising that women conscious of their social distance from a culture of poverty shrank from any contact with the new facilities of surveillance and regulation.

It is difficult to know how the growing discourse of inspection and control affected those men who, while charged with violence, were acutely conscious of their status and respectability. There is an impression, at least, that lower middle- and middle-class cases were

51

characterized more obviously by a greater literal obsession with authority, in which violence could be provoked by quarrels over issues such as child discipline and accompanied by lectures on the supreme power of husbands.[83] These are the same themes which occur frequently in middle-class cases in the Divorce Court, discussed in Part II. The same group betrayed men's readiness to agree to separation and maintenance orders in order to limit publicity stemming from court proceedings. In 1903, in a case headlined 'Business Man's Persistent Cruelty', an ex-councillor's son, who had become unemployed, had treated his wife so badly that she was 'frightened for her life'; but the court was prevented from listening to the 'painful' features of the case when the defence hastily agreed to the wife's maintenance allowance of 12 shillings.[84] Working-class defendants were less willing to agree to maintenance payments without a fight, but the court's frequent condemnation of their unmanliness, whether for cowardly violence or abdication of the responsibilities of a breadwinner, advertised an increasing willingness to submit such men's private behaviour to public scrutiny. Men's domestic conduct had become a vehicle for questioning traditional views of masculinity and its prerogatives. There is conflicting evidence to suggest both that many men were aware of the new climate, and that the incidence of domestic violence continued unabated, though increasingly in the context of more private, secluded domesticity, less susceptible to neighbourhood observation. Faced with these contradictions, the agenda of reformers, which will now be examined, ranged from vengeful punishment of offenders to palliative redress for the women victims, and ultimately, for a minority, to more fundamental abolition of gender inequalities.

CONTROLLING VIOLENCE: THE LIMITS OF REFORM

On the eve of the First World War there were reasons to think that the concentrated criticism directed against violent husbands might be producing some effective reforms. The controversy and flood of reformist publications stimulated by two years of interviews by the Royal Commission on Divorce certainly raised expectations of change. Yet, in the courts especially, an impression of inconsistency and vacillation persisted, and it was possible to find examples of unregenerate leniency, even encouragement, of wife-beating on the Bench, which hinted at continued resistance to change. The following exchange was reported in 1914 under the heading 'Controlling a Wife':

A man complained to Mr Symmons, the magistrate at Woolwich police court, that his wife was 'most violent' towards him, but he had up till now refrained from striking her.

Mr Symmons said that was manly, but a Lord Chief Justice had laid it down that a man could thrash his wife with a stick so long as it was no thicker than his thumb. He was not there to quarrel with that dictum, and he advised the man to control his wife – take reasonable means to control her.

The Applicant: 'Thank you sir. Now I know what to do.'[85]

Symmons's attitude was exceptional as well as misleading. His long-outdated view drew on surviving understandings in popular culture rather than the state of the law. In the 1760s Blackstone observed that a husband's physical 'power of correction' over his wife had been doubted for a century, and that while a wife clearly had 'security of the peace' against her husband, the 'lower rank' remained fond of 'the old common law' and exerted their 'antient privileges' of physical restraint. Despite clear rulings against violent 'chastisement' in the nineteenth century, legal and popular misunderstandings persisted, often with reference to long-antiquated laws about the thickness of sticks. In 1850 John Stuart Mill and Harriet Taylor claimed it was the 'universal belief among the labouring class, that the law permits them to beat their wives – and the wives themselves share the general error', despite any permissive laws being long obsolete.[86] Any lingering doubts were dispelled in *Regina* v. *Jackson* (1891), which further prohibited a husband from incarcerating his wife, but popular misunderstandings were more enduring.[87]

Symmons's advice contrasts dramatically with some of the more rigorous punishments handed out in police courts to wife-beaters which we saw in the previous chapter. But it highlighted stubborn attitudes among many magistrates who refused to treat personal violence seriously. This awareness had inspired Frances Power Cobbe's feminist campaign of the late 1870s against 'wife-torture'. It informed the influential paper of Serjeant Pulling on crimes of violence at the Liverpool Social Science Congress of 1876 and dominated discussion of wife-abuse throughout 1877 and 1878 in Lydia Becker's *Women's Suffrage Journal*.[88] It was a simple matter, after enumerating dramatic cases of brutality and lax sentencing, to highlight the double standard in sentencing maintained by many magistrates. A husband could 'kick his wife well nigh to death with heavy ironed clogs', and yet be simply bound over to keep the peace or summarily sentenced to token imprisonment. 'But when a wife beats her husband, the magistrates mark their sense of the enormity of the offence by committing her for trial at the sessions.'[89]

After the 1878 legislation, which allowed magistrates to grant separation and maintenance orders to wives of husbands convicted of aggravated assault, feminist criticism came to focus more explicitly upon magistrates who refused to grant the orders, and who effectively condemned abused wives to submit to continued violence. After a decade of the law's operation, critics were convinced that its administration by magistrates effectively negated the intention to offer some financial autonomy and freedom from abuse to wives. Reviewing a succession of cases illustrating judicial neglect, Mabeel Sharman Crawford concluded that judicial discretion had operated overwhelmingly against the interests of desperate women. 'Many a disfigured wife of a convicted tyrant has cause to say, as she left the magistrates' court, that when she asked for bread, she had been given a stone.'[90] Moreover, lax sentencing and refusal to grant legal relief to wives contrasted with magistrates' zeal in punishing minor offences against property. Matilda Blake's study of cases led her to the conclusion that the men of the Bench held a woman's life 'at a less value than a purse containing a few shillings'.[91]

Perusal of local newspapers afforded the critics countless examples of this kind in support of their case. Many magistrates did, indeed, give scant attention to the plight of abused and neglected wives, along with other forms of personal cruelty, especially to children and animals, so the evidence was easy to produce. For feminists it offered a dramatic illustration of the process by which men of all classes seemed to conspire in the oppression of women and would continue to do so until women became enfranchised. Violent husbands, Matilda Blake observed, were mostly poor men, but supposedly chivalric gentlemen of the upper classes, appointed by a male legislature chosen by a male electorate, acquiesced in their crimes, yet were quick to impose harsh punishments on those who took to garrotting respectable men in dark streets; such a state of mind, she argued, 'must vitiate all the relations of men with women, whether of their own ranks or of those beneath them', leading to the moral and physical degradation of men as well as women.[92]

These criticisms were powerful and persuasive, and they have been drawn upon extensively in recent analyses of feminism and marriage.[93] Essentially they illustrate the ability of stubborn magistrates, particularly unpaid justices of the peace, to frustrate legislative intentions. But it is difficult to know how generally representative these exposures were, and the picture is not as clear as most of the criticisms might suggest. Indignation against wife-abuse was also expressed by some men on the Bench, especially paid, stipendiary magistrates in urban police courts, not all of whom were as reluctant to grant separation and maintenance orders as were many of the vilified unpaid justices of the peace.

Mary Shanley has pointed out the problematic nature of much of the evidence of judicial leniency, insofar as critics rarely observed whether the wives who were refused orders had actually requested them in the first place.[94] This was clearly relevant to the outcome of cases in the Preston Police Court, where the 1878 legislation was initially explained carefully in court, and the first case in which an order was requested was adjourned for two weeks while the magistrates considered the new law.[95] In the years surveyed between 1878 and 1895 the magistrates granted orders in only 4 cases out of 55 in 1888 and 13 cases out of 44 in 1893, which might possibly suggest a growing willingness to make use of the 1878 law. But most of these cases make clear that the order was made only after an explicit request from the wife or her counsel, and in these years there were no cases reported in which a wife's request was refused if, as the law required, her husband had been convicted of aggravated assault. In most cases the order seems to have been made as a matter of course following conviction and the wife's request. The Preston experience may have been untypical, but more likely it demonstrates the continued coexistence of polarized attitudes towards marital violence. The evidence from rough music rituals gave some insight into these contradictions among working-class communities, but their persistence among governing elites requires some further explanation.

The pressure for reform achieved some success in 1895, when the Summary Jurisdiction (Married Women) Act permitted a wife to apply to magistrates' courts for separation and maintenance orders on the grounds of a husband's 'persistent cruelty', relieving wives of the need to prove aggravated assault.[96] For their legal definition of cruelty magistrates were referred to the shifting interpretation prevailing in the Divorce Court, which by this time no longer depended exclusively upon severe physical violence, thus widening the scope for wives' relief.[97] In Preston the new legislation undoubtedly led to an increase in wives' requests and magistrates' granting of separation and maintenance orders, as women routinely summoned their husbands for 'persistent cruelty'. In 1903 the court granted 30 orders out of 66 reported cases, and in 1913, 16 out of 24, despite the fact that at this time the police court missionary was facilitating the adjournment of more cases to encourage reconciliations.[98] National figures cited at the Divorce Royal Commission from 1910 confirmed that the granting of orders was substantial. There were 6,559 joint separation and maintenance orders granted to wives in 1907 in England and Wales, but without further information revealing the number of summonses this information tells us little about the extent of the relief offered to women who sought help.[99]

Despite the numbers registering a clear current of concern, the Royal Commission Majority Report tapped the equally strong sense of dissatisfaction with the facilities available to ill-treated wives. For much of the trouble it blamed unpaid and poorly qualified justices of the peace in the courts of petty sessions; these tended to be laymen who were primarily interested in petty criminal offences, and whose treatment of marital cases, unlike that of legally trained stipendiary police-court magistrates, was arbitrary and ill-informed. In some cases these magistrates granted separation orders too hastily, on slender grounds, but in others they made them too difficult to obtain, leaving wives at the mercy of brutal husbands. (For these reasons the Commission opposed the extension of divorce jurisdiction to the courts of summary jurisdiction.) But the Report also criticized the existing legislation, stressing that well over half of those separated, however dire the circumstances, were soon forced to resume cohabitation 'largely through pressure caused by the increased cost of living separately'. Successive witnesses testified that most women were unable to live and support their children on the inevitably small maintenance payments, and were thus forced to risk further ill-treatment. There was, in any case, an upper weekly limit of £2 placed on maintenance orders, which confined their operation to the 'poorer classes'.[100]

These views reflected similar ideas in much of the feminist and socialist criticism of the previous thirty years as well as the experience of police court magistrates and missionaries. All of them drew attention to the unique conditions of domestic life among the poor, where, however deplorable it might be, violence was not always the unforgivable crime it was judged to be among others. Those with close experience of living conditions among the poor were most emphatic about the ways in which poverty dictated low expectations of conjugal behaviour, resulting in women's high threshold of tolerance of rough usage so long as a bare living could be maintained.[101] The London police court missionary and prison reformer, Thomas Holmes, was convinced that the 1895 legislation prompted far more women to request separation orders, and magistrates to grant them, than before, since women could now obtain maintenance without sending their husbands to jail. But poverty continued to force such women to return to their husbands, and for many more not only poverty, but the stigma of separation, fears for their children and dogged commitment to their 'marriage lines', deterred them from seeking relief. Close acquaintance with these attitudes explained why some courts refused to jail husbands in their wives' interest, or went to such extraor-dinary lengths to encourage reconciliations rather than separations, and Holmes himself used them to justify his opposition to easier facilities for divorce among the poor.[102]

For feminists like Anna Martin, though, who had herself lived in a poor community, cultural determinants were heavily outweighed by political ones. Only women's full political and legal equality, and espe-cially their right to enforce legal contracts – like maintenance orders – against their husbands, would ultimately deter men from their 'careless and contemptuous ill-treatment'. She was among the few to insist that poor women's long-suffering tolerance of their own abuse was no excuse for doing nothing about it or for remaining content with half measures.[103] She rightly discerned that this had been the stumbling block in the many attempts to deal with domestic violence, which had so often foundered on an inability to deal with the ubiquitous individualism of the poor as well as their poverty. Lack of adequate relief for poor women undoubtedly owed more to culture and economics than it did to complacent magistrates.[104] Her analysis, though, which was derived from observation of poor communities, located the problem of violence firmly among the poor.

In this preoccupation with the moral economy of the poorest marriages, contemporary critics and reformers themselves contributed to the myth that the problem of violent conflict was confined to the very poor. Violence became one of the touchstones here for distinguishing the 'rough' from the 'respectable'. This, it should be stressed, tells us more about perceptions of the observers than the observed. Ellen Ross has shown how, among working-class women themselves, distinctions between rough and respectable were far more subtle and infinitely variable in different neighbourhoods. The maintenance of good relations with neighbours, housekeeping skills and cleanliness of her children were key factors in maintaining a woman's neighbourhood reputation.[105] It might take more than local knowledge of domestic violence for a woman to lose caste among her peers. But these subtleties only rarely informed the judgements of outsiders.

Middle-class outrage against wife-abuse among the poor certainly had a long pedigree, and many of the arguments expressed on the eve of the war can be found already fully developed by the mid-nineteenth century. As early as 1842, during debates on women's employment in coal mines, there was criticism of male miners whose wives were 're-duced to mere slaves, and then beaten by those who have sworn to cherish them'; here neglected domesticity was defined as the problem, and the transfer of wives from the pits to their proper place in the home was expected to provide the remedy.[106] But reactions ranged more widely, from vengeful demands for deterrent punishment, particularly flogging of offenders, which we saw in the response to the Haynau incident, to earnest attempts to understand the contexts of violence and reconstruct working-class marriage and serious reformist efforts intended to afford some relief to women victims. What is particularly interesting about this sustained discourse is that from the start it derived from feminists as well as from a wide range of non-feminist critics and writers. Moreover, while there were important differences of emphasis between feminists and others, the similarities are far more striking. Each demanded more severe punishment, each sought ameliorative reforms at the judicial level, and, with few exceptions, each sought understanding through analysis of the cultural determinants of violence among the poor.

By 1851 virtually the full range of later feminist arguments had been developed in a series of newspaper leaders written by John Stuart Mill and Harriet Taylor. These pieces, which reflected a heightened public interest in domestic violence in the late 1840s, foreshadowed the argu-ments on wife-beating soon to be elaborated by Taylor in her article, 'The

Enfranchisement of Women', and in Mill's later book, *The Subjection of Women*. They give some insight into the kind of cases Mill had become familiar with when, in Parliament in 1867, and in *The Subjection of Women* in 1869, he castigated the merciless abuse heaped on their wives by brutal tyrants.[107] As early as 1846 Mill and Taylor were exposing cases which illustrated judicial leniency towards male brutality. Poor women, they argued, could not expect justice from a bench or jury of men, and thus tolerated protracted 'torture' without appealing to the law.

> If justice *is* invoked, it is generally by the outraged feelings of neighbours, and if the unhappy sufferer deviates into making her inquiries known in a police court, at the next hearing she usually retracts everything; for whoever heard of a really severe punishment inflicted upon a man for any amount of brutal ill-treatment of his wife? She knows well that if the case is too clear and strong to allow of dismissing the man with a reprimand, and the woman with a piece of kind advice to be gentle and submissive, the utmost he will have to undergo is a month or two months imprisonment, to be followed by a resumption of all his former power, and her imagination can well suggest with what consequences to her.[108]

Complacency on the bench, in the face of gross assault as well as outright murder of wives, contrasted with magistrates' severity when dealing with minor property crimes. Mill and Taylor exposed one case which imposed a flogging in case the offender failed to pay a stiff fine within three days for the theft of a watch. They used the case to call for the abolition of flogging, but still noted that, if flogging was to be used at all, it should be reserved for wife-beaters. 'To such ruffians as these the degradation of corporal punishment would be very suitable. It does not make them brutes, it only stamps them as what they are.'[109]

Like later reformers, Mill and Taylor turned to the overcrowded and degraded physical conditions of the poor to explain the prevalence of domestic violence. The 'depraving influences' and 'moral evils' stemming from wretched conditions and daily suffering led the culprits to believe their actions perfectly legal and the victims to 'regard their suffering and debasement as the regular course of things, which the law sanctions and the world allows'. Worse still, violence bred violence, and the women victims sought compensation by tyrannizing over those within their own power, their children.[110] It was a grim picture, which, like later assessments, failed to explain the extensive incidence of violence among the more prosperous working class. But it did, at least, recognize that a factor in poor women's toleration of violence was the demonstrable failure of the law to provide them with real protection, and here, at least, some change could be effected.

Judges and magistrates were manifestly incapable of applying 'vigorous measures of repression to this growing evil', so in default of the judiciary Mill and Taylor appealed to the Legislature. More severe penalties 'for killing or ill-treating a wife or child' than for similar offences against others were central to their programme, so that wife-beaters could anticipate genuinely deterrent sentences and wife-murderers could not expect to have the charge reduced to manslaughter on the grounds of unintended consequences and provocation. But their research had shown conclusively that savage sentencing alone was inadequate to protect wives from vengeful husbands. Conviction for 'gross maltreatment', therefore, needed to be accompanied by legal separation and enforced maintenance from the husband.[111]

Much later experience was to demonstrate the inadequacy even of these measures, but it is striking how Mill and Taylor anticipated Frances Power Cobbe's demands by more than a quarter of a century. Unlike Cobbe's more successful demands of 1878, though, theirs preceded only half-measures, when the Aggravated Assaults Act of 1853 enabled magistrates to sentence men summarily to up to six months imprisonment for aggravated assaults on women and children, and to act on the evidence of other witnesses if the wife refused to testify.[112] Its inadequacy was underlined in a letter written by Mill in 1854, when he noted a recent case of wife-assault and attempted murder by a man who threatened to 'do worse when he went home'. After a week's remand, the magistrate, in the face of a son's allegation of his mother's 'provocation by her ill-temper', released the husband, gave him some money donated by a 'benevolent gentleman' and warned his wife 'not to make such free use of her tongue in abuse of her husband'. Was this, Mill asked, what Parliament intended in its recent efforts to protect wives?[113] His question was to echo through the rest of the century, and underlined the weaknesses in legal-judicial remedies.

It is interesting to compare Mill and Taylor's analysis to that of a contemporary without the impulse of the same feminist ideals. J. W. Kaye, Mill's successor at the India Office,[114] wrote in 1855 advocating divorce law reform, and claimed that the 1853 legislation had provided 'ample protection for the time' to poor women suffering from personal violence.[115] But a year later, after a debate in Parliament on a bill advocating the flogging of wife-beaters, Kaye had second thoughts, and devoted a long article to violent 'outrages' on poor women. Unlike Mill and Taylor, Kaye acknowledged that sexual antagonism was common in most marriages, with tension bordering on violence rarely far from the surface, even among the middle and upper classes. But poverty and appalling living conditions rendered the problem intolerable among the poor. It was thus incumbent upon the more fortunate to understand the temptations suffered by the poor, which led wives to provoke husbands and husbands to respond with violent outbursts. Kaye even argued that such brutalized conditions required compassion to be extended to the beaters as well as the beaten. For the wife, faced with an impossible task of housework and child-care in miserable housing, it was a miracle if she was not always in a 'chronic state of irritation'. In this state of resentment she encountered her husband, 'who is bringing home his own load of aggravations, and who has no conception of, and no sympathy with hers. Each regards the lot of the other as one of comparative ease and felicity.' In this atmosphere the wife, driven by her 'sense of superiority', which rendered her 'harsh and exacting', inevitably turned to nagging, and her husband, spurred on by drink, 'closes the argument by knocking her down, and kicking her as she lies at his feet'.[116]

After this analysis Kaye insisted that legislative remedies could offer little hope of protecting wives from violence. Prison sentences for husbands penalized women by depriving them of a livelihood and exposing them to later revenge. For the same reason he opposed flogging. He had already detected signs of a male backlash against women taking their complaints to the courts, and cited one case of a gathering of men outside the police court, loudly intimidating a woman victim.[117] Flogging would only increase such threats, might urge neighbouring women to ostracize the wife 'who swears her husband's back into a jelly', and thus deter injured women even further from bringing complaints. To prevent violence the reform of the social conditions which provoked it was essential. Some improvement could be expected from wider employment opportunities for women, affording them greater independence and lessening the temptations to imprudent, financially motivated marriages. But ultimately Kaye urged that the solution rested with wives themselves. Though anxious not to say 'that her sufferings are brought upon herself by her own sins of omission', that is, blaming the victim, he nevertheless saw poor women's own deficiencies in background and training as the root causes of violent discord. The great majority were unfit for 'making home happy'; their gossiping and idling led to neglect of homes and husbands, compounded by ignorance of cooking, darning, washing and household management. Competent housewives would be the best deterrent against violence, and taking his cue from a recent prescriptive text for working-class wives, Margaret Brewster's *Sunbeams in the Cottage*,[118] Kaye urged the rich to teach household skills to the poor without, like Mrs Pardiggle, patronizing them. Together with more spacious, suburban housing, and public nurseries to offer much-needed infant care, women's self-improvement and domesticity offered the key to reformed working-class marriage.[119]

These themes recurred in most discussions of domestic violence well into Edwardian years. In Parliament they appeared with predictable regularity each time members advanced new proposals to increase punishment for wife-beaters or provide relief for women victims. Central to all these arguments was the moral economy of poor families, which often led wives to defend their own attackers, and invariably meant that the husband's punishment might fall even harder on the wife. Hence, in 1853 in the debate on the Aggravated Assaults billl, advocates of longer summary sentences stressed the deterrent effect of certain, speedy punishment, which limited the intimidatory pressures exerted on wives to withdraw charges if magistrates sent the case to the Assizes. They also opposed an amendment to impose flogging on the grounds that it would deter women from complaining. Lord Palmerston, for example, spoke of the certain retribution complaining wives would face from both husbands and the local community if thhey exposed men to the lash, itself a brutalizing measure. By contrast, thhe supporters of flogging insisted on the economic hardship imposed on wives when husbands' wages were withdrawn for six months, invariably forcing them and their children into the workhouse, and, again, deterring complaints. Flogging was the only appropriate treatment for such degraded brutes as wife-beaters.[120]

Advocates of flogging made a further unsuccessful attempt to amend the law with a bill introduced by Lewis Dillwyn, the MP for Swansea, in 1856, when, they claimed, the new legislation had been ineffective, producing an average of only one conviction a day in the metropolitan districts. Again horrific details of the worst cases were repeated from the newspapers; again the chief attention focused on the plight of the long-suffering wife who tolerated appaallling amounts of rough usage, but who was herself penalized when she finally complained.[121] But Dillwyn himself betrayed a further preoccupation when he referred to a meeting of women at Leicester who had sent a petition condemning such a 'barbarous and obsolete mode of punishment', which would only result in 'further brutalizing and demoralizing those that came under its lash'. Dillwyn dismissed such complaints as irrelevant because the issue was 'a man's question' above all else.

> It concerned the character of our own sex, that we should repress these unmanly assaults; and he believed that upon the men who committed them they had a worse and more injurious effect than they had upon the women who endured them.[122]

Middle-class manliness, denoting protectiveness and benevolence to women, as well as undisputed power, was thus compromised by the unruly men of the lower classes. Such uneasiness about men's conjugal reputation, implying a challenge to the legitimacy of husbands' patriarchal rule, helps to explain the sustained attempts to reform men's behaviour in marriage, particularly when feminist criticism kept forcing the issue onto public notice. As we will see in Part II, other publicity could easily expose errant behaviour of middle-class husbands as well, and these concerns of legislators with the 'character of our own sex' hint at wider preoccupations. Might they, for example, mask displaced fears about their own behaviour? The evidence for such connections is never explicit, but the strength of the preoccupation suggests its plausibility.

By the 1850s virtually all the arguments had surfaced that were to be used two decades later in the campaign to give greater protection to women. These arguments, emanating from the mainstream press and Parliament as much as from feminists, focused overwhelmingly on the context of the culture of poverty, despite occasional admissions that the problem was much more socially pervasive. A further legislative attempt to introduce flogging, by Lord Leigh in 1874, rehearsed all the same arguments, and recited appalling cases of poor husbands '"digging" the women with wooden clogs tipped and heeled with iron'.[123] Only the poor were capable of such atrocities, and reconstruction of the marriages of the poor offered the only obvious solution to the problem.

Such arguments, of course, could be used to justify inaction as well as reform. For the more cynical, like the *Saturday Review*, the impenetrable culture of the poor, where 'wife-beating and child-starving are facts that cannot be interfered with', meant that there was little more to be done beyond flogging of the worst offenders, if only because it suited the 'law of retaliation'.[124] By 1877, shortly before Cobbe's campaign effected more substantial reform, Edward Cox, the Recorder of Portsmouth, who stressed his considerable experience of dealing with domestic cases on the Bench, voiced his impatience with the entire obsession with wife-beating. It had, he complained, become a pet subject of journalists 'looking for subjects to write about and sighing for a sensation'. They invariably pontificated about the need to inflict the most extreme penalties, particularly flogging. His own experience convinced him that the sensational and gushing leading articles were founded on fantasy, for it was a rare case that matched the 'pen and ink picture of the loving wife and submissive slave brutally beaten by her brutal husband'. Instead the 'suffering angel' was invariably a virago

> who has made her husband's home an earthly hell, who spends his earnings in drink, pawns his furniture, starves her children, provides for no meals, lashes him with her tongue when sober and with her fists when drunk, and if he tries to restrain her fits of passion, resists with a fierceness and strength for which he is no match. He is labouring all day to feed and clothe her and when he returns home at night this is his greeting.

All the critics, Cox insisted, rarely bothered to inquire into the provocations that led to the subsequent violence. Unprovoked brutal assaults on helpless women deserved high punishment, but 'happily for the honour of manhood they are very rare'.[125]

Cox's forthright victim-blaming was not unusual in analyses of domestic conflict, nor was the traditional model of combative marriage on
which it was based. At the time of the Licensing Act, in 1902, there was
further discussion of the problem of the drunken wife destroying the
home, neglecting her children and driving her hard-working husband to
violence in his desperation to be rid of her.[126] But what is more striking is
the similarity of much of Cox's analysis to that of reformers who later
attacked his views. Frances Power Cobbe, for example, saw the brutalized victim, rather than the combative virago, as the essence of the
problem, but she too confined her analysis to the very poor.[127] Each
stressed that because violence was rooted in the context of the 'wretched'
homes of the poor, it needed special judicial handling, which might not
be appropriate to other classes. For Cox all the wives who in court blithely
denied their husbands' violence after their anger had subsided pointed
to the only responsible course for magistrates in such cases, which was to
encourage reconciliation, rather than to sentence the husband and de-
prive the wife of a livelihood. His own practice in court was invariably to
lecture the couple at length, warning them of the consequences of their
quarrels, until he extracted promises of amendment. Binding the husband over in recognizances of good behaviour usually ensured that the
couple did not reappear in court, and, for Cox, that was the only
responsible judicial course to follow.[128] We have already seen that the
same policy was followed by other magistrates, eventually aided by a
force of police court missionaries, on very similar grounds, always with
reference to the special conditions of marriage among the poor.[129] Its
outcome, of course, was the precise form of lenient sentencing which so
many reformers deplored.

Frances Power Cobbe's campaign of 1878 was crucial in shifting the
emphasis in discussion of wife-abuse from punishment and reconciliation to protection and financial independence for the wife, although even
this echoed Mill and Taylor's earlier proposal. We saw earlier how her
argument stressed the model of wife as victim among the poor; unlike
Cox, she had never discovered the 'Ideal Wife-beater', a man driven to
blind rage by a drunken harpy. By contrast she was able to produce a long
list of the atrocities brutal husbands had recently perpetrated upon their
defenceless wives.[130] Her strategy was brilliantly effective in mustering
the crucial support so vital for successful reform. But it also provides an
instructive example of the interplay between feminist agitation on the
one hand, and opinion in the mainstream press, founded on more
conservative and paternalist assumptions, on the other.

Cobbe's well-known article, 'Wife-Torture in England', appeared in
the April 1878 issue of the *Contemporary Review*, and has been widely
credited with being the inspiration for the Matrimonial Causes Act of the

same year, giving magistrates the power to grant separation and maintenance orders to assaulted wives.[131] Her active involvement with the bill, extending to direct organization of its drafting and sponsorship in Parliament, was certainly crucial to its form and success, but most of this had been effected before her article appeared, the debates mainly occurring in February and March, and Royal Assent being granted in May.[132] Cobbe noted in April that Mr Alfred Hill, a Birmingham JP, had already prepared a draft bill,[133] and it is clear that well before April she had been exposing the same evils and agitating for reform. By January 1878, her letters to the *Spectator* had stimulated a debate on wife-beating in its correspondence columns.[134] It seems likely that this attracted the attention of Henry Labouchere, the editor of the decidedly non-feminist weekly, *Truth*, where an earlier summary of Cobbe's article was published anonymously under the title 'Wife-Torture'. In barely three columns this listed many of the same cases detailed in the later piece, stressed the same sadistic characteristics of the culprits and proposed the same protective reforms for wives.[135] It drew on similar themes which had already appeared in the *Women's Suffrage Journal*, to which Cobbe was a contributor. But Cobbe's choice of Labouchere's journal to publicize her views needs some explanation.

On the surface Labouchere was a most unlikely ally for a feminist campaigner like Cobbe. In Parliament and in his journal, 'Labby's' radicalism concentrated on needling the privileged classes, but never extended to any sympathy for women's rights activists, and certainly not for purity campaigners. He is best known for his amendment to the 1885 Criminal Law Amendment Act, which added a two-year prison sentence for acts of male homosexuality to a bill concerned with the age of consent and white slave traffic. F. B. Smith has plausibly attributed the apparent incongruence to Labouchere's intentions to sabotage the entire bill by rendering it ridiculous.[136] This is quite consistent with his stinging attacks on the unladylike activities of Josephine Butler and other purity campaigners in their disruptive tactics against the Indian Contagious Diseases Acts.[137] His hostility to women's suffragists was mostly crude and frivolous, and never engaged seriously with their arguments ('sex will be abolished, and we shall have an uprising of sexless beings . . .').[138]

But in other respects Labouchere's muck-racking journalism lent itself aptly to Cobbe's campaign. One of his chief targets for regular vilification was the 'Great Unpaid', those magistrates who summarily inflicted severe sentences for minor property crimes but imposed derisory fines for the most brutal forms of personal violence. Like Cobbe, too, his attacks extended to inadequate sentencing for cruelty to animals.[139] But his greatest venom was directed at those magistrates who failed to take wife-beating seriously. Many of the cases he exposed were sent in from his 'lady readers', and other correspondence from both sympathetic and offended magistrates suggests that his charges gained a wide currency.[140] He welcomed both the 1878 and 1895 reforms (the first 'a step towards cheap and easy divorce') as measures likely to repress wife-beating and offer wives some escape from brutal husbands, but also asked whether it was 'not time that magistrates also amended their ways, and ceased to treat aggravated assaults with such misplaced leniency?'[141]

Labouchere's merciless lampooning of the 'Great Unpaid' predated Cobbe's campaign and continued for years beyond the controversies surrounding the reforms of 1878 and 1895. His exposure of inconsistencies in sentencing for domestic assaults and petty property crimes echoed similar feminist outrage regularly expressed in the *Women's Suffrage Journal*.[142] A typical contrast came from the Malling bench in 1892, where a husband who brutally assaulted his pregnant wife was given a fine of £1 plus costs or fifteen days, and was bound over to keep the peace, while his wife was refused a separation order; at the same time a man who had poached two rabbits was fined £2 plus costs or one month. Labouchere observed:

> It will be seen that a considerable amount of brutality is required to constitute an aggravated wife assault in the eyes of the Malling magistrates, even though the victim be in a condition which should protect her from the violence of all except the most savage and callous of husbands, in fact their worships treat the poaching of a couple of rabbits as a rather more heinous crime than a ruffianly attack on a pregnant woman.[143]

By 1892 Labouchere's revelations had become sufficiently frequent to justify a routine feature, which he dubbed his 'Legal Pillory', and hoped would give greater prominence to 'magisterial follies and eccentricities', thus encouraging reform in the magisterial system.[144] Week after week parallel columns effectively contrasted magistrates' token sentencing for savage assaults on women, children and animals with long prison sentences imposed for petty theft, 'sleeping out', and on runaway apprentice sailors in Grimsby. With such routine reports it is not surprising that Labouchere seized every opportunity to expose any personal misbehaviour of magistrates which called their judicial suitability into question. When, in 1895, the Divorce Court granted the wife of a Kidderminster carpet manufacturer a judicial separation from her husband for violent attacks causing serious injury, Labouchere noted that

> the gentleman accused of this brutality is a Kidderminster magistrate, an ex-Mayor of the borough, and a County Councillor for Worcester. His constituents will doubtless, in due course consider the question whether he is a worthy representative to return to a public body. For my own part, I shall watch with special interest to see what sort of justice Mr Green deals out to wife beaters.[145]

It was left for feminists like Matilda Blake to make the political connection between poor working-class wife-beaters and their far from guiltless lenient judges, appointed by male legislators elected on an exclusively male franchise.[146] Labouchere saw little merit in such connections. But his more implicit connection between a defective magistracy and leniency to rough usage among the poor was no less effective for that. It was, for him, appalling evidence of the failure of some men of all classes to live up to proper standards of manliness, measured by chivalrous protection of the weak, especially women, whom husbands promised to protect in return for obedience. In this light his praise for all the protective matrimonial legislation urged by feminists, his savage indictment of incompetent magistrates obsessed with the sanctity of property and his scorn for the political dimensions of feminism were perfectly consistent. But his regular publicity was only the most strident among weekly and daily newspapers expressing outrage against the marital misconduct of poor working-class men and their lenient treatment by the courts. It gave popular articulation to the anxieties of both feminist and paternalist reformers, which had been developing in intensity since mid-century. The process is an interesting example of how, in the intersection of feminist and paternalist agendas for reform, each enabled the other to be heard more effectively.

The outcome of this conjuncture, though, was less successful than might have been expected. The late-Victorian and Edwardian outpouring of reformist literature on marriage in journals like the *Westminster Review*, the revelations of social investigators and the agonizings of conscientious magistrates and court officials at the Royal Commission on Divorce, with few exceptions continued to treat violence as a problem unique to the very poor. Reform, they argued, could only be effective if it recognized the constraints of the moral economy of poor families. For this reason the proposed solutions all worked within a context which assumed that reconciliation was preferable to separation. This approach had always dominated legal and judicial thinking on marriage, and while significant breaches had been made in it by Edwardian years, as late as 1937 the extension of grounds for divorce were accompanied by extension of the machinery of conciliation to 'keep failing marriages alive', which was the only effective political rationale for successful divorce law reform.[147] Against this ideology, the voices of feminists like Anna Martin, who demanded more fundamental legal equality for women as a precondition to effective marital reform, made little progress.[148]

We have seen that some writers, like Edward Cox, blamed women's behaviour for precipitating marital conflict among the poor. But the great majority of critics, regardless of their political colour, were united in identifying men's misconduct as the fundamental source of the trouble. The long history of reformist literature on domestic violence is very largely that of a discourse which progressively defined male behaviour as a social problem to be analysed and regulated, whether by ameliorative reform, more severe punishment, cultural change or thorough-going sexual equality. For paternalists the stimulus came from threats to traditional standards of manliness, which were most crucially defined by humane and protective treatment of women. For feminists violence was a symptom of more fundamental sexual inequality. For both the misconduct of poor working-class men provided fertile ground for analysis, protest and reform, but the exclusive focus on the lives of the poor eventually had to confront disturbing evidence that domestic violence was socially more diffused. The evidence presented by the Women's Co-operative Guild at the Royal Commission on Divorce demanded help for those most ignored by protective legislation: the 'more intelligent and thrifty' respectable working-class women, more likely to be wives of skilled workers.[149] Moreover, criticism of a callous and lenient judiciary made uncomfortable connections across the social spectrum which suggested that the problem extended well beyond the very poor. Commentators preoccupied with the failings of middle-class marriage and the inadequacies of divorce legislation for women, as Part II will illustrate, were acutely conscious of this, although the critique of middle-class husbands never made violence a central metaphor for marital conflict to the same extent it did for the poor. At a deeper level all this was part of a wider discourse which called the fundamentals of male power in patriarchal marriage into question. But as an attempt to control domestic violence the narrowly defined class dimensions of the debate, confining most of the analysis to the purportedly unique culture of the poor, doomed the reforms to be little more than half measures.

Part II

MIDDLE-CLASS MARRIAGE

INTRODUCTION

The marriages discussed in the following chapters range broadly over time from the early nineteenth to the early twentieth century. Changes affecting the structure and ideology of the middle-class family were accelerating rapidly over these years, so we should expect the experiences we encounter to be marked by diversity. The traditional idea and practice of the unity of work and household where the wife was an informal partner, her legal personality absorbed in that of her husband (by the common-law doctrine of couverture) was rapidly giving way to a family ideal governed by principles of separate spheres, in which, while married women's legal status remained unaltered at first, family life was elevated in importance, and the home, overseen by dependent wives, provided a refuge for husbands, as household heads, from the separate place of work.[1]

In this Part we will see examples of both these models, some which fall between the two ends of the spectrum, and some which resemble more modern structures. Clergymen, for example, spent much time at home, and their wives, though usually thoroughly domesticated, were often intimately caught up in the work of the parish. The variations in the division of labour within the family were thus complex, and we cannot assume too easily that marital conflict was invariably the consequence of the most obvious structural gendered inequalities. Nevertheless the evangelical emphasis on domesticity elevated motherhood and the moral power of women to a point that was inconsistent with their total subordination. This could not help but feed doubts about husbands' supreme authority, which emerged whenever feminists challenged women's subordinate legal status in campaigns over child custody, married women's property and divorce.

What follows, though, is concerned less with the famous campaigns than with more ordinary women whose challenges to their husbands' authority did eventually make an impact upon public perceptions of marriage. The process is most obvious in the cases from the Divorce Court, where wives who accused their husbands of cruelty eventually influenced judges to liberalize the law and others to debate it. When judges shifted their focus in dealing with legal cruelty from the nature of the offence to its effect on the victim, they began to concede the demands of aggrieved wives for some recognition as autonomous individuals. The women's demands, while more implicit and less sensational, paralleled the dramatic claims of Sophia Jex-Blake and others for recognition as 'persons', in such struggles as that for admission to medical education.[2] Other examples of conjugal tensions illustrate ways in which contradictions flowing from the inequalities of separate spheres provoked women's resistance from the outset. As with working-class marriages, private contest soon translated into public discourse and fed the reforming agendas of conservatives and feminists alike, who, when faced with husbands' abuse of power, could find themselves in surprising agreement about the need for reform. Criticism of men's tyrannical abuse of their familial power, combined with a heightened appreciation of the benefits of marital companionship, was bound to lead to some questioning of standards of masculinity in marriage. The fact that most critics restricted their reform proposals to civilizing men's patriarchal power rather than eliminating it, limited the scope of the changes which followed, but for all that the critique reflected profound changes in attitudes to marital authority and laid the groundwork for more far-reaching campaigns and changes in the future.

The most important demographic change affecting middle-class family life in the second half of the nineteenth century was, of course, the beginning of the sharp decline in the birth-rate. This change, like others, was variable, and initially most pronounced among professional families like those of doctors and the clergy.[3] The change was undoubtedly linked in some ways to the higher standards of marriage and motherhood which accompanied the evangelical imperative. Smaller families accompanied higher expectations of companionate relations and more intense parental focus on fewer children, for which more exacting standards of domestic behaviour were essential from both partners. These developments may often have formed a shadowy, unstated, set of assumptions behind many of the marital grievances expressed by wives in the Divorce Court. Complaints directly relating to birth-control practices are rare, but it is helpful to keep in mind the wider demographic context during the more explicit discussion of middle-class marital conflict which follows.

COMPANIONATE MARRIAGE AND THE CHALLENGE TO PATRIARCHY

PRESCRIPTIVE LITERATURE AND THE RISE IN EXPECTATIONS

The comfortable assumption that marital violence was a problem peculiar to the lower orders often left middle- and upper-class commentators basking in their own complacent sense of self-congratulation. Only in the later years of the nineteenth century did some awareness of the incidence of violence among the middle class begin to develop. Even Frances Power Cobbe, who did so much to expose the savage treatment meted out to their wives by poor labourers, was ambivalent about the conduct of educated husbands. Admitting that wife-assault existed among the upper and middle classes 'rather more' than was generally recognized, she nevertheless felt it was mostly innocuous, rarely extending 'to anything beyond an occasional blow or two of a not dangerous kind'. Still she saw the most puzzling paradox to be the indifference of civilized men, habitually protective of their own women, to the suffering of the abused women of the poor:

> How does it come to pass that while the better sort of Englishmen are thus exceptionally humane and considerate to women, the men of the lower class of the same nation are proverbial for their unparalleled brutality, till wife-beating, wife-torture and wife-murder have become the opprobrium of the land?[1]

This did not mean that middle-class marriage escaped critical scrutiny; indeed, the virtual industry of marital prescription throughout the nineteenth century was premised on assumptions that many husbands and wives found the advice difficult to follow, and that companionship and harmony in marriage was an elusive goal. But the problems defined by prescriptive writers were of a different order to those found in the 'dingy courts' of London and Lancashire. In 1856, when the prospect of divorce law reform was in the air, J. W. Kaye, in his discussion of domestic violence among the poor, found little to admire in the marital behaviour of wealthier men:

Men of education and refinement do not strike women; neither do they strike one another. This is not their mode of expressing resentment. They may utter words more cutting than sharp knives; they may do things more stunning in their effects on the victim than the blows of pokers or hammers; they may half kill their wives by process of slow torture – unkindness, infidelity, whatever shape it may assume – society will forgive them. The law, too, has nothing to say to them. They are not guilty of what is recognized as an assault, because they only assail the affections – only lacerate the heart. They speak with horror of the 'brutal wretches' who inflict on women blows, less painful at the time, and less abiding in their effects. But is their treatment of women any better than these ruffians? Have they any higher sense of what is due to womanhood? . . . If we would see the worst type of man's cruelty to woman, we must not go into the police courts, where women with dishevelled hair and disfigured faces give painful evidence against their husbands, but into the best streets of London after nightfall, where the unspeaking and unspeakable evidence meets us at every turn.[2]

For Kaye the common source of evils perpetrated by rich and poor alike was 'an utter disregard for the sufferings of women'.[3] This was more than a simple lament for the tragedies of a minority of hard cases. His criticism hints simultaneously at a higher standard of marital expectations and a sense that companionate marriage among the middle and upper class too often was seen to have failed to live up to popular ideals. The same recognition informed debates on divorce law reform[4] and the sustained outpouring of marriage advice literature. By the 1850s idealists, as well as reformers, had succeeded in constructing middle-class marriage, and the behaviour of husbands and wives, as a problem, ripe for scrutiny, debate and reform.

The discovery that companionship and mutuality in bourgeois marriage was problematic was not unique to the nineteenth century. Marriage advice literature since before the Reformation reflected similar preoccupations and contradictions; Puritan concern for husbands' dominance, for example, vied with ideals of shared domesticity.[5] This should not be surprising if Jeffrey Minson is right to claim that the very notion of criticism and reform of the family was coeval with the origin of the family itself.[6] But despite the continuity some clear changes of emphasis emerged in the nineteenth century. It is not simply that the change was relative rather than absolute, although that certainly seems to be true of the greater intensity with which Victorians came to debate marital conduct. But by the 1850s a great deal more evidence of marital discord, such as daily news of divorce cases, was becoming available for discussion, so that private behaviour became a subject of everyday public scrutiny.

The long continuity in the discourse of marital prescription presents some difficulties for the much-discussed transition from patriarchal to companionate marriage advanced by Lawrence Stone and others.[7] But at this point my concern is less with Stone's conception of the changing nature of actual married life than with the particular direction taken by prescriptive literature on marriage by the nineteenth century. Susan Okin has argued that, whatever changes may have occurred in actual family life, there was a 'distinct shift in ideology' towards the ideal of the 'domesticated sentimental family', or companionate marriage, by the eighteenth century. She found that eighteenth- and early-nineteenth-century political theorists took for granted this ideal of the family, selectively ignoring seventeenth-century individualism and reinforcing patriarchal relations by constructing women's nature as sentimental and domestic.[8] Prescriptive texts, moulded for more deliberately propagandistic purposes, served a similar function, especially in their persistent emphasis on the virtues of separate spheres and their assumptions of husbands' supreme authority.

Recent research has done much to clarify the role of early-nineteenth-century prescriptive texts in the formation of domestic ideology and the promotion of separate spheres. Most valuable is Davidoff and Hall's analysis, in *Family Fortunes*, not simply of writers' preoccupation with women's training for domesticity and subordination, but also with the 'social power' they could exercise in the domestic sphere. By the middle of the century the foremost popular exponent of this dualism, of the 'tension between subordination and influence, between moral power and political silence', was Mrs Sarah Stickney Ellis, who, Davidoff and Hall show, purveyed a democratized notion of domesticity to all strata of the middle class.[9] Her series dealing with the women, mothers, wives and daughters of England was only the most popular of a long list of publications including short stories, serialized novels, other advice books and periodicals, all promoting a proper training in domesticity for women.[10] This training, though, had to prepare women as well for the hazards of relationships with men, and Ellis devoted much of her advice to methods for promoting harmony between the sexes and avoiding the worst forms of marital conflict. In doing so she offered a persuasive diagnosis of the tensions of married life commonly experienced among the middle class.

The discourse of female subordination, which pervaded so much advice literature, was premised on assumptions about male perfection which were bound to strain credibility. Ellis was at her most eloquent in her descriptions of the 'power and sublimity . . . approaching what we believe to be the nature and capacity of angels' in a 'noble, enlightened, and truly good man'. It was a high privilege, a 'perpetual feast' to 'dwell within the influence of such a man', and listen to his conversation, 'but to

75

be admitted into his heart, – to share his counsels, and to be the chosen companion of his joys and sorrows' required humility and gratitude. But after this high rhetoric the reader was hurriedly brought down to earth with the reminder that if all men were so faultless 'these pages might be given to the winds'.[11] For women yet to marry the crucial distinction was between reasonable and unreasonable men. The former were 'impartial and comprehensive', open to persuasion and conviction, but the unreasonable acted simply according to their will and were beyond argument or opposition. Once cursed with such an unreasonable husband, a woman had little choice but to make a study of 'the patience of Job', or, in the famous phrase from *The Daughters of England*, to 'suffer and be still'.[12] Precisely for that reason she devoted an immense proportion of her writing, fictional and didactic, to the education of girls for what she insisted was the most crucial decision of their lives, the choice of a suitable husband. One serious error in that quest would result in a lifetime not of pleasant submission, which should be the norm, but of patient suffering and unhappy martyrdom.

A woman who chose wisely, though, still had to navigate a treacherous conjugal path, for even the noblest men had faults, which would soon imperil married life. The blame for this was shared by 'foolish and indulgent mothers' and the culture of public schools, 'where the influence, the character, and the very name of woman was a by-word for contempt'.[13] Hence, men, selfish by misguided training, instinct and the dictates of a demanding public occupation, required ministration by dutiful wives who were capable of anticipating their needs if harmony was to prevail. Conflict was never far from the surface, and Ellis enjoined wives to avoid it by recognizing 'the inalienable right of all men, whether ill or well, rich or poor, wise or foolish, to be treated with deference and made much of in their own houses'.[14] Ellis, and her literary colleagues, seem to have concluded that for women this was the crux of the problem, since they so often lamented the failure of women to practise the kind of deference that would pacify their selfish husbands.

Wives' deference to their husbands, though, was inseparable from the context of their nominal responsibility for management of the domestic sphere, for household organization and weekly budgeting, and this invariably raised questions of the propriety of managing husbands themselves. A household which was run on principles of strict economy, for example, could be undermined by men's habitual fondness for 'personal indulgences', which, Ellis thought, were fair recompense for their labours. But the wife was left with a dilemma:

It would, indeed, be a hard thing to refuse to the husband who returns home from his desk, his counter, or his fields, the best seat, or the choicest food, with any other indulgences his circumstances may afford. Here, however, in certain families, exists a great difficulty; for some men, and I need not say they are of the *unreasonable* class, are determined to have the indulgences, and yet are unwilling to incur the expense. From their habit of disregarding things in detail, and looking upon them only as a whole, they are utterly unconscious of the importance of every little addition in the shape of luxury, to the general sum; and thus the wife is placed in the painful dilemma, either of denying her husband the gratification of his tastes and wishes, or of bearing all the blame of conducting her household expenses on too extravagant a scale.

Ellis usually followed such passages with soothing words about the need to respect all husbands, foolish or wise, to minister to their dignity as well as comfort and so on, but she could not escape the tendency for women in such difficulties to resort to humouring and manipulation. An 'artful woman' could practise a 'mean and degrading system' of management of her husband. Through control of her temper, 'servile and flattering subserviency in little things', she could avoid conflict and get her own way, 'when a single rash or hasty word, especially if it implied an assumption of the right to choose, would have effectually defeated their ends'.[15]

Much as Ellis deplored the 'utterly revolting' habit of managing and manipulating husbands,[16] like other prescriptive writers she had to face the implication that dilemmas arising from their management of a household led them to deceive the husbands they had vowed to obey. She acknowledged, for example, that many women lived in sheer terror of their husbands, fearing to take any initiative in the household lest they should disapprove, but argued that, by nature rather than circumstance, wives were just as likely to defy them and get their own way,

for there seems to be a natural tenacity of purpose – a certain wiryness in the spirit of woman, proportioned to her wishes, whatever they may be; so that, by hook or by crook, as the saying is, she manages for the most part to bring about the event upon which her heart is set.[17]

There was a tension here between the natural moral power of women, which Ellis praised, and their tendency to deceive and manipulate. But so much of her writing acknowledged that the 'unreasonable' characteristics of men warranted some management, and that increased happiness required that 'men should let these things [i.e. domestic matters] alone', that it is hard not to conclude that she felt that management was preferable to open conflict or defiance.[18] Defiance, indeed, was the deadly sin of wives' conduct, lowering them as well as their husbands, and much of her advice was directed to the folly of wives who refused to submit to their husbands and humour them in a way which might ensure the harmonious coexistence of separate spheres.[19]

Ellis's consistent emphasis on submission to husbands is ironic in the light of her private views. Before her own marriage she often referred sardonically to the 'lords of creation', but was more frank about the faithful and enduring affection binding some women to their 'lordly inferiors who nothing but themselves have ever loved, and to whose capricious and selfish wishes they are willing and delighted to administer'.[20] On the eve of her own marriage, at 38, to the missionary, William Ellis, she questioned his ability to cope with her strong will and accustomed independence, and was quick to rebuke him for the 'unreasonable' demands he made on her time.[21] Five years later she informed a friend that the writer, Anna Jameson, an 'irreproachable woman', had separated from her husband. 'There seems to be no luck with authoress wives,' she commented; 'Mary Howitt and I have stood it out yet – but there is no saying what may come!'[22] Such prospects were the harsh backdrop against which Ellis moulded her prescription to wives of patient submission, even to the most selfish husbands. It was their task to create a higher standard of companionship in marriage, to forestall the ever-present reality of power struggles between husbands and wives, constant bickering, and mutual antipathy; it was also their duty to suppress the very discontents and desires for purpose and independence that Ellis herself was unable to resist. Her austere prescriptions actually reflected women's heightened expectations of the quality of marital companionship, but, by contrast, her discouraging descriptions of marital experience mirrored the more realistic contradictions in a form of companionate marriage still based on separate spheres and patriarchal authority.

Writers before and after Ellis, as Davidoff and Hall have shown, went to great lengths to construct a domestic idyll based on sexual difference and the complementary virtues of benevolent manliness and compliant femininity.[23] But again much of the prescription relied upon a negative reading of marital behaviour, marking a general concern that more young women and men were entering the lower middle class, and thus needed advice on domestic conduct to promote family harmony.[24] For Elizabeth Sandford the common sight of 'ill-assorted marriages', mostly based on wives' failure to cultivate the 'feminine' virtues of obedience and dependence on their husbands, was sufficient incentive to dispense her advice. It was woman's duty to make the sacrifice of adaptation, she wrote. 'She must, in a certain degree, be plastic herself, if she would mould others.'[25] Ann Taylor's advice to both husbands and wives to cultivate domestic virtues together, to exercise forbearance and respect for each other's spheres, raised the constant spectre of the consequences of failure. The 'uncouth' sight of husbands and wives 'struggling for power' contrasted with the admirable 'influence' of a wife 'acquired by amiable conduct and self-command'. A woman 'who can tyrannize over her husband' would do the same with children and servants, and a man, who should certainly be 'master in his own house', would nevertheless bring his home to misery if he treated his wife as a slave, failed to support her attempts at economy, was extravagant, took his pleasures away from the home circle, and failed to take her into his confidence about his business affairs.[26]

Some writers acknowledged the great difficulties for both spouses in living up to their exalted ideals. Most advice to women on the choice of husbands, for example, usually expanded on the difficulties for men of accommodating domesticity to the demands of a profession. One such guide insisted that only consistent religious principle could prompt a man to the necessary patience, tenderness and attention demanded by domestic life, dispose both parties to 'mutual concessions and forbearance, and prompt them to share each other's burdens with alacrity and ease'. This posed a problem for a woman seeking a husband, who needed to find some proof of his 'domestic inclinations' and his ability to spend time at home, yet not be tempted to marry a weak man 'in the hopes of governing him'. In that event her own authority would simply erupt in 'numberless petty instances of tyranny and caprice' to her own disadvantage, while the quality showing her to best advantage was 'a modest submission of her understanding' to the man of her choice.[27]

Few professions, though, according to the same writer, afforded the conditions to ensure that a man could adequately cultivate and share his domestic pleasures. Military men were too subject to dissolute temptations and frequent absences, the income of physicians was too uncertain, the law 'begets an unpleasant spirit of cavilling and contradiction' inconsistent with nursing the 'finer feelings'; if successful, lawyers, too, were unlikely to be often at home. Finally, a country gentleman was too prone to be more attached to his dogs, horses and hunting than his wife, and would be oblivious to her needs. This left the clergy, and the clergyman author had no hesitation in recommending his profession to be the most suitable source of domesticated husbands. Their calling was the most regular and retired, exempt from the bustle and competitiveness of the world, preserving innocence, sensibility, integrity and virtue. A clergyman could best appreciate and enhance married happiness, with leisure for 'the tender offices of friendship, and the little sportive playfulness of amusing conversation'; more importantly he would have time to superintend the instruction of his children, 'calling their latent powers into exercise and action'.[28] The preference for men's regular presence at home was at odds with messages in some prescriptive texts written by women, who recognized the potential aggravation that could be provoked by men constantly interfering with the running of the household, raising, again, the delicate issue of management of husbands.[29] But the issue of men's domestic presence remained one of symbolic importance for the health of companionate marriage.

If only clergymen could fulfil women's heightened expectations of companionship in marriage, then the prospect was bleak for those seeking partners worthy of the new standards of domesticated manliness. The advice may seem comic to us, but it underlined the more general emphasis in prescriptive literature that greater emotional expectations made marriage a much more hazardous venture for both parties, where self-control became a prime qualification for success. The catalogue of defects which writers drew on to illustrate the dangers symbolized the greater stress on emotional compatibility: in men, a tyrannical abuse of their legitimate authority, in women overt defiance or subversive management and manipulation of husbands for selfish ends. While increased attention was being given to proper standards of manliness, there seems little doubt that the mass of writing promoting domestic ideology during the first half of the nineteenth century focused more on women's behaviour, deploring excessive self-assertion and independence. Some such criticism may well have been a nervous response to controversies stimulated by women like Caroline Norton, who voiced their complaints in public and were mostly vilified for it.[30]

All this was prime grist for the mill of mid-Victorian satire, when no caricature of marriage was complete without the traditional defiant, nagging wife wearing the breeches, and a diminutive, hen-pecked husband. *Punch* best exemplified the early-Victorian version of the genre in its abrasive satire of the 1840s, particularly in Douglas Jerrold's highly popular series, 'Mrs Caudle's Curtain Lectures' in 1845, warmly endorsed for its verisimilitude by William Thackeray.[31] Another frequent contributor, Thackeray himself, professed some admiration for women who usurped male power, but asserted simply in 1849, 'Every woman manages her husband: every person who manages another is a hypocrite.'[32] The inversion of authority was further developed and exaggerated in his novel of 1853, *The Newcomes*, in the character of Sophia Newcome, who effectively managed her husband's business as well as his home.[33]

Satirists might inflate women's domestic influence and power, but, like prescriptive writers, they were silent on the deeper contradictions in domestic ideology between women's moral influence and their legally sanctioned subordination.[34] There was, indeed, a long tradition of feminist protest against women's subservience in marriage, stemming from the seventeenth century, which sought to make female equality compatible with the companionate ideal, and was pursued with fresh vigour by Owenite feminists in the early nineteenth century.[35] Some of the Owenites' early successors, like Marion Reid, also linked their protests to radical demands for political equality,[36] but a few concentrated on structural inequalities in the marriage relationship. Ann Lamb, for example, lamenting the lack of companionship and friendship in marriage, blamed the husband for his 'perpetual fault-finding, and blame-giving for the things she cannot help', driving the wife to find 'her situation all but unendurable, – the very antipodes of her inexperienced expectation'. To bring mutual happiness a more enlightened social system would abolish 'the one rule of "Wives, *obey* your husbands!" no matter how silly . . . the command may be'. A wife's duty, in practice 'the obedience of a Turkish slave', contrasted with the commonly abused authority of her husband, who

> deems himself free to do as he likes; to spend his money and time as he pleases, and to scold his *patient Griselda*, should she dare to remonstrate about extravagance, waste, indolence, or idleness. *Her* business is to love! suffer!! and obey!!! the three articles of a woman's creed.[37]

Lamb's radical and forthright critique, similar to some of the well-publicized grievances of Caroline Norton, foreshadowed the late-Victorian marriage debate, in which feminists and moralists alike came to scrutinize the abusive conduct of husbands more fully.[38] But at mid-century the circulation and influence of these views was limited compared to the mass of marital prescription promoting domestic ideology, in which women's defiant conduct received most attention, and negative appraisal of husbands' behaviour was nuanced.

All these criticisms of marital behaviour provide some evidence, albeit inconclusive, of a higher set of expectations of marriage for both men and women by the mid-nineteenth century. Writers like Ellis spoke from personal observation when they lamented, in 'ill-assorted marriages', the failure of too many husbands and wives to live up to each other's hopes. We have yet to test the reliability of their observations of actual behaviour, but it is significant that their lessons in proper marital conduct were conveyed through enumeration of deviant bad habits rather than a simple catalogue of abstract principles. Formulated this way, their precepts for emotional compatibility elevated private behaviour to a matter of public importance and discussion on a quite unprecedented scale. Such a discourse, focused on standards of conduct, could not help but move from advice to reform and regulation, and it is no accident that such a mass of prescriptive literature preceded the widening of facilities for divorce and separation in the 1857 Divorce Act. Divorce Court judges, as we will see, were as much interested in regulating marital behaviour as they were in dispensing relief to wronged spouses.[39]

A rise in emotional expectations of marriage, as Roderick Phillips has demonstrated, is easier to assert than to chart with precision. Expectations clearly vary between marriages, and over the life of individual marriages, as well as collectively over the *longue durée*. But the height-ened early-Victorian concern with private behaviour evident here is consistent with Phillips's general argument, which sees the Victorian period as the key period of change. The change marked a shift in emphasis from material to affective expectations, from marriage as an economic relationship to a companionate institution requiring stability, and, with higher expectations, an increasing probability that marriages would break down on grounds of incompatible behaviour.[40] Guidebooks promoting domestic ideology provide one impression of these changes in expectations by the 1850s; we need to turn now to the kind of marital experience brought to light through the Divorce Court to test the mean-ing of such changes for individuals.

CASE STUDIES IN CONTESTED AUTHORITY

In November 1848, Robert Bostock, a retail druggist in Kennington, South London, and his wife, Charlotte, engaged in one of a long series of violent quarrels. On this occasion, although Charlotte had not been physically assaulted, Robert's behaviour to herself, their children and a neighbour had been so threatening and violent that, on the prompting of her brother, Charlotte consulted a solicitor, who advised her simply to keep out of her husband's way as much as possible. As a result Charlotte, as she later described it, 'stayed entirely in the nursery with her children', but in the middle of the next night was disturbed by Robert knocking on the door, groaning 'my lastt hour has come' and claiming illness. Charlotte then called in two nearby surgeons, and later a third, who advised her, in writing, that her husband suffered from

> intermitting paroxysms of excitement during which he has threat-ened the life of his wife, and has struck and ill-treated his children; we therefore recommend that a proper attendant should be em-ployed to act in the evennt of any sudden emergency.

A 'keeper' was thus brought into the house for a week, which Roberrt claimed was entirely his wife's doing under the pretence that he was of unsound mind. He added that the surgeons had told Charlotte that his life was in her hands, that she had a solemn duty as a wife to soothe and not to vex and irritate him, and that Charlotte had declared that one of them had talked to her like a father and 'affected her to tears'. Both husband and wife agreed that when, soon after, Robert went to Brighton for his health, Charlotte wrote him affectionate letters, because, as she stated, 'she always wished to write affectionate letters, as her endeavour was to try to soothe and not to irritate him'.[41]

These domestic tensions were recounted in detail by both partners in one of the first petitions for judicial separation, based on a charge of cruelty, to go to the new Divorce Court in 1858. This brief glimpse alone conveys hints of some of the dilemmas facing women in troubled marriages, as well as some stock responses of husbands and wives in domestic crises. Robert Bostock was well versed in the far-reaching authority and privileges his status conferred on him, and he could rely on professionals, whether lawyers or doctors, to draw them to his wife's attention. Charlotte, by contrast, negotiated a narrow and hazardous course between resistance to excessive authority and submissive affection designed to 'soothe' her husband's bruised dignity. Authority and abuse, defiance and submission, vied for relative advantage in marriages where law and custom weighed heavily on the side of husbands, but where in daily life wives might improvise a different set of rules from day to day to promote domestic harmony. The frequency with which such domestic dramas were detailed to the Divorce Court underlines the fragility of marriages where implicit understandings about the nature of the contract could break down so easily. The richly documented cases described below provide a window on the dramas of sexual politics acted out in the home at a time when patriarchal authority was facing subtle pressures to adapt to new ideals and changing conditions.

The Bostocks were married in 1827, and in thirty years of marriage they had had thirteen children, of whom eight, five sons and three daughters, survived. For most of the marriage they had lived at about four addresses in South London, mainly in Kennington. Robert's retail chemist business, in which Charlotte sometimes assisted, had been established for him by his father, who had expressly refused to allow his son to pursue his own preference to enter the Stock Exchange, like his brothers. The business, which Charlotte claimed Robert disliked, failed twice, first in 1834 and again in the late 1840s after he had inherited a substantial £10,000 from his father in 1847. The circumstances of the failures remain obscure, but Robert's father, James, a stock jobber, seems never to have trusted him financially, pointedly choosing his two other sons as executors and insisting that the £2,000 advanced to set up the business should be deducted from his inheritance. Whatever the fate of Robert's inheritance, and to judge from his later will it mostly went into East India railway stock, it seemed to have little bearing on the Bostocks' domestic life-style. Before and after 1847 they lived a relatively spartan lower middle-class existence, apparently never employing more than two servants, often less, plus a shop assistant, and money was at the heart of much of their domestic strife.[42]

Charlotte's background is less easy to trace. With a brother serving as a major in the Indian army her family was undoubtedly middle-class, but without resources to spare for a daughter's dowry. She acknowledged that she brought no money to the marriage and that it was 'one of affection' on Robert's part, who claimed, probably correctly, that his father had opposed it in 1827.[43] What she did bring to the marriage, over time at least, was considerable business skill and assistance. She and Robert each referred to her routine work in the chemist shop; in 1848 during ill-health Robert went to Brighton, left Charlotte in charge of the business, and asked her to attempt to sell it. By 1856 she was sufficiently competent financially to act as an executor to her aunt's will. Robert's regular complaints about Charlotte's absences were generated as much by the loss of her assistance in the family business as by her alleged neglect of household duties.[44]

In her petition Charlotte alleged a long series of violent assaults by her husband from shortly after the marriage, each of which was the end product of much dispute and recrimination, mostly over domestic issues. There was no hint here of the more sensational divorce charges of adultery or drunken violence, and alcohol was never mentioned by either party. She alleged that he had struck and injured her on the head while she was holding an infant, that he beat her and threw her to the floor, that he broke down bedroom doors when she locked herself in with her children, once with a sledge hammer, that he attempted to strike her with a club, threatened her with a knife and pistol and on several occasions threatened to murder her. The violence, she claimed, was regularly accompanied by his

> abusing her in the most degrading language, and [he] applied to her the most opprobrious epithets, amongst other things calling her a cow and declaring that she was worse than any strumpet that walked the streets, that all women were damned Bitches and devils and that [she] had made his home a Rabbit Warren.

Robert denied all these accusations, except to admit that he had once 'boxed her ears', and another time had taken her by the waist and laid her down on the floor when she threw some glasses at him. More significantly, he attributed the source of their conflict to Charlotte's behaviour:

> though he admits that having been twice unsuccessful in his business of a chemist and druggist, and his family having been numerous, which required him to enjoin on his wife strict economy in her expenditure, but which she neglected to observe, he was, on account of her extravagant habits, and her disregard of his remonstrances thereon, greatly annoyed, and he has on many occasions expressed himself as feeling angry and vexed with her.[45]

The Bostock family economy was indeed a central bone of contention, one of the chief aggravations being regular doctors' bills, which, on some occasions, Robert refused to pay. But there were other tensions. Robert accused Charlotte of neglecting her family duties through excessive visiting and lying in bed reading novels (which she denied). There was further conflict over the visits of her mother and he accused her of never being happy unless she had one of her 'fancy men' around, his way of referring to the attendance of doctors.[46] Robert's economic resentments and territorial jealousies were familiar themes, not far removed from the disputes of working-class couples. But as the years passed and the children grew older, he betrayed a growing sense of resentment that his authority in the family, which he took very seriously, was being increasingly defied. This is best illustrated by some relatively trivial incidents discussed at length by both parties, where the violence was relatively muted but the conflict intense.

Shortly before the events described above, in November 1848, the Bostock family were having dinner between 2 and 3 p.m. when a friend of Charlotte's, a Mrs Silva, called to visit. Charlotte and her eldest daughter soon afterwards left the table and accompanied their guest upstairs, while Robert attended the shop. At about 5 p.m., as it grew dark, Charlotte called for tea and asked the servant to bring up a lamp, a recent present from her eldest son, remarking to Mrs Silva 'I must show you a present I have had from my son Chig'. Robert was, he claimed, reading with the lamp downstairs and refused to part with it, but shortly afterwards the shop-bell rang and while he was attending to a customer Charlotte had the lamp brought up. Robert then went upstairs 'in a very excited state' and attempted to retrieve the lamp, but met the resistance of Charlotte and her eldest son. As Robert put it, 'he thereupon addressed Mrs Silva and requested, if she was a friend of his, to come downstairs and have tea with him, since his wife and his son were against him'. A scuffle ensued between Robert and his son, the lamp glass was broken and Robert's face was cut. He then went downstairs and, in his own words,

> fetched the staff which he had as one of the special constables in the riots at the commencement of the said year [i.e. in April 1848], and threatened to take his said son and those who sided with him into custody.

The special constables appointed during the Chartist demonstration of 1848 no doubt took pride in the public acknowledgement of middle-class respectability thus signified, but it is intriguing to see the implications this could have for family politics. Robert's domestic authority and respect as household head failing him, he fell back in some desperation, indeed pathetically, on his public authority and official status. But even that status of was of little avail, for a further scuffle ensued and Charlotte alleged that a blow with the constable's staff intended for her was deflected by Mrs Silva, who received a badly injured and permanently marked arm. Not surprisingly no one was taken into custody.[47]

Some years later, in September 1853, another family scuffle erupted when Charlotte and her eldest children neglected to invite Robert to attend the theatre with them. He claimed that his two eldest daughters appeared in evening dress and evaded his questions as to where they were going. Charlotte, significantly, denied this part of the story, insisting that they had 'never had evening dress and that there was great difficulty to get even the necessary clothing for them'. Upon discovering their intention Robert 'complained at their not having treated him with proper respect in not having informed him of their intention, nor asked him to accompany them'. Upon their return he renewed his complaints, asking under whose protection they had been (they had gone with the eldest son, Chignell) and claiming that they 'had all come in reeking hot from the streets'. This provoked another family scuffle, Robert struck one daughter, was attacked by another, who tore his coat, and a struggle ensued between him and a younger son, only terminated, according to Charlotte, by Robert's threat: 'Come, let us go out into the garden and fight it out with knives.' That night, as on numerous other occasions, Charlotte slept with her daughters behind a bolted door, which Robert later burst open and, according to her, 'was in a fearfully excited state, and continued walking about until half past four o'clock, all the time abusing her and her family'. The 'Rabbit Warren' that Robert had complained about earlier had decisively joined forces with Charlotte, rendering even his violence ineffectual. All the same the emotional wounds festered, and soon after that occasion Charlotte left for six weeks, one of several separations before the final one in 1856.[48]

In his long affidavits of answers and 'responsive allegations' to Charlotte's charges, Robert took every opportunity to declare his own grievances, while attempting to satisfy the legal requirement in court that Charlotte might not only have provoked his outbursts of violence, but had subsequently condoned, and thus negated, whatever legal cruelty had been established. He complained, for example, that she used very irritating language, calling him a dirty, stuffy old man, and saying that he 'smelled like a labourer', a class insult that may also have carried gender connotations, since in the early years Robert was evidently conscious of his difficulty in fulfilling the role of the middle-class male provider. Another allegation about an event which took place in 1843 casts some light on his attitude, and Charlotte's too, to their quarrels at the time they occurred. After a dispute Charlotte accompanied him to St Anne's Chapel in Clapham and, according to Robert, agreed that he should send a note to the clergyman, Reverend Charles Bradley,

> requesting him to offer up in that part of the service called the
> general thanksgiving, their special and united acknowledgements
> for mercies recently received, meaning thereby their reconciliation,

and that they both on such occasion received together the Holy Communion.

For Robert his right to make a public declaration of what he considered to be their 'reconciliation' was never in doubt, but for Charlotte that became the crux of the issue. She objected to the airing of their domestic affairs in public, insisting that he had never informed her that any such note had been sent to the minister until she was in the church and then unable to prevent the announcement. For all its apparent triviality, this incident and the different construction placed on it by each partner, went to the heart of their opposed notions of the reasonable limits of authority and subordination. Charlotte felt not only that Robert had exceeded his rights, but that she had a perfectly legitimate right to veto such a public declaration.[49]

More dramatic illustrations of these contrasting perceptions emerged in some of the Bostocks' violent quarrels, which each described at length. In July 1845, Charlotte went to stay with her mother one night in order to see her brother, just returned from a twenty-year absence in the army in India. Not for the first time her absence caused great aggravation at home. Robert required her assistance in the business and was much inconvenienced by her 'neglect of her family duties'. After her return next day during supper he 'reproached' her and the argument became violent. Charlotte claimed Robert struck and beat her, threw her on the floor and gave her a badly bruised and swollen face; Robert alleged that he did no more than 'take her by the waist and . . . lay her down on the floor', but then added that her behaviour had been 'very provocatory and violent' and that she had thrown two glass tumblers at his head. But Charlotte's provocation, he insisted, was more than physical; he admitted to 'being greatly annoyed and vexed at [Charlotte's] absenting herself from home on other occasions', and claimed that she had promised to return the same night because of his lack of a business assistant, but that she sent no message, causing him to sit up waiting till a late hour; moreover, she returned late the following evening 'which occasioned him great annoyance'. Charlotte's version implied that the whole grievance was inflated out of proportion, since she had explained that she would stay overnight if, as happened, her brother was delayed, and she had sent her daughter home to inform Robert. But in her final affidavit she gave an expanded and illuminating version of their physical struggle. Robert, she stated,

> struck her repeatedly and violently, when she told him that if he did so again she must protect herself, that he did again strike her, whereupon she threw a tumbler at him, that he struck her again, when she threw another, and [he] still continuing to strike her, she then threw a piece of bread at him, when [he] knocked [her] off the

chair on which she was sitting onto the floor, and continued to strike her while on the ground.[50]

Even allowing for conflicting versions and legal intent in these accounts, this episode offers a revealing glimpse into the dynamics of the Bostocks' domestic politics. Charlotte was not unaware of Robert's simmering resentment over her frequent absences from the home and shop, though for all his self-conscious assertions of authority he seemed powerless to prevent them. As well, she was not beyond resorting to physical as well as verbal defiance, although at other times her most frequent and effective weapon seems to have been simply to ignore him and lock herself in her daughters' bedroom, or, if that failed, to leave the house again, which Robert regarded as further provocation and defiance. Her final departure occurred in 1856 after a series of apparent murder threats, or at least so she interpreted them, when Robert referred to the recent Corrigan murder case, in which a husband had stabbed his wife to death, and 'threatened to serve his wife as Corrigan had done his wife'.[51] We cannot know how regularly husbands used such widely reported events to threaten their wives, but, like the 'Jack the Ripper' sensation years later, they easily lent themselves to this kind of terrorism, in the process reinforcing the authority of husbands who made the connection.[52]

If such acts on Robert's part suggest a measure of desperation, they also underline the considerable distance Charlotte had travelled in thirty years of marriage in refusing to tolerate the excesses of her husband's behaviour. While she usually came off worst in most of their physical battles, there were limits to her willingness to accept the unrestrained exercise of his authority. But her defiance was long in gestating. If the violence dated from early in the marriage, a pattern of Charlotte's resistance only emerged after a decade of married life, and more persistently as her children grew into early adulthood and gave her moral and physical support. Robert's resentment fed on all these tendencies, driving him in 1850 to turn his two eldest sons out of the house.[53] By that time his actions had begun to betray some glimpses of an embattled patriarchal authority under siege, an authority with undisputed power, even sanctioned by the opinion of professionals, but without the means to enforce absolute compliance from his family. If Robert betrayed signs of mental disturbance and 'paroxysms of excitement' he remained typical in taking his family authority very seriously, apparently more seriously than his wife. Had he, one wonders, read more carefully than Charlotte the popular injunctions of Mrs Ellis and others about the imperatives of wives' subordination?[54]

None of this should be read as Charlotte's rejection of the legitimacy of Robert's authority, which she never questioned and indeed went to great lengths to acknowledge. In her response to his charges of extravagance she insisted that she accepted her role as subordinate and delegated household manager, protesting only that she was not extravagant because 'he never gave her the opportunity of being so'. His unjust parsimony with the housekeeping money, she implied, marked his failure to fulfil his role as a judicious and understanding provider.[55] There were, to be sure, glimpses of other sides to this relationship, quite apart from Charlotte's obvious attempts to persuade the court that she had acted as a dutiful and affectionate wife. As late as 1855 Charlotte wrote from Hastings, 'My room has a four-poster bedstead and a nice feather bed, and I fancy I shall sleep so soundly tonight; I only want you with me; I cannot bear sleeping alone'.[56] The many 'affectionate letters' cited by both sides in court and Charlotte's acknowledged endeavour 'to soothe and not to irritate him' suggests a more complex relationship than the image of perpetual violent dispute portrayed by the legal texts. They may also suggest either that she had thoroughly internalized the feminine civilizing mission prescribed by writers like Mrs Ellis, or that, faced with a difficult husband, she developed a system of 'humouring', or manipulation, to ensure his good temper. Her proclaimed distaste for sleeping alone, for example, sits awkwardly with her frequent attempts to escape from him by sleeping with her daughters behind locked doors.[57]

Very likely the apparent contradictions in the behaviour of both Charlotte and Robert were explained in part by the determination of each of them to avoid losing face. Intense struggles over the possession of a lamp and visits to the theatre and public declarations about their relationship from the pulpit reflected the resolve of each not to back down. Whatever the truth, Robert's theoretical supremacy was rarely an overt issue, but Charlotte attempted to juggle an acceptance of his authority with evasion and resistance. More simply, she defied him whenever she considered his behaviour to be unreasonable. This theme, as we shall see, was a common one in middle-class Victorian marriages.

If the wife's actions in the Bostock marriage were characterized by resistance, the husband's betrayed a persistent and desperate attempt to assert patriarchal supremacy, and the latter feature loomed large in many of the more richly documented cases after mid-century. As the untrammelled rights of husbands became an increasing focus of public scrutiny and regulation, their behaviour reflected a close knowledge of and preoccupation with their marital rights, which some plainly understood to be under attack. What is striking is the extent to which their preoccupation with authority, when challenged, so often moved to the point of neurotic obsession. This was apparent in the case of *Curtis* v. *Curtis*, another suit for judicial separation heard by the Divorce Court in 1858.[58]

The Curtises were married in 1846. John Curtis was a civil engineer and Frances the daughter of a barrister and Justice of the Peace. Her

wealthy parents, it emerged, had disapproved of the marriage, consider-
ing their son-in-law's station, in one of the new professions, to be
beneath their daughter's; at the outset there was a quarrel over the
marriage settlement and throughout the marriage John objected to what
he felt was inappropriate interference from his father-in-law, Mr Flood.
Frances's marriage in the face of her parents' opposition gave an early
hint that she was accustomed to getting her own way, but she was to
encounter more difficulty in asserting herself against a husband who was
unwilling to let his rights and authority be infringed. Five children were
born of the marriage, of whom three had survived by the time Frances
Curtis filed for a separation in 1858.

Frances's long petition alleged violence early in the marriage, partly
occasioned by disputes over the children, and there was also some
violence alleged to the children in the mother's presence. John denied
these accusations, except to admit that he had once, during a dispute
with Frances, 'boxed her ears'.[59] Some of the alleged assaults were
occasioned by disagreement over John's desire to emigrate to Australia,
which Frances flatly refused to do. Other accusations focused on John's
treatment of the children, once in stopping a young baby crying by
squeezing its throat, and later pouring a bucket of iced water over an
infant suffering from chicken-pox. Disputes over child-care, clearly,
constituted a running sore in the Curtis household, and hint at John's
close involvement in domestic matters. In a letter to her mother Frances
insisted that he was obsessively 'wrapped up' in his children.[60]

From early in the marriage, though, there was sustained antagonism
over the couple's class differences. John objected to Frances's going to
parties, particularly at her parents' house, because he could not afford to
return the invitations, and insisted that he was considered and treated by
her family as socially inferior. Frances admitted that her family often
spoke of John's occupation as 'engineering rubbish', though at the trial
she claimed that it was not meant offensively. These differences frequently surfaced during other disputes. The fact that religious and
political discussions led to heated arguments, one allegedly stirring John
to spit in Frances's face, hint at the depth of their differing political and
social outlooks, not to mention Frances's refusal to bow to Mrs Ellis's
advice to keep her opinions to herself.[61] In the heat of an argument she
once taunted him by saying that he had spoiled her prospects, that she
had married a 'low fellow' and that 'the only compensation he could
make to her for having induced her to marry him was to die'. He
responded with jealous, though unfounded, accusations of infidelity,
which aroused Frances to suggest that each of the children may have had
a different father, provoking John to a physical attack. The later conflict
between the couple needs to be seen in the light of these class tensions,
evident in John's claim at the hearing that he had always worked very

hard 'in order to put his wife into the position she thought she was entitled to occupy'.[62] John, like Robert Bostock, was quick to equate class insults with slurs on his masculinity, embodied in his implied inadequacy as a middle-class male provider.

Stress, or 'irritability', allegedly resulting from John's hard work and family conflict, brought on a mental breakdown, diagnosed as 'brain fever', late in 1850, during which he was confined in an institution and put in a strait-jacket. But within a few months he was pronounced fully recovered, and resolved to improve his prospects (and, presumably, escape the influence of his wife's family) by leaving England. Frances fiercely resisted his proposal to go to Australia, despite some proven violence and threats to take the children away from her. But by July 1851 John had finally induced Frances to leave England with him, this time for New York, largely by means of a further threat to remove the children from her custody if she stayed behind. In New York their quarrels continued, particularly over care of the children, despite Frances's loss of her 13-week-old baby within two months of their arrival. As other witnesses testified, John took a very close interest in the welfare of his children, but he seemed unable to do this without trespassing on Frances's domestic role.

The fullest evidence we have about the nature of the relationship, and Frances's perception of it, is contained in a long and revealing letter she wrote to her mother in March 1852. After informing her mother that she was again pregnant, she described a recent quarrel which followed her permission to let her children play with two others under the supervision of her servant. When John discovered this he 'was evidently much put out and excited, and asked me what I meant by allowing strange children, of whom I knew nothing, to play with his children'. He added, angrily, that 'all the misery of his life had arisen from immoral habits learnt from other children' and insisted that she separate them immediately, but the dispute escalated further:

> unfortunately, on his going on to be much excited, and to talk as I thought very disgustingly, I got angry, and said I refused to talk of such things, as I thought it corrupting. This only made matters worse, and at last I said, 'Really, if things go on in this manner I shall be obliged to put my children under the protection of the Government.' I said it thinking it might do good to shew a little spirit, and also from being really angry and disgusted; but the words were hardly out of my mouth when I saw the mistake I had made; and really, my own mother, the persecution and humiliation I have undergone since have been enough to break a heart of stone.[63]

The 'persecution and humiliation' experienced by Frances reduced her status in the household to that of a child. John refused to accept her apology, and prevented her from saying prayers with the children,

> and went on perpetually at me the whole evening; next, he made me beg his pardon over again in the presence of my servant, explaining to her that I had been impertinent to him, . . . then this morning there had been the same thing over again, – scolding, scolding, scolding without end, and I can conscientiously say without pro- vocation, pointedly helping the servant to bread at breakfast before me, and at last, on my making some slight remark, sending me out of the room to finish my breakfast in my bedroom.[64]

Still dissatisfied with the sincerity of her repentance he next told her that he would 'devise some punishment' for her, and accordingly gave full charge of the children to the young servant and forbade Frances to go near them. When the children ran into the room 'he sent them off, telling them repeatedly that mamma was naughty'. During John's absence she man- aged to see the children 'by stealth, and telling lies when he comes in, and pretending I have not seen them'. But by now she was looking ahead to a possible legal solution:

> I would to God he would do something that would set me at liberty. I often wish he would strike me, but that he never attempts, – indeed, he seemed much kinder for a while; but the plain fact is that he carries the idea of his authority to a mania.[65]

There were further quarrels over Frances's reading material; John burnt a copy of *Harper's Magazine*, telling her 'not to bring books into his house until he knew what they were about' (despite this she urged her mother to continue to 'send the papers: they help to keep me sane'). After further admonishment for entertaining visitors without his knowledge she concluded that humouring was the best policy. 'You see it is necessary in everything to flatter his amour propre if he is to be kept in tolerable humour.' But she continued to have reservations about a policy of duplicity: 'It is so impossible and wicked to be always deceiving and telling lies.'[66]

Paradoxically, this letter was produced at the hearing by John, in order to argue that Frances's reference to his refusal to strike her proved she had never suffered personal violence. But the judge was struck far more by evidence of John's abuse of his authority, and particularly by his dis- placement of Frances from her 'proper position in her house', which became the basis of the court's decision in her favour.[67] It was no accident that in her letter to her mother Frances chose to stress, as 'cruel and outrageous', the loss of her authority over those deemed to be her social subordinates, marking the implicit importance attached to her class identity. The ultimate domestic outrage, from this point of view, was inversion of roles between middle-class mistress and servant, an act only possible for the servant-employing class, and this seems to have legitimated the sense of grievance for the court as well as for Frances.

For John Curtis, who shortly afterwards suffered another attack of 'brain fever', his extreme and obsessive measures formed part of a coherent system designed to keep the material world at bay. As a husband and father he saw his authority being challenged by outsiders: his father-in-law persistently threatened to have him placed in an institution; his wife's relationships with others compromised his absolute control; doctors called to treat his ill children, with treatment of which he disapproved, brought unpredictable influences, as did his children's playmates (which recalled unspecified ghosts from his own childhood) and his wife's reading material. To justify his actions he invoked religion, prompting Frances's diagnosis that he was motivated by 'a feeling of fanatic enthusiasm, and thinking that I belong to the world and not to God'. But he never doubted that it was his proper role to be the absolute divine representative and arbiter in the Curtis household. The long tradition of religious sanction for domestic tyranny still carried much force with middle-class husbands, but by the 1850s it had come to seem perplexing to wives like Frances: 'the extraordinary mixture of arrogance, self-love, love of power, with religious feeling and enthusiasm, is too much for me to understand'.[68]

Much of John's action might be dismissed as the product of severe mental disturbance, were it not for the fact that his preoccupation with authority and control persisted long after his recovery. Soon after the receipt of Frances's letter to her mother, her father went to New York and procured John's confinement in Bloomingdale asylum. Frances returned with her father to his home in Ireland, where she stayed, apart from John, for five years. John wrote from Bloomingdale shortly after his incarceration, full of remorse for his past conduct, which he attributed to 'extreme anxiety, coupled with the disadvantageous circumstances and impressions under which we mutually laboured', and insisted that despite the past his love and affection for her remained unaltered.[69]

After a few months, when John's mother secured his discharge from Bloomingdale, he obtained employment in Spain and made no contact until 1856, after which he began to press Frances, without success, to return to him. When he visited her in Ireland in 1857 a violent scene took place, climaxed with John's curses on Frances and her father. Frances's reaction to this was to flee with her children to her sister's home in Hornsey, Middlesex, where she adopted an assumed name. John's response was to place placards in her father's neighbourhood, announcing that his wife had 'left the protection of her said husband, and absconded . . . without [his] knowledge or consent . . . taking with her his three children', and offering a £10 reward for information leading to their recovery by the 'deeply afflicted father'.[70] Six months later, according to Frances, he discovered her Hornsey address, broke down a bedroom door and attempted to drag the youngest child away, and was only forestalled by police intervention. This event led to Frances's petition for separation, but throughout the proceedings litigation continued over custody of the children John had ignored for four years.[71]

The experience of Frances Curtis, like that of Charlotte Bostock, suggests that any serious resistance she chose to make against her husband's unreasonable behaviour would encounter a formidable battery of legally entrenched and publicly sanctioned patriarchal powers, powers which lost little of their force because a husband might be mentally unbalanced. Frances's escape from John's rigid system of confinement in New York was only possible because of her father's professional and social position; Frederick Flood, the barrister and JP, at least, understood the workings of the law better than John Curtis. But that did not prevent John from taking his marital grievances into the public domain, confidently declaring his wife's misconduct and appealing for help to retrieve his children. Much of the conflict in these marriages arose from the close involvement of husbands in their wives' domestic affairs, symbolized dramatically by John Curtis's humiliating replacement of his wife as household manager by a young servant. All these themes were displayed even more vividly in the case of *Kelly* v. *Kelly*, heard in 1869 and 1870, one of the best-documented and legally significant Victorian separation cases.

Frances Kelly petitioned for a judicial separation from her husband, Rev. James Kelly, the Anglican vicar of St George's Church in Liverpool, on the ground of cruelty. This leading case, which sustained press interest for some five months, constituted a turning point in the law of matrimonial cruelty, since it established clearly that non-violent cruelty might justify a decree, and departed from the earlier strict requirement of physical violence.[72] But the significance of the case extends well beyond legal precedent, since the charges and defence delved so deeply into the domestic relations of the Kellys, and James Kelly, especially, provided such a richly detailed account of his version of the events and elaborate justifications of his own actions. All this provides a rare glimpse, not only into the realm of sexual politics in the domestic sphere, but into the workings of the mind of one husband who took his authority very seriously.

The Kelly case raises some obvious questions about the reliability of divorce records for analysis of marital relationships, since such a large part of the material originated from the husband's extraordinary efforts to prove his innocence of the charge of cruelty. James Kelly was so convinced of the rightness of his own actions, and his wife's culpability, that he wrote a fifty-page affidavit justifying his behaviour, reproducing early correspondence from his wife and others, and, refusing legal counsel, conducted his defence in person, including an appeal to the full court and later litigious challenges to alimony rulings.[73] Ironically, much of this material worked to discredit his own case. Lord Penzance, the 'Judge Ordinary' or president of the Divorce Court, commented that the case was unique in depending so little on the truth or falsehood of each party's evidence; neither spouse, he claimed, willingly deviated from the truth in their factual accounts, nor was there much essential contradiction about the nature of the salient facts.[74] As we shall see, much of this was due to James Kelly's unwavering self-righteous conviction of his own correct and superior behaviour.

The Kellys were married in 1841 and had one surviving son, born in 1845. The dispute that prompted Frances Kelly to leave her husband in January 1869, had begun only in 1867 over a financial dispute, but the case brought to light other illuminating quarrels from much earlier in the marriage. Sometime in 1849, while they were living in London, Frances lost an infant son. During the child's illness she engaged a nurse, and at about the same time she invited her close friend, Emily, to stay with them. Frances's letters, copied by James in his affidavit, reveal a highly charged emotional atmosphere in the household and her grief over the loss, which continued for some months. Not surprisingly, though, other tensions began to develop, and it was these to which James later drew attention in his attempts to prove that his wife was prone to make false accusations against him and to defy his authority. Soon after the child's death, Frances began to suspect an excessively intimate relationship between Emily and her husband. Whatever her evidence, and whatever her feelings, it is clear that she accused them of adultery, and, even after making abject apologies, she revived the accusation more than once. On one occasion, according to James, a noisy scene erupted 'before servants and friends and neighbours', passers-by and a police-man knocked at the door suspecting a breach of the peace, and his reputation in the neighbourhood became akin to that of 'the song of the drunkard'. Frances also convinced her nurse of the truth of her suspicions, which provoked tension between Emily and the nurse, and Emily apparently left the house on two occasions to escape the hostility.[75]

It is impossible to be certain of the accuracy of Frances's allegations, or of what suspicions she may have continued to harbour, but her letters strongly suggest that she came to accept that all her accusations were false. Any remaining doubt stems partly from the recurrence of her accusations between 1849 and 1852, but more importantly from the fact that all her letters of apology were written at the express insistence of James, who refused to respond with any unconditional forgiveness. His demands resulted in a succession of repetitious confessions of guilt and self-hatred from Frances. Repeatedly, she asked him, if he could not forgive her, to at least pray for her before the congregation, but her confessions invariably referred back to earlier exchanges in which James had been demanding repentance and applying discipline as if to a child. She could not expect her confession to be believed, she told him, and

> you were right in saying the evil spirit has not been crucified. I have myself brought on this dreadful misery. . . . Have pity upon me my dear husband, and forgive all the vile things I said the other night. It was rage dictated them. I do humble myself before God, on account of it, and will take meekly whatever treatment you think right. I have no doubt but that you will spurn this from you. I shall not wonder at it. Only give me your prayers that the Lord may work.

After a subsequent quarrel she wrote,

> You wished me to write down what I was saying to you today. Well then, I wanted to tell you how truly I grieve for my sinful conduct in professing to have abjured a sin I was indulging in. . . . But, my dearest husband, you have often said we know not what grace to the uttermost was with the Lord. I beseech you then, manifest it now to me. Give me once more an opportunity of proving my penitence and of erasing in some measure from your mind the awful opinion you have of me.[76]

Other lectures from James provoked similar responses. When James 'put the case' before her 'in plain words' she shrank from her earlier suspicions. So much of her self-denigration referred back to James's earlier harangues and demands for meek apology that it seems clear that her letters were written virtually under his instructions. 'You spoke the truth when you said I had lost *self*-respect. . . . Surely I never knew what the indulgence of sin could lead me into. It is powerful indeed thus to *learn* what the evil of one's heart is.'[77] But none of this seemed to produce the forgiveness that Frances begged for. Further remorse and expressions of self-loathing resulted only in further demands for self-abasement, with which Frances complied. 'Truly,' she wrote, 'I have been led captive by Satan – you say, truly, I am unworthy the name of Christian. I am not worthy of the position I occupy.' She had been shown 'the corruption of the depth of iniquity in my heart'.[78] Under James's urging, Frances wrote similar letters of apology to Emily, urging her to return to the house; she also wrote to her nurse, to whom she apologized for leading her into her own sin and urged her to make similar repentance.[79]

What is striking about this correspondence, apart from the extremes of Frances's self-vilification, is the relentless and unforgiving nature of James's assertion of his authority and demands for submission. The uncompromising divine sanction he claimed for this regime contrasted with Frances's appeal to a more tolerant and forgiving authority. But there are only faint hints that Frances may have protested at the severity of her treatment. In one letter she admitted that she could not expect, for the present, to be restored to his confidence, but it was his saying

> I never could possess it again, that I wished you to retract. There would be comfort in a ray of hope. But since you declare this to be impossible, I must submit to it as the punishment of my sin.[80]

At about the same time she begged him to delay the dismissal of an 'obnoxious servant' during her illness, when she felt unequal to further 'fatigue and anxiety'. She reminded him that he had always been kind to her in illness, but concluded with further self-criticism. 'I do abhor and loathe myself. Severe as have been your expressions of horror, they have been less than I deserve. I hate myself if you don't hate me.'[81] After eight years of marriage Frances was, indeed, capable of some self-assertion, as the origin of the episode itself demonstrated, but she was not yet prepared to defy his absolute assertions of authority and demands for submission under pressure.

A further twenty years of marriage with James seem to have taught Frances that there was little to be gained by meek submission while he demanded total obedience. Frances alleged in her petition that most of £5,000 bequeathed to her by her sister had been lost by James in an investment in 1867. He informed her of the loss, claiming that he had not mentioned it before to protect her from the 'corroding care' of his financial worries. A dispute followed, during which James reminded Frances of his past 'carefulness' when 'alas! I too often criticized our weekly expenditure'. The losses were such that James insisted that they must move to a less imposing house 2 miles distant, provoking Frances to further protests, which he alleged were 'heartless' and warranted an apology. But despite her demands he refused to provide any further information.[82] In order to ascertain her rights and those of her son under her sister's will Frances wrote to her brother-in-law, Colonel Thornbury, who informed her that in law the money was entirely at James's command, and that she and her son had no legal claim upon it. Further correspondence with Colonel Thornbury, and with Frances's brother, ensued, all of which was discovered by James, who had secretly opened her locked drawer and copied the letters. From that time James instituted a campaign of harassment of his wife, which seems to have been designed to extract precisely the same kind of abject confession he had forced from her in 1849. At the same time he quarrelled with his son, now 22, who was forced to leave the house, and since Frances supported her son the antagonism increased.[83]

Frances's refusal to humble herself on this occasion resulted in a prolonged period of conflict during which, the Court noted, James's actions went far beyond the bounds of a husband's reasonable authority as currently understood, provoking a breakdown in Frances's health and eventually inducing her to leave him.[84] His correspondence monotonously conveys his paranoid obsession with the notion that his wife was plotting against him, and he extended the same accusations to Frances's doctor, solicitor, and Colonel Thornbury. He continued to open her letters, called her a vile traitor and apostate and told her that she was no more fit than a prostitute to associate with modest women. He refused to sit at meals with her, insisted on a separate bedroom, and, when they were together, spent the time 'putting her sin before her', accusing her of treachery and being a traitor to her lawful husband.[85]

James's most dramatic form of punishment, though, was his entire displacement of Frances as household manager, 'entirely deposed', in the words of the shocked judge, 'from her natural position as mistress of her husband's house.' He gave her no money, no control over household expenses, which were now delegated to a housekeeper, and any item of dress or other needs were to be requested in writing. She was no longer allowed to go out alone, particularly to visit the poor in Liverpool, as had been her custom; on rare occasions when she was permitted out without James a male servant was deputed to follow her and she was barred from receiving her usual friends as visitors. The management of the household was given over entirely to a newly hired housekeeper, the wife of the manservant, and James warned the woman to take no orders from his wife.[86]

James's regime of incarceration and, in Lord Penzance's words, his treatment of Frances 'like a child or lunatic', was intended to produce confessions akin to those in 1849, but while he succeeded in breaking down her health, he could no longer elicit self-abasement.[87] Instead, as Frances's health declined, there were successive outbursts of conflict between Frances, James and the servants hired to control her. There were quarrels in front of servants over the use of Frances's cutlery; James forbade contact between Frances and the laundress lest the laundress might be used 'to post illicit letters which might not be written by a dutiful wife', and his insistence on using the housekeeper as an intermediary in all such communications provoked regular outbursts between her and Frances. On one occasion Frances called her a 'bugger', pushed the parlour door on her and crushed her fingers. A few weeks later, when Frances repeatedly removed some items hung on the hall rail at James's direction, he intervened, and, 'as a little measure of discipline', attempted to remove her two bird-cages, wresting one from her hand, causing a scuffle, during which one cage was dropped and a bird released. Only when she allowed the articles to remain on the hall rail did he permit the cages to be returned. There was further friction over James's censorship of Frances's reading; he insisted that the only books he refused her were those 'she appeared to demand as a matter of right, at the very time when she was indulging in acts of the grossest insubordination and rebellion against his authority'. He commented that he often left newspapers for her to read, but that he had felt that her desire to read them, or, as he more often noticed, novels, 'in the midst of such domestic affliction' was 'truly mournful'.[88]

James's determination to extract repentance for what he deemed to be 'treachery, treason and conspiracy' was mostly played out in the household before the limited audience of family and servants, but before long it broke those bounds. He lectured her on a wife's duties, read the marriage service to her and called in two fellow clergymen to explain the religious basis of a wife's obedience. Twice, after a particularly bitter argument, Frances attempted to escape by climbing out of a front window, scandalizing James by attracting the attention of neighbours and passers-by. But James himself was no less capable of exposing his domestic troubles to public gaze. In January 1869, only a week before Frances left James for the last time, he insisted that she accompany him to one of his morning church services. Just before the service was to begin, Frances left the church, pursued into the street by James, who attempted to force her to return, fearing, he claimed, that she was headed 'in the direction of the dirty courts, whither she had gone on a former occasion'. James's version was that he simply linked arms with her and 'endeavoured to lead her quietly back to the church'. Frances's account was that he seized her by the arm and 'dragged her in the street' towards the church. Whatever the truth, a scuffle resulted, the shrieks and shouts attracted a 'mob' and James declared that his wife was 'in a fit'. Her resistance proved too much for him, so he returned alone to the church, leaving Frances in the charge of his manservant, where, James alleged, she 'began to harangue the crowd, mentioning him by name'. After the servant induced her to return to the service Frances claimed that James referred to her in his sermon 'as a woman possessed by the Devil and as resisting her husband who wished to prevent her going to some low place'.[89]

It is impossible to trace the varied sources of James's neurotic obsession with his authority, but in the final years of the marriage it was clearly intensified by the increasing steadfast resistance he encountered from Frances. In one of the early letters she wrote to Colonel Thornbury, which so incensed James, she asked whether he advised 'patient submission to this slow assassination', but asserted that 'I feel satisfied I am doing right in resisting.' To James such resistance represented unnatural rebellion against his authority, and he went to extreme lengths to prevent his wife from taking it beyond the household. He refused to allow her to see her doctor without him because he feared she would discuss 'not her bodily ailments but her fancied sense of legal wrong'. Similarly, he escorted her to a solicitor 'to prevent if possible the indecent clamour about her rights'.[90] Throughout all this, Frances, though seriously affected in her health, insisted on the justice of her case, and seemed to wish for no more than mutual forgiveness and reconciliation. After she had left him she wrote suggesting that they

> bury the past in oblivion; let bygones by bygones, forgive and forget mutually, and seek to spend the little time that remains of this life on earth together in peace. . . . I never thought you had done anything dishonourable, and certainly I never tried to prove it. . . . You are under a complete delusion as to my conduct. My desire is to act toward you with the submission, obedience and even affection of a wife.[91]

Frances's long lesson in the necessity of resistance was here subdued by the language of prudent forbearance and submission. It is striking testimony to the pertinence of Rosalind Coward's proposition that 'not only is identity a construct, but it is also continuously and precariously reconstructed.'[92] For James, though, forgiveness or forbearance continued to have no place in his strict Calvinist system of patriarchal rule. Repeatedly he rejected Frances's apologies, asserting that 'it was not my duty as a Christian to be so satisfied. There ought to be a weeping out of the offence, with sorrow.'[93] Significantly, the judge, Lord Penzance, commented that he had used religion to sanction a 'harsh and cruel retaliation', while forgetting its 'leading precepts', humility and forgiveness.[94] His defiant appeal against the Court's first ruling against him, his long affidavit supporting his case and his determined arguments in court without any legal counsel, all testified to his refusal to bend in the interests of companionate understanding. In court he betrayed some awareness of the strange, obsessive figure he cut in public, when, after a two-day address during the appeal, he 'complained of the obloquy and ridicule from which he had suffered since this suit was instituted'.[95]

James Kelly's obsessiveness and paranoia cannot help but invoke suggestions of mental illness; indeed early in the dispute one of his servants thought 'Master must be mad' and Penzance felt Kelly's behaviour was unparalleled in its combination of an inflexible will and the power of self-deception.[96] Similar tendencies in the Bostock and Curtis cases are enough to hint at the regular propensity for men's obsession with control to skirt the borders, at least, of mental illness. More significant, though, is the fact that in all these cases the object of each husband's obsession was his sense of his own unlimited authority, expressed in the desire for mastery, determination to control outside influences like doctors, and the illegitimacy of his wife's defiance, sometimes extending over many years. It was no accident that by the second half of the nineteenth century husbands' obsessive assertion of their well-understood rights was accompanied by rejection of the language of mutual forbearance and a nervous protest against the 'indecent clamour' about the rights of wives. If these husbands were mad their behaviour remained a powerful indicator of the marital tensions of their time, for, as we shall see, the 'indecent clamour' was in the process of becoming a subject of open public debate.

It is striking that most of the antagonism evident in these marriages was of a uniquely middle-class character. Wives' slurs on their husbands' cleanliness and breadwinning capacities, like husbands' use of servants to humiliate their wives by subverting their household management, all linked gender identity to class identity, and thus worked as more potent insults. Husbands' confidence in their domestic sovereignty, too, drew on widely understood class understandings of their patriarchal powers, whether by reference to professional opinion or religious sanction; their readiness to expose their marital quarrels and sense of mastery to public gaze underscored their confidence. But this patriarchal construction of men's authority was a gendered understanding, sharply distinguished from the more companionate construction of their wives, who appealed to a less Calvinistic, more forgiving, religious authority, and had a more flexible understanding of the limits of absolute authority and submission, and the legitimacy of resistance. Like Douglas Jerrold's Mrs Caudle, these women were not likely 'to wear chains without shaking them'.[97] We have already seen how husbands might take their more authoritarian cues from prescriptive literature. It remains to be seen how far these 'hard cases' represented more common patterns evident in Victorian middle-class married life, in the Divorce Court, in conjugal behaviour more generally, and in the prescriptions, criticisms and ideals that informed the Victorian discourse on marriage.

4

CRUELTY AND DIVORCE

THE PUBLIC FACE OF MIDDLE-CLASS MARRIAGE

The vivid window on marriage which was opened to the public by press reports from the new Divorce Court after 1857 was one vital factor stimulating changes in attitudes to marriage by the end of the century. It contributed to a process which rendered the private unit of the family a more public property subject to regulation, opening marital behaviour of both sexes to more regular scrutiny. Paradoxically, at the very moment when the transformation of marriage from an economic institution to a private relationship was being consolidated, its privacy was compromised by intrusive scrutiny and surveillance. This was facilitated by the contemporaneous spread of literacy, newspapers and reading habits that encouraged a shared newspaper culture among the middle class.[1]

At the same time one should not confuse all the apparent novel revelations of conjugal troubles with experiences that were uniformly new and specific to mid- and late-Victorian social conditions. In 1831 Diana Belcher, married to her husband, Edward, a navy captain, for less than a year, wrote to him to explain why she wished to separate. 'In addition to all,' she told him,

> I dread the system of tyranny which you have prepared me to expect on your return, part of which is your declared intention of removing the faithful attendant of sixteen years' standing, who nursed me in all my illness, and is so much attached to my person and my friends.[2]

Her complaint was a familiar one; if anything was to rouse middle-class wives to resist excessive domestic control by their husbands it was arbitrary dismissal of their treasured servants, who had often been lifelong companions. Frances Kelly later experienced similar difficulties with her husband, and in cases brought to the ecclesiastical courts before 1857 this, like other issues involving servants, was a regular cause of wives' protests.[3] The heavy hand of husbands' rule in the home, as well as wives' outraged defiance of it, was not unique to the nineteenth century.

102

Marital stability and breakdown, too, as we have seen, had always been taken seriously, by authorities and the community generally.[4]

But if sexual antagonism was not new to the era of the Victorian Divorce Court, a much wider public profile of marital breakdown, stemming from greater publicity, was. Central to the change was increased access to the court, so that a minority, at least, of most social classes, could seek relief from a troubled marriage. But access to the court came with the considerable penalty of public exposure, where close dissection of one's marital troubles took place in the press, with all the attendant risks to the respectability even of an innocent party. Press reporting of the court's proceedings was generally seen as a salutary deterrent to marital misconduct, although concern was voiced regularly about the effects of publicity on morality until reports were restricted in 1926.[5]

The ramifications of publicity, though, were far-reaching, as themes from the court's deliberations entered the realm of public discourse, stimulating popular literature and feminist reformers to more intense analyses of marital relationships. Most importantly, the public focus now extended beyond the sensational dalliances of the aristocracy and the rich, for the Divorce Court heard cases from a wide range of middle- and working-class petitioners. *The Times* concluded from its assessment of the social composition of reported cases that they constituted 'a strange revelation of the doings of the middle classes in this country'.[6] Marital breakdown across the social spectrum thus assumed much greater significance, and behaviour to one's spouse gradually became a matter of more conscious reflection and social consequence, for both litigants and the public. While much of the publicity continued to dwell on the sensations of adultery in high places, more routine reporting examined the everyday tensions involved in cruelty charges. A brief survey of the social profiles and sexual antagonisms revealed in cruelty cases should help to shed some light on this changing public face of marriage.

One of the most enduring myths about the early Divorce Court is that it catered solely to the wealthy.[7] It is true that the costs of an action, from about £40 for an undefended case and £70 to £500 for a defended case, theoretically put the court beyond the means of most of the working class and lower middle class. But recent research has demonstrated convincingly that for many the financial barriers were not insurmountable, quite apart from the *in forma pauperis* provisions which allowed free legal service, tightly means tested, to petitioners without resources.[8] The most ambitious research, by Gail Savage, reveals that in the first decade of the act working-class petitioners made up 23 to 31 per cent of the total, the lower middle class 19 to 23 per cent, and the gentry-professional classes 42 to 56 per cent.[9] In addition, 40 per cent of divorce petitions and 90 per cent of judicial separations were filed by wives; in the former their

Table 4.1 Husbands' occupations in surveyed cases citing cruelty (160 identifiable out of 188)

Occupations	1858–66	1882	Law reports	Total cases
Working-class				
Unskilled:				
Unemployed	1	1	-	2
Labourers	6	4	1	11
Servants	1	-	1	2
Shop assistants	1	-	-	1
Merchant seamen	-	1	-	1
Sub-total	9 (13%)	6 (8.8%)	2 (8.7%)	17 (10.6%)
Skilled tradesmen	12 (17.4%)	10 (14.7%)	3 (13%)	25 (15.6%)
Total	21 (30.4%)	16 (23.5%)	5 (21.7%)	42 (26.2%)
Lower middle-class				
Clerical	1	10	2	13
Shopkeepers	8	3	-	11
Commercial travellers	1	1	-	2
Farmers	6	-	1	7
Merchant marine commanders	3	1	-	4
Artists, musicians, actors	1	2	1	4
Total	20 (29%)	17 (25%)	4 (17.4%)	41 (25.6%)
Gentry, professional, managerial, employers				
Managerial, employers	13	18	1	32
Professional	4	7	6	17
Army officers	3	5	-	8
Independent	2	3	1	6
Titled independent	3	-	1	4
Unspecified middle-class	3	2	5	10
Total	28 (40.6%)	35 (51.5%)	14 (60.9%)	77 (48%)
Total identified	69	68	23	160
Unidentified	14	12	2	28

Sources: Principal Probate Registry, PRO files J77, also law reports and *The Times*; see appendix 1.

success rate was identical to that of husbands, at 68 per cent, in the latter it was greater, at 36.76 per cent compared to 30.18 per cent.[10] Clearly, the new court was not the exclusive preserve of upper-class men.[11]

Savage's research was based on a comprehensive sampling of all petitions brought to the court by 1868. The research for this chapter, based on a much smaller and less systematic survey, draws mainly on petitions which cited cruelty, either alone for a judicial separation or in combination with adultery for divorce, and can make much less claim to statistical representativeness.[12] Nevertheless the occupational profiles are broadly in line with Savage's findings. Table 4.1, based on three separate surveys of cruelty cases, yielded 26 per cent working-class petitioners, 25 per cent lower middle-class and 48 per cent gentry, managerial, professional and entrepreneurial. The cluster of working-class and lower middle-class occupations, amounting to nearly half the petitioners, mirrors a similar pattern of occupations at the upper end of the Preston police court survey, where gentry and professionals were mostly absent.[13] The less affluent obviously resorted to the police courts in much greater numbers, but were still prepared to use the Divorce Court when circumstances allowed, and in some cases the petition expressly detailed earlier summonses and convictions of husbands by police court magistrates.

This small sample of cases citing cruelty is, of course, distinguished from other surveys by the overwhelming preponderance of women petitioners. The legal double standard provided obvious reasons for this, since a woman suing for divorce needed to prove an additional offence beyond adultery, whereas a man could divorce his wife for adultery alone. Because aggrieved wives were thus less able to obtain a divorce, many turned to the narrower claim for a judicial separation, which did not permit remarriage. In both cases cruelty proved to be the most common offence, although alternatives such as desertion, incest and bigamy could also be cited. Table 4.2 suggests that between 1858 and 1882 women may have made increasing use of cruelty charges against their husbands, for both divorce and judicial separation petitions. The bulk of these were straightforward charges of violent treatment, but by 1882 there was also a slight though increasing trend for wives to respond to husbands' charges of adultery with cross-suits charging cruelty, which allegedly conduced to their adultery. Moreover, the cases where husbands charged their wives with violent cruelty, as opposed to responsive allegations of violent provocation for their own cruelty, were rare; for a divorce the charge was superfluous once adultery was proved, though it was included in a very few petitions to build up the main charge. The few cases where a husband petitioned for a judicial separation from an allegedly violent wife were highly untypical, like the 82-year-old Earl of Devon, who charged his middle-aged wife with merciless beatings in the isolation of Powderham Castle.[14] Despite the relatively small number of cases in the survey, then, a focus on cruelty charges has the advantage of illuminating a wide variety of wives' grievances and husbands' responses, like those we saw in detail in the previous chapter. In the more richly documented and defended cases, where each side went to great lengths to deny charges, allege provocation and vindicate their behaviour, we can obtain rare insights into marital relationships as wives and husbands reconstructed them.

Table 4.2 Cruelty charges in Divorce Court survey

	1858–66	1882
Total petitions in survey	241	141
Petitions citing cruelty	83 (34%)	80 (57%)
Cruelty charges in wives' petitions (divorce and judicial separation)	50%	80%
Wives' divorce petitions citing cruelty	56%	75%
Cruelty charges in husbands' petitions	3 (1.25%)	2 (1.42%)
Cross suits with cruelty (mutual accusations of cruelty and/or adultery)	6 (2.5%)	10 (7.1%)

Sources: Principal Probate Registry, PRO files J77: 1, 2, 3, 4, 13 (1858–66), 274, 275, 276, 277 (1882); see appendix 1.

If contemporary and later assumptions about the greater brutality of working-class men were correct, one would expect to find a marked class-specific behavioural contrast amongst husbands charged with cruelty. It is true that among the twenty-two husbands in the survey who had previously appeared before magistrates on charges of violent assault against their wives, the majority, fourteen, were clearly working-class. The exceptions were a publican, two farmers, two shopkeepers, a commercial traveller, and only one, a solicitor, among professionals. But this tells us more about working-class monopoly and middle-class avoidance of the magistrates' courts than it does about private behaviour. Threats to murder, brutal attacks bordering on murder, wilful communication of venereal disease, and relentless persecution, in fact all the violent behaviour commonly associated with husbands summoned in the lower courts, was recounted by those working-class wives who brought their husbands to the Divorce Court.[15] In the realm of male brutality, though, democracy reigned supreme in the court, as upper- and middle-class husbands seemingly attempted to surpass the working-class in the viciousness of their assaults.

Among any sample of divorce cases it is a simple matter to locate the more dramatic and sensational cases of marital discord involving frequent adultery, sexual cruelty and extreme brutal violence bordering on murder. Adultery cases, especially, were usually those which attracted most attention when reported in the press. The most famous, such as the Mordaunt case, which implicated the Prince of Wales, dominated high-society gossip, just as they have dominated more trivial recent historical studies of divorce.[16] The less sensational cases, though, were more socially revealing. Contrary to popular belief, upper-class men were as likely, among those appearing in the court, to strike their wives with pokers and similar weapons, throw them downstairs, threaten murder, beat them during pregnancy, enforce sexual intercourse after childbirth, and indulge in marital rape or enforced sodomy, as were those lower in the social scale.[17] Army officers and independent gentlemen often fulfilled to the letter the stereotype of the dissipated upper-class roué, sexual adventurer and fortune hunter. Their wives often lived in fear of their lives, like Elizabeth Denton, whose husband, at home and on their travels on the continent, beat her regularly, and once 'threw her down on the bed, and threatened to throw her out of the window, smash her head and kill her'; in addition he frequently insisted on committing sodomy, often succeeding, despite her resistance.[18]

If anything distinguishes upper-class from middle-class cases in this study, it is upper-class men's association with a more traditional and aggressive concept of masculinity, defined in opposition to the domestic. Their employments and recreations – especially the male preserves of hunting, gambling, drinking and sexual adventure – confronted wives' more companionate expectations, often with disastrous results. Elizabeth Boynton, the wife of an army captain, suffered numerous beatings, some during illness and pregnancy; he assaulted her in a Brussels street, attracting a large crowd, and locked her in a hotel room. Most of their disputes stemmed from George Boynton's preference for horse-racing and the company of his regiment, even after his retirement. His defence counsel admitted that the quarrels mostly arose from 'the husband's weakness for sporting, and the wife's weakness for dress, admiration and gaiety'. But despite her large marriage settlement, Elizabeth was regularly deprived of money, which went to support George's gambling. Her most telling grievance emerged from being forced to 'sit at table with a low person, apparently a trainer', whose 'vulgar conversation' with her husband, about 'bad girls' George had known, astonished her servants and forced her to leave the room.[19] Some of the complaints such wives made of their husbands suggest the wide gulf of expectations distinguished by gender and convey hints of a regular domestic battleground. Anne Smith, for example, charged her husband, an army lieutenant, with annoying her with his smoking, particularly in the dining room. She complained that he had 'during the whole of his married life neglected the duties of a husband and refused to accompany her to any places of amusement'.[20] There was little evidence, in these cases, of the Christian manliness, promoted by Evangelicals, which was so fundamental to domestic ideology.[21]

These sources, though, reveal more than the brutal habits of errant upper-class men. It is precisely in the more mundane cruelty charges, which required careful investigation and extensive evidence in court, often precipitating intense argument and cross-examination, that we see the most subtle differences in husbands' and wives' expectations of marriage. Most of the charges, in order to prove legal cruelty, were based on acts of physical violence, often extreme violence, but the violence itself conveys less than the resulting arguments over provocation and alleged failures to live up to appropriate standards of behaviour.

It is hardly surprising to find that most cruelty cases, like those explored in the previous chapter, reveal a veritable domestic battle-ground, with quarrels between middle- and upper-class husbands and wives being developed over the years of a marriage almost to the point of ritualized sexual antagonism. On one side we see husbands, with the backing of a still confident and publicly sanctioned patriarchal authority, going to extreme lengths to enforce obedience. Here we find the closest consistency with traditional domestic ideology, and most husbands seem to have been acutely conscious of the ideological support system that sanctioned their authority. More significantly, perhaps, they also reveal a regular pattern of frustration of husbands in the exercise of their power, and it may often have been that frustration which resulted in physical acts of violence – or cruelty – which brought them to the Divorce Court. If they interpreted their wives' resistance as provocation or their wives had ever forgiven them and hence 'condoned' acts of cruelty, the resulting arguments could stimulate more intimate examination of their behaviour.

Many middle- and upper-class wives, undoubtedly, submitted over years to extremely harsh treatment and violence, and any attempts at resistance might involve even greater risks of physical abuse. But, like Frances Kelly, not all their grievances were confined to acts of physical assault. The area we still know least about is that of sexual cruelty, although the alleged frequency of marital rape, particularly, stimulated the activities of some feminist reformers by the late nineteenth century, and has recently received considerable attention from feminist historians.[22] This cannot be directly tested from divorce records, for the simple reason that marital rape *per se* was not an offence in criminal or divorce law; only violence associated with it might be successfully pleaded to sustain a charge of cruelty.[23] But other frequently cited grievances hint at the unstated sub-text of sexual tensions. The fact that so many assaults were described as having taken place in bed, with no explanation of precipitating arguments, suggests an obvious sexual battleground, where women might resist but run a high risk of becoming physical victims. We cannot be certain, for example, why John Bayley seized his wife, a clergyman's daughter, by the shoulders 'and forcibly held her down upon the bed, and thereby greatly terrified' her, but the regularity of such charges is heavily suggestive.[24] Much the same applies to similar charges of husbands' breaking down doors to force their wives to return to their own bed after they had sought refuge with a relative, although such demands could result as much from husbands' fury at defiance of their authority as from immediate sexual demands.[25]

More explicit charges of sexual cruelty tell a more obvious tale, providing vivid evidence in support of John Stuart Mill's allegation that the law of marriage could deny Victorian wives any role but that of 'the personal body-servant of a despot'.[26] Charges of forcible sodomy, which was a marital offence, and could be supported by medical evidence, appeared where marital rape could not, and were calculated to outrage judges against a crime 'so heinous and so contrary to experience'.[27] The pleading and hearing of such charges was a delicate matter; even the charge in the petition might be couched in guarded language; wording such as 'disgusting, degrading and unmanly conduct on the intercourse between himself and your petitioner', and treatment 'with the utmost cruelty and indelicacy in other respects which she forbears to mention' left no doubt of the charge.[28] In some cases the judge ordered the court cleared of women and children for the hearing.[29] But the main impression to emerge from the hearings was the domination by husbands, not so much through superior strength as claims to power through authoritative knowledge. Mary Norris, for example, who attempted to resist her husband's 'peculiar' intercourse after the first occasion, neglected to complain of it because he persuaded her that 'it was usual between man and wife', and that 'he had a right so to treat her if he pleased'.[30]

Similar impressions emerge from the frequent charges of wilful communication of venereal disease, which was sufficient to establish a charge of legal cruelty. In isolation the charges convey little more than fairly obvious examples of the double standard of sexual behaviour, but in the context of other allegations they underline the vulnerability of young, sexually ignorant wives, to their husbands' manipulation. Bernard Brocas infected his wife, Jane, with syphilis during her pregnancy, and when painful symptoms appeared persuaded her that it was merely the result 'of being in the family way, and that all women in that state suffered in the same way'. When her condition worsened, she consulted a doctor, who advised against any sexual intercourse, which was very painful to her, but 'in spite of her entreaties' Bernard insisted on his rights. He also assaulted her shortly before her child was borne. Jane left him to stay with her father, Sir John Rose, and returned when Bernard promised to treat her more kindly, only to be infected a second time and suffer several violent assaults. After the death of her father, who had offered her some protection, Bernard's conduct worsened. He left her without food and threatened even harsher treatment, claiming, she alleged, that now that her father was dead 'she should be obliged to bear whatever he chose to inflict upon her'. When she pleaded with him not to sleep with her because of his disease, he declared 'that he would "use" her as long as he chose. That no resistance of hers should prevent it, for he would tie her down, not that he cared for her but that he chose to make "use" of her.' Jane also alleged that Bernard insisted on acts of sodomy with threats of violence.[31] Even if her testimony was exaggerated, it is clear that the evidence of infection sustained her more general charge of sexual victimization.

No explicit allegations of rape, which was not a marital offence anyway, were necessary in such petitions, where allegations of blatant sexual persecution were so conspicuous. It is impossible to know how often such grievances formed an unstated and unprovable agenda behind the more common charges of physical assault. But the frequent evidence of wives' resistance generally should caution us from leaping to the simple assumption that they were invariably victims, even in sexual contests. The Norris case, for example, which involved a sodomy charge, apparently arose from a habit of tests of strength. Mary Norris admitted that on one such occasion 'we did try strength and I was the strongest then', and other evidence suggested that the couple frequently indulged in rough physical play, and that violent acts sometimes occurred after they had been 'romping together'. Some such 'romps' might easily get out of control, and if play moved to uninhibited aggression she would very likely be left at her husband's mercy. But the practice of rough play and banter in itself hints at a less one-sided relationship than the offence itself might suggest.[32]

It is less certain what to make of other more obscure sexually related cruelty charges. When Louisa Birch, who had had three children in less than two and a half years, charged that her husband, a civil engineer, had 'insisted on using against the wish of your petitioner French Letters when he had connection with her, and thereby incurred the risk of injuring her health', she may have been seeking desperately for any charge to support her case, which was not legally strong. The court ignored the charge, but her solicitor took it seriously enough to include it in her petition, suggesting that mechanical methods of birth-control may still, as late as 1872, have been regarded as unnatural and dangerous among some sections of the middle class.[33] Possibly it echoed the same fears of those wives who complained that their husbands beat them during pregnancy and attempted to force them to have abortions.[34] Certainly it supports the general impression that sexuality, pregnancy and childbirth were issues of frequent contention in middle-class marriage.

It would be misleading, though, to leap from that finding to the assumption that the more mundane charges invariably masked an unstated form of sexual cruelty. Husbands who responded to the regular demands to spend more time at home could provoke countless disputes over genuine domestic issues with no sexual resonance. Whether the tensions arose over finances, contested authority over servants and children, or conflicting interpretations of their mutual obligations, the resulting conflict was usually intense and enduring. Because petitions citing cruelty needed to focus on acts of violence or persecution they necessarily dominate most of the texts. But in the complex arguments and presentation of evidence one of the most common patterns to emerge is wives' ultimate resistance, either sustained and consistent resistance or opposition coming late in the marriage, to what many described as a system of tyranny, or, more simply, as unreasonable behaviour. There is an obvious tautology involved in highlighting such resistance in divorce cases, since the very step of petitioning for a divorce or separation from nineteenth-century marriage was itself an act of resistance or defiance – the last desperate attempt, for those able to afford it, to escape from an intolerable marriage. But the records often indicate levels of resistance which predated the divorce petition by many years; they also reinforce the impression from the case studies that, for many wives, submission to their husbands, while in principle an explicit article of faith, in actual practice was hedged about with limitations based on what they regarded as reasonable or unreasonable behaviour.

The most overt form of defiance by wives was itself physical violence, either in desperate self-defence or last resort, or, occasionally, taking the offensive against a violent or unreasonable husband. Richard Dyer, an accountant in the civil service, was divorced by his wife, Amelia, in 1859 after twenty-five years of marriage, during which each of them maintained the other had been violent. But the kind of incidents which were proved to have provoked the wife's violence were either the violence of her husband, or, more interestingly, actions of his which she felt to be unreasonable, one case being his refusal to hire a wet-nurse for her after the birth of her fourth child. The petition makes it clear that Amelia felt a wet-nurse was a quite reasonable request rather than a luxury and that Richard had exceeded his reasonable authority in denying her.[35]

Defiance cannot exist without authority and power, and wives' defiance invariably arose from simmering resentments on both sides about the contested exercise of men's power.[36] The apparently trivial nature of many of the quarrels which led to violence underlines the depth of those resentments, and it is not surprising that the violence so often appears out of proportion to the presumed insubordination of wives. Elizabeth Waddell precipitated one fight with her husband, a Customs clerk, by venting her irritation when he ordered her to clean his boots while lying in bed intoxicated. She 'told him to clean them himself and threw them at him' and was repaid with a violent blow, giving her a black eye and a cut lip.[37] Similarly, when Pleasure Butler, the wife of a lock manufacturer in Wolverhampton, was aroused by his abuse of their daughter at the tea-table, she slapped him with the back of her hand, precipitating such a furious beating, which knocked her against the fender, that the servant and neighbours, possibly concerned about her pregnancy, came in to help and put her to bed.[38]

Cases of wives' violence being clearly proved, even when they charged their husbands with cruelty, were not uncommon. Some, like Charlotte Bostock, would simply throw back missiles already hurled by their husbands. More often they would attack them with the most easily available weapon, the poker, or occasionally an umbrella or walking-stick, and a great deal of scratching and biting was admitted as well.[39] More revealing, though, was physical resistance which was humiliating rather than violent. A husband's wounded dignity did not readily recover from the pulling of his whiskers – a frequent target among Victorian husbands – or the emptying of the contents of a chamber pot over his head. The chamber pot, like the poker, was an ever-present temptation should a bedroom fracas turn violent, and it was a weapon used by husbands as well as wives. But the polluting indignity of such an act was hardly consistent with a husband's rightful authority in his own household.[40]

Acts of violence and humiliation, though, were not the most typical forms of wives' resistance. More common were the less physical acts of defiance and self-assertion by wives which husbands often confidently charged as provocation for their own resort to violence. Defiance to many husbands served as a warrant for violent retribution and later as grounds for a defensive charge of provocation in the Divorce Court (which rarely succeeded unless the wife herself had resorted to violence). In 1858 George Blake, an army lieutenant, denied beating his wife during her pregnancy, but went on to blame her for all their troubles because she had 'neglected her household duties and disregarded his advice and wishes and thwarted and opposed him, and was unmindful of and acted in a way wholly incompatible with her conjugal duty of submission to [him]'.[41] After ten years of marriage Emma Baker sued her husband, Thomas, a draper in South London, for divorce, partly because of a succession of violent quarrels. The most common cause of the quarrels was proved to be Emma's complaints about her husband's habit of staying out late at night and her refusal to get up at 4 a.m. to make coffee for Thomas and a friend he brought home. The judge, who granted Emma's petition, apparently agreed that such a demand was unreasonable, but it seems that her husband or his counsel did not think that it was an excessive demand to make of a wife and regarded it as sufficient provocation for violence.[42]

Such disputes, trivial on the surface only, go to the heart of middle-class sexual antagonism, for they reflect deeply felt and conflicting understandings of mutual obligations in marriage. Most husbands found it difficult to abandon expectations of literal and unquestioning obedience and service, while their wives more often tried to establish a threshold of tolerance of their husbands' conduct, beyond which they resisted what seemed to be unreasonable. As we saw in the previous chapter, husbands' 'unreasonable' behaviour encompassed more than violent treatment. Passionate convictions about child-rearing, for example, could provoke fierce quarrels, as mothers subverted the harsh disciplinary regime of fathers. Robert Mytton, a barrister, accused his wife, Annie, of inciting the 'undutiful and disobedient conduct' of his 3-year-old son, as Annie, along with the servants, protested against his threatening treatment. Long periods of isolation locked in a bedroom, verbal hectoring as Robert promised to 'master' him and give him a 'good whipping', and a terrifying display of anger as he shook a heavy life-preserver at his head, all provoked Annie's protests. Her intervention was seen by Robert as aggravating disobedience against his reasonable correction. He demanded her absolute submission, without much success, and read out the marriage service to her to 'insist on the duties and obedience of a wife'. His disciplinary regime then extended to Annie, as he attempted to censor her reading, persecuted her during illness, deprived her of food and accused her of bad management of his house and children. His sense of power is conveyed in his taunt to her that she would never goad him to strike her 'because I know the law', but he also betrayed his frustration against the alliance of the household, including servants, against him, and, during fierce quarrels, accused her of 'prigging' his money extravagantly, failing to earn her bread in any way and being a burden to him.[43]

The Mytton case hints at one of the most common grievances of husbands and wives, arising from economic tensions, particularly in the handling of household finances. Husbands routinely charged their wives with extravagance with the housekeeping money, and wives answered that their husbands were unreasonably parsimonious in providing money for household expenses which they did not understand. We have already seen the Bostock household haunted for years by that central bone of contention. But charges of wives' extravagance were invariably accompanied by wider complaints of violent language, an irritating manner, deficient housekeeping, 'neglect of business' in a family enterprise and general defiance.[44] Wives' efforts to make ends meet commonly provoked violence if they trespassed on their husbands' business sphere. There was a thin line between financial interference in emergencies and more general subversion of a husband's sense of control, as Ann Hoit, a builder's wife, discovered when she provoked a severe beating by selling off her husband's building materials to supplement the housekeeping money, which she claimed was inadequate to feed and clothe the family.[45] There is a clear parallel here with tensions among working-class couples provoked by women's survival strategies, such as pawning, which could blur gendered understandings of economic roles and provoke violence.

Where traditional roles were inverted and wives became the main breadwinners, the chances of violence were even greater, and the results illuminating. The evidence of greater combativeness among those wives who adopted or maintained an active economic role in a family business or outside the household recalls the commonly stated observation that a working-class wife's best protection against a violent husband was an income of her own.[46] Small retail businesses often survived only through a wife's intervention and management if a husband neglected it and turned to heavy drinking. She could then be subject to regular demands for money, accompanied by threats and violence.[47] Much the same pattern occurred when women established schools and other businesses after husbands ceased to support them, or where widows married again after inheriting a business.[48] Unless the wife's property was protected by a marriage settlement their husbands had the right to claim what was legally theirs, yet most of these women, well before the Married Women's Property Acts, doggedly refused to yield their income and livelihood. Eliza Brunell, for example, inherited a public house in Weymouth from her first husband. On the morning after her second marriage in 1857, to Theodore, a 'photographic artist', a furious quarrel erupted over her refusal to pay his debts, and until he left her, with debts still unpaid, he conducted a series of savage beatings and humiliated her in the street. Yet, despite Eliza's legal vulnerability to Theodore's demands, she never paid his debts, and managed her business despite his harassment. The fact that he rapidly followed his assaults with adultery, as well as the rape of a young girl for which he was imprisoned, made Eliza's divorce a simple matter.[49]

Cases like Brunell's, even without its extremes, invariably attracted the court's sympathy for the wife, who had supported herself in the face of her husband's unmanly failure to provide. For men like John Curtis, whom we saw in the previous chapter, the role of a successful breadwinner was inseparable from their sense of manliness. Not all men were similarly moved, as Robert Mytton's taunting of his wife with her failure to earn a living suggests. But the court was in tune with prevailing ideas of respectable masculinity in legitimizing wives' defiance of these feckless husbands.

One of the most eloquent statements husbands could make about their marital power was that made by John Curtis and James Kelly when they deposed their wives from domestic management.[50] Control of children, servants and household arrangements, though theoretically delegated by husbands, was a hallowed preserve of women's distinct sphere, so it is not surprising that wives brought such grievances to the Divorce Court to support a cruelty charge, and that the court took men's aggressive invasion of women's realm seriously. Separating a mother from her children was serious enough,[51] but wholesale removal from household management could climax long years of antagonism, and was likely to have been planned carefully by husbands, rarely in a fit of spontaneous pique. After many quarrels, during which John Duncan abused, beat and degraded his wife, Mary, in front of her servants and children, he deposed her from all domestic responsibility, told the servants to take no instructions from her, barred the children from her company and her from his bed, and insisted she eat alone. In her place he put a daughter from his first marriage, Mary's stepdaughter, a drastic and humiliating act in itself.[52]

The ultimate humiliation, no doubt, was the elevation of a servant to the wife's position, which was central to James Kelly's elaborate system of mastery. But without going to those lengths, servants could be called upon to augment a wife's sense of degradation. Another clergyman, James Cooke of Suffolk, responded to his wife, Frances's 'insulting, offensive and irritating language' in his family's presence by deposing her from all domestic management, putting her 16-year-old daughter in her place, and banishing her to a tiny servant's room. He crowned the indignity by calling the servants to hear him find fault with her, declaring that 'her conduct and management were such that he would not bear it any longer.' On other occasions, in the presence of children, servants and guests, Frances's 'irritating' language prompted him to drag her chair away from her and send her from the room. Significantly, when James insisted that if she was to stay in the house she should return to his own bedroom, she refused, in the judge's words, 'unless she was treated as a wife, and restored to her proper position downstairs, and in the management of the house'. After Frances left him this condition remained central to the fruitless negotiations about her possible return to the home.[53]

Servants, as such incidents demonstrate, were a defining feature of the dynamics of middle-class family relationships, and their presence distinguishes middle-class marital conflict most sharply from that among the working class. For wives, whose gender identity was intricately bound up with class identity, servants could be used to threaten both simultaneously. For husbands, female servants also provided the prospect of sexual adventure, and in some cases adultery and 'undue familiarity' with servants was combined with further humiliation of wives. Emily Swatman complained that her husband persistently wooed the servants in her presence and encouraged their disobedience to her.[54] Other women charged that men drove them to do servants' dirtiest and most menial work, like Jane Hudson, married to a farmer, who stressed that she 'had been accustomed to good society and to the comforts and indulgences befitting her condition in life as the daughter of an independent gentleman'.[55] Most often, though, servants, like children, appear as women's allies, witnessing violent treatment, rescuing them from dangerous assaults, intervening to drive off dangerous husbands, and providing safe refuge from further violence, sometimes by sleeping together in a locked room. Their close relationship with a wife could lead them to be assaulted or terrorized along with her,[56] and in one case a servant, known to be a sympathetic witness, was intimidated by the husband, for which he received a contempt of court warning.[57]

Servants, then, were far more than a threatening alien presence below stairs to be kept apart from or patronized by respectable employers, as some accounts have represented them.[58] Certainly the size of many middle-class homes provided greater opportunities for conjugal seclusion, and much argument and violence may have taken place in bedrooms just to ensure greater privacy. But as witnesses to marital behaviour servants were ubiquitous and missed very little. They might attest to the adultery of either partner at home and even give evidence on the state of the bedsheets to confirm venereal discharges.[59] No husband or wife could be unaware that they lived under a kind of perpetual observation, which rendered their privacy a relative matter. Under ordinary circumstances the presence of servants, as social inferiors, might not 'matter',[60] but in an atmosphere of conflict servants rapidly became deeply implicated, as observers and participants, ensuring that the differences of their employers were played out on a larger stage. Once in the Divorce Court they became parties to that public gaze which stripped middle-class marriage of any pretence to privacy.

The public gaze was central to the process of marital regulation. One practical purpose of the new Divorce Court had been to provide relief from unbearable marriages to a slightly wider cross-section of society than the previous regime had catered for. But it had a further, less explicit, purpose, to regulate the worst kinds of marital misconduct, and to make husbands and wives more moral. Once the court was established it became an invitation to publicity, and friends and relatives of aggrieved parties sought to vilify their partners in the press and inform the Queen's Proctor of decrees obtained under false pretences.[61] But the most consistent publicity came in the daily reporting of cases, from the sensational to the mundane.

From the beginning the propriety of publicity prompted some soul-searching and regrets. Opponents of reform attacked public curiosity in the court as well as the act itself; Sir George Bowyer, for example, feared that the court had also become a 'school of divorce', as prospective litigants flocked to hearings and devoured press reports to learn how to do it, their minds inevitably becoming tainted in the process.[62] By contrast *The Times*, which discussed the issue regularly, supported regular publicity, though it admitted that its chief evil 'lies in looking to it for a succession of exciting narratives; and when the public gets rid of this propensity the Court will do its business with cavil from no one'.[63] By 1910, when the Royal Commission on Divorce canvassed the issue of publicity, there was a large body of opinion in favour of rigorous censorship at the discretion of judges.[64] But the moral lesson of marital misconduct punished always remained adequate justification. Despite his own misgivings, Sir Cresswell Cresswell, the first president of the Court, concluded that

> a calm consideration of the state of feeling that results from matri-
> monial quarrels, and of the utter disregard of public opinion, and of
> the shame and disgrace which must attach to them, often mani-
> fested by both parties, must produce a beneficial influence upon all
> who are not blinded by their vindictive feelings.[65]

Not all divorce cases reached the press, of course, but the daily diet of reports was wide enough in scope to expose the full range of marital discord, from sensational adulteries to savage violence and the calculated though frustrated campaigns for mastery of the Reverends Kelly and Cooke. Revelations of sexual infidelity lent themselves to the laments of moralists and the imagination of novelists. By contrast the 'unreasonable' behaviour of husbands surveyed here produced a different kind of reaction, which inspired feminist attacks on marriage and a full-blown campaign of reform within two decades. The sustained resistance of wives to their husbands' varied attempts to maintain absolute control was usually quite explicit in the reports. But less explicit was the conditional nature of their resistance, their limited threshold of tolerance for ill-treatment, and their determination to insist on a reasonable standard of conduct. Their private correspondence, like that of Charlotte Bostock and Frances Kelly, invariably held out the hope of reconciliation if only their husbands would moderate their rigid expectations of obe-dience. Annie Mytton, whose lawyer husband had persecuted her and her child relentlessly, concluded her letter to him after a brief reconciliation:

> Your loving wife – always – if only you would behave as you did in
> the last three or four days and renew that period of happiness all
> would be well. For the sake of those few days of happiness how
> much I could forget![66]

The frequency with which husbands promised to amend their behaviour if their wives would return to them, only to renew the same treatment after forgiveness and reunion, suggests that Annie Mytton, and thou-sands like her, could be grasping at straws in their companionate tolerance and expectations.[67] The rigid, patriarchal standards which inspired so many husbands' violence and intervention in domestic affairs died hard, but after 1857 public exposure provoked increasing criticism. We need to turn now to one of the first sites of criticism and regulation, the Divorce Court itself.

THE CONCEPT OF MATRIMONIAL CRUELTY: JUDICIAL INTERVENTIONS

The judiciary, one might expect, should have been the last body to display sympathetic understanding of dissension and sexual inequalities in marriage, much less legal adaptation to them. The notorious conservatism of the law, its reliance on precedent, and, on that account, its instinctive defence of the status quo, should, logically, have enlisted the elderly, upper-class male monopoly of judges on the side of traditional notions of patriarchal supremacy in marriage. Ideologically, indeed, most judges involved in divorce law continued to declare their commitment to a patriarchal model of marriage, and to lecture wives on their duty of submission and restraint. Yet, faced with overwhelming evidence of what they came to agree was the 'unreasonable' behaviour of husbands, their rulings shifted progressively in wives' favour and towards a more companionate model which demanded restraint and forbearance from husbands. This is most apparent in their modification of the law of matrimonial cruelty. Subtle but important changes in the common law effected by judges, in both the Ecclesiastical and Divorce courts, reflected not only their own domestic ideals but the range of expectations, grievances and attitudes brought to the courts, where issues of what constituted reasonable marital behaviour were often of crucial moment. There was, in effect, a delicate process of interplay between marital experience exposed in the courts and the judicial rulings which effected significant changes to the law of matrimonial cruelty by 1869. The changes that did evolve also implied a recognition from the bench that matrimonial legislation, after the reform of 1857, was inadequate to cope with the wide extent of sexual antagonism in middle-class marriage, an acknowledgement, in effect, that the 'hard cases' we have already seen were the tip of an iceberg.

The nineteenth-century divorce law is often presented as a paradigm of Victorian conservatism in social and political attitudes: slow to change, limited in application and reflecting rigid inequities of class and gender, it illustrates the less progressive dimension of the Victorian reforming impulse.[68] Under ecclesiastical jurisdiction before 1857 it provided no more than separation from bed and board (divorce *a mensa et thoro*), and prohibited remarriage of either party, absolute divorce (*a vinculo matrimonii*) being restricted to the wealthy minority able to finance a private act of Parliament.[69] With the Matrimonial Causes Act of 1857 the new Divorce Court permitted absolute divorce, but enshrined the double standard of morality in law by allowing relief to a husband for his wife's adultery alone while requiring a wife to prove aggravated adultery, which required a compounding offence such as cruelty, desertion, incest, or bigamy. The old divorce from bed and board, without right of remarriage, re-labelled 'judicial separation', continued to be administered by the new court in virtually unaltered form, and both kinds of relief inherited the old body of principles and rules from centuries of ecclesiastical decisions. Under both ecclesiastical and secular jurisdictions access was limited, with some exceptions, to those able to afford substantial legal fees, and no significant changes were made to the legislation until 1923 when the double standard was abolished and 1937 when grounds other than adultery were admitted for a divorce decree.[70] By most contemporary standards the law was indeed conservative, reflecting widely held, though by no means universal, convictions about male superiority and female submission in marriage. More liberal voices opposed the double standard, particularly, from the time of the passage of the 1857 act through Parliament, while divorce reformers in some American states and British colonies, before and after 1857, felt that patriarchal marriage was secure enough to withstand more adventurous measures of reform.[71]

For all its importance as an indicator of general attitudes, the rigidity of the law tells us little about the practice of the courts. Historians have only recently begun to probe beyond the history of the law itself to the more complex social history of judicial decisions, and the nature of the marriages which came under its scrutiny.[72] We have already seen how divorce records can open a dramatic window on to the sexual politics of marital relations, but they can also illuminate the process of change in judicial attitudes. In this respect case records show the operation of the law of matrimonial cruelty to have been of special significance.[73] Before and after 1857 it was one of the most crucial grounds for women, either as a single justification for judicial separation or, in combination with adultery, for divorce. Legal arguments from both spouses over what constituted cruelty provided the courts with vivid insights into the nature of domestic relationships.

As in other spheres of matrimonial law, judicial attitudes affecting legal cruelty were slow to change. English judges, for example, never accepted the American arguments in favour of mental cruelty that produced such a radically different divorce law by the late nineteenth century.[74] But judicial conservatism masked an evolution in decision-making which was of central importance for women seeking relief from intolerable marriages. Indeed, since legislators in 1857 had shown reluctance to do much more than increase access to the old divorce facilities, confining themselves to an act of administrative rather than social reform, any changes which were to be made to the double standard necessarily had to come instead from evolution in case law.

By the late eighteenth century the ecclesiastical courts had generally come to equate legal cruelty with extreme violence, although the degree of violence required to justify a decree had become less savage since the Restoration; the emphasis had evolved from a clear risk to life to a pattern of 'grave and weighty' acts resulting in pain and suffering. The only clear exception to this rule was the general acceptance of 'wilful communication' of venereal disease as legal cruelty, which required proof that the offending spouse was aware of the infection, the disease was actually communicated, and the victim was unaware of the offender's condition.[75] J. M. Biggs, the legal historian, found that violence was present in all cases alleging cruelty up to the end of the eighteenth century. The statement of this state of the law delivered by Lord Stowell (Sir William Scott), together with an expansion in its interpretation, in the case of *Evans* v. *Evans* (1790), formed the basis of innumerable judgements well into the twentieth century:

> The causes must be grave and weighty, and such as shew an absolute impossibility that the duties of married life can be discharged. In a state of personal danger no duties can be discharged; for the duty of self-preservation must take place before the duties of marriage, which are secondary both in commencement and in obligation; but what falls short of this is with great caution to be admitted. . . . What merely wounds the mental feelings is in few cases to be admitted where they are not accompanied with bodily injury, either actual or menaced. Mere austerity of temper, petulance of manners, rudeness of language, a want of civil attention and accommodation, even occasional sallies of passion, if they do not threaten bodily harm, do not amount to legal cruelty: they are high moral offences in the marriage state undoubtedly, not innocent surely in any state of life, but still they are not that cruelty against which the law can relieve. Under such misconduct of either of the parties, for it may exist on one side as well as the other, the suffering party must bear in some degree the consequences of an injudicious connection; must subdue by decent resistance or by prudent conciliation; and if this cannot be done, both must suffer in silence.[76]

After this essentially negative definition, Stowell stressed that the court had always insisted upon proof of danger to life, limb or health. It had been 'always jealous of the inconvenience of departing from it', and he had heard no one case cited in which the Court has granted a divorce without proof given of a reasonable apprehension of bodily hurt. I say an apprehension, because assuredly the Court is not to wait until the hurt is actually done; but the apprehension must be reasonable; it must not be an apprehension arising merely from an exquisite and diseased sensibility of mind.[77]

This more positive definition, as Biggs noted, contained great potential for expansion in the law relating to cruelty, since to actual physical violence it added 'threats' of violence, which could in time be extended to include not only verbal threats but also non-violent conduct which might arouse a fear that violence could follow.[78] Stowell himself began to stretch the concept soon afterwards, when, in *D'Aguilar* v. *D'Aguilar* (1794), he affirmed that 'words of menace intimating a malignant intention of doing bodily harm, and even affecting the security of life' constituted legal cruelty. The husband had resorted to some violence, but his threats had been regular and extreme enough to provoke 'such fear and terror as to make the life of the wife intolerable. If rendering life intolerable be the true criterion of cruelty, what can have that effect more than continual terror, and the constant apprehension of bodily injury?' Here Stowell came close to opening the way to a new definition of cruelty in his stress on 'rendering life intolerable', which shifted the emphasis away from the strict definition of the offensive act towards the consequences for the victim.[79] But at this stage the emphasis remained focused upon a narrower construction of the interpretation of violent threats.

Stowell's judgement in the Evans case was vitally important to the subsequent direction of the law of matrimonial cruelty; no case was cited more often to justify varying decisions of judges in both ecclesiastical and divorce courts. Its influence was threefold. First, for those judges intent on holding to a strict construction of cruelty, Stowell's negative definition served well, and during the first half of the nineteenth century the main criterion continued to be bodily injury 'either actual or menaced'.[80]

Secondly, for those judges interested in expanding the definition, the Evans case invited them to ponder the meaning of a 'reasonable apprehension of bodily hurt' and to probe in greater detail into domestic relations to discover conduct which might be construed as equivalent to a threat of violence. This preoccupation, as we will see, eventually prompted 'reforming' judges to place a greater stress on the consequences of marital conduct, such as ill-health, rather than its nature and intent;[81] their rulings certainly went well beyond anything Stowell construed from strict violence or threats. In view of the consistent reluctance of Parliament to legislate on legal cruelty, such changes, indeed, could only come from the judges, who, as one legal historian commented, embarked upon a 'conscious circumventing of established precedents, thereby rendering the older decisions obsolete'.[82]

But thirdly, it is significant that throughout this period of erratic change most judges readily echoed the kind of homilies Stowell delivered to the spouses before him, whether or not he granted their petitions. When he rejected Mrs Evans's petition in 1790, for example, he added his hope that she 'has not to learn, that the dignity of a wife cannot be violated by submission to a husband'.[83] Similarly, in 1801 he rejected Mrs Oliver's allegations with the admonition that 'having assumed the relation of a wife, she is bound to execute the duties that that relation imposes; and particularly to abstain in future from inordinate pretensions and exaggerated complaints'.[84] Provocation, as he reminded Mrs Waring in 1813, could disqualify an abused wife from legal remedy, since 'if the conduct of a wife is inconsistent with the duties of that character, and provokes the just indignation of the husband, and causes danger to her person, she must seek the remedy for that evil, so provoked, in the change of her own manners.'[85] Matrimonial law under Stowell and his contemporaries could afford to be liberal in dealing with cruel excesses, but a strict law of patriarchal supremacy was regularly upheld as the central principle governing marital relations. In effect these homilies constituted a working judicial definition of patriarchy, emphasizing the ultimate benevolent sovereignty of husbands and humble submission of wives, which, implicitly or explicitly, continued to dominate judges' rulings for more than half a century.

It is a nice historical irony that Lord Stowell's rulings should have played such a prominent part in encouraging moralizing homilies from the Bench and the judicial assertion of principles of husbands' supremacy, wives' submission and the need for domestic forbearance. In 1813 at the age of 69 he married his second wife, Lady Sligo, only to leave her for the peace of his club and Doctors' Commons after barely a year of shared domestic strife.[86] 'Physician heal thyself' was an alien notion to Stowell, but that did not cause his successors to dispute either his broad definition of cruelty or his strict insistence on wifely submission. In 1844 Dr Lushington, refusing Lady Dysart's plea for a separation from a marriage with a long history of violent quarrels, some of them apparently equally matched physically, commented that a wife could secure her own safety 'by lawful obedience and by proper self-command'.[87]

Homilies urging wives to seek security in submission were commonplace, especially during the first half of the nineteenth century. They testify to deeply held judicial beliefs in a patriarchal model of marriage. But those beliefs did not prevent the same judges from reinterpreting Stowell's definition of legal cruelty very much to the advantage of wives in search of relief. From an early reluctance to consume the court's time deliberating on 'mere domestic quarrels',[88] judges moved increasingly to more detailed investigations of marital relations, and in the process were forced to confront the routine drama of sexual politics as it was acted out in the home. Their altered concerns and judgements reflected changing expectations and standards of marital conduct, which prompted them to turn increasingly, if hesitantly, to a companionate model of marriage. When Lord Penzance (Sir James Wilde) dismissed Mrs Hudson's plea for separation from a drunken husband in 1863, his advice to her was not that she must submit to her husband but rather that she seek 'such remedies as may be found in the force of the natural affections and domestic ties'.[89] The shift in vocabulary was symptomatic not only of a hesitant move by judges towards a companionate model of marriage, but of their increasing tendency to scrutinize those 'mere domestic quarrels' which Dr Lushington preferred to ignore in 1831.

'Mere domestic quarrels' were, no doubt, far removed from the more dramatic cases which tended to capture public interest, but significantly they were the driving force behind changes in the common law. The more sensational cases, as we have seen, especially those exposing the sexual dalliance and brutality of the upper class, attracted most attention when reported in the press. They presented few legal difficulties for judges once the charges were proved, since the proven violence usually satisfied a generally agreed and objectively judged standard. On the other hand more common and mundane cruelty charges, like many of those detailed in the previous chapter, and which required more detailed judicial scrutiny within the context of particular relationships and class assumptions, are revealing of problems arising from the exercise of authority in marriage, which changing attitudes in society were causing to be judged differently in the courts.

Close judicial scrutiny of routine conjugal relationships stemmed from worries over precisely those themes we have already identified in the previous analysis of divorce records. Wives who chose to resist their husbands, whether physically or passively, effectively challenged authority which enjoyed the backing of a confident and powerful ideological support system. A legal system which encouraged husbands to equate wives' resistance with provocation and forgiveness with condonation of acts of cruelty could produce knotty legal complications, and the resulting charges and counter charges might involve ever more detailed examination of their domestic lives.[90] Wives' resistance, as we have seen, was frequently qualified by their sense of what constituted legitimate submission to their husbands, but their submission was hedged about with limitations based on their definition of reasonable or unreasonable behaviour. Precisely the same preoccupation with husbands' 'reasonable' behaviour exercised judges in their deliberations over the definition of legal cruelty. In the process they gave some legitimacy to women's heightened expectations, and moved closer to the concept of companionate marriage which most petitioning wives took as their governing model.

It was against a background of defiant wives and rising expectations, then, that the first presidents of the Divorce Court, Sir Cresswell Cresswell and Lord Penzance, made decisive changes in the law of matrimonial cruelty. By 1869 their rulings developed to the point where the traditional requirement for violence was no longer necessary to substantiate a charge of cruelty. Before the 1857 Divorce Act the tendency had largely been to continue to apply a literal interpretation of Lord Stowell's 1790 judgement. In 1854, in the London Consistory Court, Dr Lushington, commenting on *Chesnutt* v. *Chesnutt* (1854), in which Mrs Chesnutt accused her husband of constant intoxication and obscene language, applied a strict interpretation of Stowell's ruling:

> Here is no charge either of bodily violence inflicted, or of threats of personal ill treatment. However disgusting the language charged, if proved, may be – however degrading habits of intoxication – however annoying to a wife, especially the wife of a gentleman and a clergyman – these facts, standing alone, do not constitute legal cruelty. If it be said that the consequences to the wife are mental suffering and bodily ill-health, I do not think that the case would be carried further. The same might be said of other vices; of gaming for instance; or gross extravagance, to the ruin of a wife and family; – all these might occasion great mental suffering, and consequent thereon, bodily ill-health to the wife; but they do not constitute legal cruelty.[91]

By contrast, Lushington's own judgements betrayed some early con-tradictions and uncertainties about the need for violence when he equated spitting in a wife's face with a threat of violence, a decade before the Divorce Act. His ruling reflected a genuine revulsion with the offence:

> Is it possible to imagine that when a husband has proved himself so utterly insensible to all those feelings which he ought to entertain towards his wife, so brutal so unmanly, that he would, when his passion was excited, restrain himself within the bounds of law, and that his wife would be safe under his control? Threats of ill-usage have been deemed sufficient to justify a separation. I am of opinion that such an outrage as this is more than an equivalent to any threat, for it proves a malignity of feeling which would require only an opportunity to shew itself in acts involving greater personal danger, but never surpassing in cowardly baseness.[92]

Here Lushington stretched the law by enabling the 'cowardly baseness' represented in the act of spitting to be equated with a threat, at least, of violence. Still, like his predecessors, his emphasis remained fixed upon the offensive act itself rather than the consequences for the victim. By contrast the process by which Cresswell and Penzance, who remained committed to the marital views and decisions of Lord Stowell, moved rapidly after 1857 from a rigid position to a more flexible interpretation, offers an interesting insight into the interplay between the law, domestic ideology and the realities of marriage.

The new Divorce Court inherited the rulings of the old ecclesiastical courts for judicial purposes, so there was no obvious reason why any dramatic changes should have been anticipated from the new jurisdiction. No doubt the formation of a new civil court, headed by permanent presiding judges trained in the common law, rather than ecclesiastical law, offered tempting opportunities to reshape matrimonial rulings.[93] It is in just such circumstances that judges might be prompted to bring the law into closer conformity with changing standards by acting according to their own lights. But a more persuasive explanation for the shift lies in the increased frequency and intensity with which middle-class wives brought their complaints of both violent and non-violent cruelty to the court.[94]

The increased frequency doubtless stemmed from easier access and comparative cheapness in the new court; the reformed divorce law opened facilities to a much wider cross-section of the middle class, and even to some beneath the middle class.[95] But there was also a widening in the kind of complaints brought by wives, which might suggest that companionate ideas were undermining their willingness to tolerate meekly their husbands' abuse of authority, even when the abuse was non-violent. By a slow process, with much vacillation and assertion of the legitimacy of patriarchal authority, Cresswell and Penzance came to share the views of many petitioning wives about what constituted actionable cruelty. From early in Cresswell's jurisdiction (from 1858 to 1863) the increase in applications for relief provoked public expressions of concern, and alarmist critics soon alleged that he was opening the floodgates to an intolerable level of licentiousness, or, at the least, that the daily revelations had 'disturbed our previous notions of conjugal felicity'.[96] These fears stemmed largely from the novelty of marital sensations, particularly involving the adultery of the upper class, which were now reported more routinely in the press. But they did nothing to prevent Cresswell and Penzance from quietly adjusting the law to fit new conditions.

Soon after Cresswell's appointment there were some suggestive straws in the wind foreshadowing changes in the interpretation of cruelty. His judgement in the Bostock case of 1858, which we examined in detail in chapter 3, made important changes to the law of condonation, which so often operated to prevent women from obtaining relief even after the most violent abuse was proved in court. Condonation, simply, amounted to forgiveness of a marital offence. A spouse who explicitly forgave an act of cruelty or adultery, or who implicitly forgave it by cohabiting with the offender afterwards, was deemed to have 'condoned' the offence, thus negating its legal force. Victims of violence who lacked alternative accommodation – which was the plight of many wives without their own resources or near relatives – necessarily would find their case hard to win, no matter how clear cut the evidence of cruelty.

In 1858 Cresswell ruled that Charlotte Bostock had undoubtedly suffered from violent cruelty for the first twenty-eight years of her marriage, but that there had been 'undoubted condonation' by her up to May 1855, and no later violence. But he then ruled that the legal force of the earlier violence could be revived, not only by subsequent violence, which was the existing requirement, but by later verbal threats of violence which satisfied the court that 'further cohabitation would be attended with danger to the party threatened'. In the Bostock case this centred on Robert's alleged threats to treat his wife as the murderer, Corrigan, had treated his, which, Charlotte claimed, prompted her to leave the house in fear of violence. For Charlotte it was a cruel irony that, having opened the prospect of winning her separation without the need to prove further violence, Cresswell then dismissed her case because of her technical failure to prove that 'the threats were such as to have caused a reasonable apprehension of bodily injury, or that, in fact, the wife quitted the husband's house on that account'. But Charlotte Bostock's failure should not obscure the genuine transformation effected by Cresswell, since his ruling shifted the court's attention from the nature of offending acts, whether physical or verbal, to their results, in this case the wife's 'apprehension of bodily injury'.[97] This was to form a consistent theme in other changes to the law of cruelty, and to open the way to rulings which would afford relief to wives whose cases would certainly have been dismissed before Cresswell's judgement.

Cases which followed the Bostock ruling established a clear tendency to widen the definition of legal cruelty. In 1859, in *Suggate* v. *Suggate*, Cresswell ruled that violence to the children in the presence of their mother could be accepted as legal cruelty despite the absence of any violence to the mother herself.[98] Two years later, in *Milner* v. *Milner*, he held that a husband who treated his wife in the street in such a way that passers-by took her to be a prostitute was also guilty of cruelty, again despite minimal violence. Cresswell's shock at this case, in fact, prompted him to forget to apply any test of violence or violent threats at all:

A man who has insulted his wife by treating her in the street like a common prostitute is guilty of at least as great an indignity as if he had spat in her face. I can imagine nothing more insulting or shocking to a woman of proper feeling than being so treated. . . . It is a case of the grossest and most abominable cruelty.[99]

A year later, in *Waddell* v. *Waddell*, Cresswell admitted what he would otherwise have dismissed as inadmissible violence because it was combined with other offensive behaviour from the husband, particularly throwing cold water and spitting in his wife's face. Echoing Lushington in *Saunders* v. *Saunders*,[100] he stressed, not for the first time, that it was the wife's social background which conditioned the gravity of the offence, and there 'was nothing to lead me to suppose that the insult to the wife would not be felt as an act of grievous cruelty'.[101] Lord Penzance continued this trend in *Swatman* v. *Swatman* in 1865, where, again, despite negligible violence, he held that the husband's behaviour, extending to regular drunkenness, carousing with the servants, entertaining prostitutes at home and drunkenly urinating throughout the house 'made up a burden which the petitioner's health was unable to bear, and under which she could not be expected to discharge the duties of married life'.[102] In all these cases the emphasis had begun to shift more consistently away from the particular offence to its effects on the victims, conditioned by social background and expectations.

Two cases, which we examined in detail, in chapter 3, may enlarge our understanding. The Curtis case, heard by Cresswell in 1858, provides an obvious pointer to the process that resulted in the decisive Kelly case which followed in 1869.[103] Much of the conflict in the Curtis household, we saw, was provoked by class resentments between Frances and John Curtis. Frances and her family showed contempt for John's engineering profession, and John nursed insecure resentments about his ability to provide for a wife with high expectations and a tendency to defy him when provoked. Cresswell insisted that John was quite within his rights in attempting to enforce his authority in the proper manner against Frances's objections. He commented, for example, that John had a 'perfect right' to improve his condition by removing his family to Australia, but no right to enforce that by violence, threats and blows. Cresswell did accept the early violence as legal cruelty but then discounted it because continued cohabitation for years after the events constituted condonation of the offence, which could only be revived by further violence or threats of violence. Other acts alleged at this stage, which were not accepted as legal cruelty, mainly dealt with John's treatment of the children, which, Frances alleged, was excessively harsh.

The case was complicated by medical diagnosis of John's mental state, which twice led to his being placed under restraint for 'brain-fever'. But for Cresswell the eventual granting of Frances's petition was based on the fact that he was not insane, and, therefore, she was all the more in need of protection from his excitable temperament. If he had been judged insane that would have ended the case, since the remedy then became incarceration rather than separation. John's performance at the trial certainly convinced the court of his sanity; he was sufficiently lucid to undertake his own defence, he hired neither a solicitor nor barrister, conducted his own cross-examinations, and, according to *The Times*, 'summed up the evidence in a very able speech'.[104]

The crucial element in the Curtis case was non-violent behaviour which Cresswell deemed to have revived the earlier violent cruelty, thus negating the condonation. This brought Cresswell to focus in detail on quarrels over control of the children, John's 'discipline' of Frances for presumed misbehaviour, and particularly his displacement of her as household manager. Frances's detailed account to her mother of John's system of control was central for Cresswell in his judgement that John's non-violent actions revived his earlier physical cruelty. He rejected John's allegation that Frances's admission of his refusal to strike her proved she had never suffered personal violence, and summarized the significance of his behaviour this way:

> she was treated with great harshness, insulted in the presence of her servant, displaced from her proper position in her house, and rendered subordinate to her own servant; not indeed on account of any immoral propensities of the respondent, but from a violent and unreasoning exercise of authority, – a course of treatment, in my mind, constituting a breach of the implied condition which the law would annex to any condonation of earlier acts of cruelty and sufficient to excite a well-founded apprehension of further violence.[105]

The legal import of John's behaviour remained fixed, as before, on the fear of further violence that it invited. But this was neither the first nor the last case where the court expressed disgust at a husband's displacement of his wife from her 'proper position in her house', and Cresswell was sufficiently impressed with Frances Curtis's assessment of her husband's 'unreasoning exercise of authority' to use it as the basis of his decision in her favour. The preoccupation, both in Frances's petition and Cresswell's judgment, with the loss of a wife's authority over those deemed to be her social subordinates, vividly underlines the importance that each attached to women's class identity. The inversion of roles between the middle-class wife and her servant, which, as we saw, so outraged Frances, seems also to have reinforced the gravity of the offence for Cresswell. Sixty-eight years earlier, in the Evans case, Lord Stowell had largely ruled out such grievances 'arising from particular rank and situation',[106] but now the dignity of class was closely tied to Victorian ideas of conjugal companionship. The offence against separate spheres was intricately bound up with an offence against class norms.

Very similar forms of disapproval are evident in the judgment of Lord Penzance, eleven years later, in the leading case of *Kelly* v. *Kelly* which established a crucial change in the law of cruelty. As we saw in chapter 3,

James Kelly's intrusion into his wife's domestic activities was more relentless and sustained than that of John Curtis. To his removal of her as household manager, he added an unremitting system of control, surveillance and incarceration. For Lord Penzance this was the salient aspect of the case. James had opened her letters, called her a vile traitor and apostate, challenged her fidelity without foundation and accused her of treachery and treason. In Penzance's words 'She was entirely deposed from her natural position as mistress of her husband's house', she was followed by a servant, and when the couple were together James spent the time 'putting her sin before her'.[107] James's unreasonable and unforgiving attitude was evidenced by his detailed production in court of a twenty-year-old correspondence recounting an earlier dispute, for which Penzance castigated Kelly, observing that the letters proved that 'in place of forgiveness for a fault so bitterly repented, he offered a harsh and exacting demeanour, withholding his confidence, and at each fresh, self-accusation insisting on further abasement'.[108]

In granting Frances Kelly her separation, Penzance, and later, on appeal, Penzance and two other judges, stressed that physical violence was not essential because the husband's actions had become a clear threat to his wife's health, which had broken down under his relentless campaign. It was, then, not the nature of James Kelly's actions – clearly non-violent – which was important, but their consequences, and that was what constituted the legal importance of the case as a landmark for the concept of matrimonial cruelty.[109] But the three appeal judges also expressed indignation at the nature of the case, far more so than in many cases involving extreme physical violence. Penzance, for example, commenting on James's removal of his wife as household manager, insisted that 'without disparaging the just and paramount authority of a husband, it may be safely asserted that a wife is not a domestic slave, to be driven at all costs, short of personal violence, into compliance with her husband's demands'.[110]

In contrast to earlier warnings to wives to secure their safety by control of their tongues and tempers, the appeal judges countered James's accusation that his wife frequently lost her temper with the affirmation that 'a wife does not lose her title to the protection of this court merely because she has proved unable to bear with perfect patience and unfailing propriety of conduct the ill-usage of her husband'.[111] In response to Kelly's insistence that his ruling motive had been simply to put sufficient pressure on his wife to ensure her lawful obedience, Penzance took the opportunity to deliver a homily on the familiar rules and limits of patriarchal marriage. Kelly, he claimed, 'invokes the theory of the law, that the wife should be subject to the husband, but he forgets to add the qualification, "in all things reasonable"'. His elaboration of this theme was a succinct statement of evolving judicial views on the limitations of female submission and male coercion in marriage:

> The law, no doubt, recognizes the husband as the ruler, protector, and guide of his wife; it makes him master of her pecuniary resources; it gives him, within legal limits, the control of her person; it withdraws civil rights and remedies from her, save in his name. Conversely, the law places on the husband the duty of maintaining his wife, relieves her from all civil responsibility, and excuses her even in the commission of great crimes, when acting under her husband's order. By these incidental means, it has fenced about and fostered the reasonable supremacy of the man in the institution of marriage. In so doing, it is thought by some that the law is acting in conformity with the dictates of nature, and the mutual characteristics of the sexes. Be that as it may, the subordination of the wife is doubtless in conformity with the established habits and customs of mankind. With all these advantages then in his favour, the law leaves the husband, by his own conduct and bearing, to secure and retain in his wife the only submission worth having, that which is willingly and cheerfully rendered. And if he fail, this Court cannot recognize his failure as a justification for a system of treatment by which he places his wife's permanent health in jeopardy, and sets at nought not only his own obligations in matrimony, but the very ends of matrimony itself, by rendering impossible the offices of domestic intercourse and the reciprocal duties of married life.[112]

Penzance's assertion of the theory of patriarchal supremacy in 1869 was no less certain than that of Stowell in the 1790s; indeed, at the same time Penzance went to great lengths in the House of Lords to ensure that married women's property reform should protect abused women without violating 'the old idea of the husband being paramount and the wife subordinate'.[113] But his qualification of patriarchy, together with his decision in Frances Kelly's favour, mirrored a change in judicial attitudes to sexual politics in the domestic sphere. Both he and his brother judges saw one of James Kelly's chief excesses of authority to be his removal of Frances from her domestic managerial role. The resulting judicial disapproval of the violation of separate spheres, which the judges saw as part of a wider system of relentless persecution, social humiliation and unwarranted interference with wifely duties, followed Cresswell's line in the Curtis case, and reflected a changing assessment of what constituted unreasonable exercise of male authority.

This far-reaching change was prompted at least in part by the kind of behaviour wives were refusing to tolerate and bringing to the courts. The evolution of judicial judgement, then, was partly an empirical response to accumulating evidence of wives' resistance or defiance of their husbands' 'unreasonable' behaviour. Even the language used by the judges tended to follow that of petitioning wives, particularly in their use of the term 'unreasonable' to define a shared threshold of unacceptable non-violent abuse. It is no coincidence that the non-violent behaviour frequently condemned was a direct product of the undue invasion and control of the domestic sphere by husbands, a uniquely middle-class offence, as the Curtis and Kelly cases illustrate. Companionate marriage might prescribe a greater domestic presence for men, but while it remained fused with patriarchal notions it could easily backfire and become simply another sphere for the exercise of a husband's absolute authority. The alterations made by mid-Victorian judges to the law of matrimonial cruelty gave tentative acknowledgement to these contradictions.

The extent to which the new-found flexibility of Divorce Court judges was a product of their learning on the job, through exposure to mounting evidence of sexual antagonism which came to the court, is underlined by comparison with decisions in other courts, where there was less direct experience of family relationships. In the Court of Queen's Bench, for example, the right of a husband to kidnap and incarcerate his wife was not rejected until the notorious Jackson case went to the Court of Appeal in 1891. Edmund Jackson, confronted with his wife's refusal to obey a court order for 'restitution of conjugal rights', simply kidnapped her, and held her in his house forcibly. His action was upheld in Queen's Bench, and only reversed when the Lord Chancellor, Lord Halsbury, argued in the Court of Appeal that 'no English subject has such a right of his own motion to imprison another English subject, whether his wife or anyone else'.[114] The case underlines the importance of close judicial acquaintance with domestic experience if even the slightest progress in legal change was to be effected. The only parallel was in the magistrates' or police courts, which dealt with many cases of wife-abuse among the poor, and we have seen how magistrates often developed a reputation among women for sympathetic treatment of their problems.[115]

The cautious nature of this alteration in case law is obvious, and perfectly consistent with the more general British conservatism already noticed in matrimonial law reform. It is also what we might expect from judges who made their commitment to patriarchal ideals in marriage so explicit. The Kelly case certainly opened the way to greater discretion for judges in interpreting non-violent cruelty and allowing for sensibilities 'arising from particular rank and situation',[116] which Stowell had rejected. But later attempts to extend the definition to include 'mental cruelty', which went beyond threats to health to include any actions which made married life intolerable, were decisively rejected, thus avoiding the judicial liberalization of divorce law which had already occurred in many

American states.[117] Despite this the changes did have wider ramifications. When, in 1895, the legislature permitted women to obtain separation, maintenance and custody orders from magistrates' courts on the ground of 'persistent cruelty', it adopted the definition already developed in the Divorce Court, including threats to bodily or mental health.[118] For years afterwards magistrates had to grapple with their own subjective interpretations of 'persistent cruelty', and the later Royal Commission on Divorce, conscious of inconsistency, urged that it be expanded to include 'grave insults and offensive conduct, though not amounting to actual physical violence'.[119] But since the magistrates provided many more separation orders than the Divorce Court provided divorce and separation decrees, that was where the implications for abused women were felt most substantially.[120]

The evolution of the law of matrimonial cruelty, for all its caution, reflects a subtle process of interplay between marital experience, ideology and the law. One of the most striking features of the process was the responsiveness of judges, though wedded to traditional patriarchal notions of marriage, to accumulating evidence of intolerable levels of non-violent cruelty. In the Curtis and Kelly cases the judges came to share wives' grievances through an appreciation of their husbands' violation not only of separate spheres, but of women's rightful place in the class hierarchy, especially in relation to subordinate servants. The sense of class violation paralleled and developed from that shown in earlier cases where men spat in their wives' faces or treated them like prostitutes. For legal historians the explanation for this legal evolution has usually been limited to a reference to changes in social attitudes to marriage and to the 'greater equality of husband and wife'.[121] But for social historians the process of change is necessarily the central object of inquiry, since it takes us beyond legal changes to the drama of everyday sexual politics acted out in the home, and to the construction of bourgeois gender roles.

It is precisely in the construction of gender roles, though, that deeper significance of this judicial scrutiny of marital cruelty emerges, for, as the prescriptive manuals and other commentaries on marriage testify, the judges were not alone in their criticism of husbands' abuse of authority. Most prescriptive writers were unable to envisage any solution beyond the language of forbearance, but the considerable power of judges enabled them to go well beyond the customary moral homily. Their increasing willingness to give wives relief from cruel husbands when companionate harmony failed served notice that men's behaviour was becoming subject to a more rigorous standard of regulation. The management of conflict, in effect, had brought the private sanctuary of the middle-class family, increasingly recognized as a locus of sexual antagonism, into the public domain. Individual conflicts were exposed in minute details of personal behaviour explored in the courts and reported in the press, and fed the debate on marriage which flourished in late-Victorian England. The courts had joined feminists, journalists and novelists in the popular cause of marriage reform, which in the later nineteenth century took on the mission of civilizing patriarchal authority and moulding a more feminized companionate ideal.

Divorce Court judges were at the heart of the process of regulation, alert to petitioners' grievances, reformers' demands and moralists' fears. Their own efforts at regulation and reform were, like divorce legislation into the twentieth century, designed to protect the institution of patriarchal marriage rather than weaken it, and the need for protection was highlighted all the more by abusive husbands who put men's authority into jeopardy. Matrimonial law had been entering the public arena as a subject of popular interest for much of the nineteenth century, sometimes through the initiative of judges themselves. The long tradition of law reporting of significant cases was an 'in house' procedure for the legal profession, rarely accessible to public scrutiny. But by the 1830s some judges sought wider publicity for judgements they deemed significant through separate publication. In an illuminating judgement, published separately in 1835, Joseph Phillimore, after dismissing a wife's plea of cruelty, justified his ruling publicly, noting that

> persons united in marriage must exercise mutual forbearance to lighten the yoke which they have imposed upon themselves; coarseness of manners, or austerity of temper, if proved, which they are not in this case, would not amount in law to legal cruelty. . . . It is my duty to remember that the general interests of society are best secured by maintaining and upholding the indissolubility of marriage, and that it is not competent to a judge to create a new precedent to meet the exigencies of an individual case.[122]

Press reporting of such cases in the ecclesiastical courts had become routine by this time, but the proceedings of the new Divorce Court in 1857, where Phillimore's successors gradually undermined his ruling, provided an unprecedented opportunity for real marital discord to vie with fiction for public attention. For all their caution in adapting the law to new conditions, the judges were instrumental in placing men's authority and private behaviour on the agenda as a subject for public debate. The new discourse of marriage reform was to succeed in bringing husbands' conduct under scrutiny, but the extent to which it really brought about a change in marital relationships is more difficult to establish.

5

THE ADAPTATION OF PATRIARCHY IN LATE-VICTORIAN MARRIAGE

EVIDENCE FROM AUTOBIOGRAPHY

The impression of domestic tyranny which emerges from the Divorce Court, necessarily based on some of the hardest known cases, is a severe and no doubt unrepresentative one. It would be a simple enough task to select an equally impressive and untypical list of Victorian 'happy marriages' to contradict the striking examples of patriarchal rigidity and female resistance we have seen.[1] At the same time it should be acknowledged that the more rigid patriarchal characterization of English husbands, especially, was common by the middle of the century. Harriet Beecher Stowe was one foreign observer who found Englishmen quite unlike their American counterparts in their insistence on obedience. Writing for an American audience about the management of conjugal tensions she contrasted American views (and particularly her own) with those of England:

> Read Mrs Ellis's *Wives of England* and you have one solution of the problem. The good women of England are there informed that there is to be no discussion, that everything in the *ménage* is to follow the rule of the lord, and that the wife has but one hope, namely, that grace may be given to him to know exactly what his own will is. *'L'état c'est moi'*, is the lesson which every English husband learns of Mrs Ellis, and we should judge from the pictures of English novels that this 'awful right divine' is insisted on in detail in domestic life.[2]

Stowe's image of English husbands, though a common one and based on some observation, was already under attack when she wrote. The reaction of Divorce Court judges, alone, conveys some idea of the intensity with which patriarchal views of marriage were being tempered by companionate prescriptions. But it is much harder to gauge the wider impact of such changing views on middle-class marriages which never reached the Divorce Court.

Autobiography can provide one set of impressions of marital experience, even though its use is fraught with methodological difficulties.

Several recent studies of autobiography as a genre and source have expanded on these difficulties. The dangers of misrepresentation, exaggeration, defective memory and an eye for a particular readership can all lead to serious distortion. Together with the vagaries of self-selection of autobiographers from among the more literate, politically prominent and self-preoccupied, these problems militate against any clear typicality or representativeness, and certainly underline the need for caution in their use. Such hazards, clearly, are not unique to autobiography; most historical evidence comes to us with similar imperfections, demanding similar critical treatment. Several recent historians, recognizing this, have made extensive use of autobiography for family history, and have been quick to detect significantly common preoccupations with aspects of family life, such as childhood, education and family relationships.[3]

It is precisely here, though, that we encounter more serious handicaps in the use of autobiography for insights into the history of gender relations. The reticence of autobiographers, not only from the working class, on issues of sexuality is notorious, at least until recently. Much the same kind of inhibition has applied to other elements of conjugal intimacy beyond generalized assertions of sentimental and idealized devotion. Marital conflict, like sexuality, was not a side of their life which most Victorians wished to expose to their progeny, let alone the public. Middle-class men, particularly, as Davidoff and Hall have shown, could have a deeply felt investment in domestic harmony, 'as the crown of the enterprise as well as the basis of public virtue'.[4] Their domestic tensions invariably remained a deeply private matter, more suited to divorce proceedings of the disreputable than to the story of a virtuous life. Sensational stories of violent marital hostilities, like those of the Bulwer-Lyttons and Nortons, stand out as exceptions to the general Victorian rule of reticence on the tensions of married life.[5] The fact that such stories attracted an eager audience, as did sensational divorce cases, was all the more reason for discretion.

These limitations, though, do not apply with the same force to the autobiographical writings of many of the literary children of the late-Victorians. From about the 1920s this post-Freudian generation began eagerly to dissect their parents' – and grandparents' – marriages in minute detail, often to seek clues to the formation of their own character in the obsessions, affections and conflicts of their families. Frequently their interest stemmed from the closer, more intense family intimacy experienced by the less prosperous middle class compared to those whose childhood had been secluded in distant nurseries and dominated by under-nurses and governesses.[6] The intended point of the story might be a heroic, oppressed mother, a defeated father, lifelong devotion or relentless antagonism. The account might well be distorted by a child's eye view, later filtered through the refracting lens of the professional

135

writer's creativity and the need to give meaning to a prosaic childhood. But after allowing for such bias, we are given illuminating insights into late-Victorian and Edwardian private life.

The clearest impression to emerge from these stories, as we might expect, is one of diversity in marital relations; few stereotypes are sustained, no myths conclusively debunked. There is, for example, no consistent pattern of meekly submissive mothers and uniformly author-itarian and repressive fathers, like that found in a recent study of earlier Victorian autobiographies.[7] But amidst the diversity one can detect a gradual adaptation of patriarchal power and authority to changing conditions. What follows, drawn from about fifteen autobiographies, is an attempt to highlight the most common aspects of the process of adaptation. Given the wide diversity in social backgrounds of these writers, no claims can be made for systematic prosopographical cer-tainty.[8] The objective here is to delve more deeply into aspects of middle-class family relationships already identified in the court records, for which the frankness of many autobiographers offers an ideal vehicle.

With these late-Victorians we find little to parallel the rigid, uncom-promising husband in the mould of James Kelly. Certainly, among the fathers of most writers the preoccupation with their authority was far from dead, but more striking is the frequent contrast writers drew between their relentless, often brutally patriarchal mid-Victorian grand-fathers and their fathers, whose relationship with both their wives and children could be far more complex, aspiring to varying degrees of companionship. Richard Church remembered his maternal grandfather, Benjamin Orton, 'as a holy terror, a perfect example of the Victorian domestic tyrant'. Solemn rituals attended his daily return from work, as his wife and children received him at the door, helped him with his coat and hat, and submitted to inspection. Nightly his wife stood by, towel in hand, while he ritually anointed his feet with olive oil. His cantankerous outbursts at the dinner table are reminiscent of Virginia Woolf's fictional characterization of her father, Lesley Stephen, in *To The Lighthouse*, when, finding an earwig in the milk, he threw his plate through the window.[9] Orton's family routinely prayed that his dinner would please him, but, on one occasion, 'He picked up the offending viand on his fork, examined it, looked angrily at his wife, and said, "What is this; an *attenuated* mutton chop?" And he flung it into the grate.' Church's mother eventually rebelled against her father's tyranny, gaining for the rest of the family 'some degree of freedom, with only a grumbling Zeus in the background, still dangerous but latent'. The freedom, though, extended less to Orton's wife, who continued to submit to his threatening rule.[10]

Similar accounts recur among those few writers who remembered their middle-class grandparents. Eric Bligh, for example, described his maternal grandfather as a 'masterful rather than a tender husband'.[11]

What is more intriguing is that, in these two cases, at least, their daughters became strong wives, fully able to stand up to their own husbands.

Most late-Victorian and Edwardian husbands, to be sure, were still a long way from relinquishing their authority. Gerald Brenan's father, an army officer, adapted his habit of military command to his domestic rule, where his family were periodically terrorized by his irritable moods and outbursts, particularly when he was frequently at home after his retirement from the army due to defective hearing. Brenan's mother attributed these explosions to his father's 'liver', but their target was always his wife. His outbursts, frequently at the breakfast table, had a ritual quality. In his 'black mood, assailed like Prometheus in his liver', he would seek a target for attack.

> This someone was always my mother. Bursting with a sense of injured impotence, craving to rend and destroy, he would find his opportunity in one of those appeasing remarks that, with incurable tactlessness, she invariably made when she saw trouble coming. Without looking up, he would snub her and then, throwing down the *Morning Post* which he had been reading, he would turn on her in the rude and contemptuous tone that came so natural to him. The tone of the Victorian gentleman addressing his wife, which even the Married Women's Property Act had done little to mitigate. She, obedient wife that she was, would take this meekly, only muttering to me apologetically under her breath that this morning he had 'a little touch of the liver'. But meekness was a spur to my father. He wanted to hurt, to injure, yet he was afraid of going too far, because he did not like scenes.[12]

From the day of her marriage Brenan's mother had learned to tolerate her husband's 'cold autocratic rudeness' and his 'exaggerated jealousy' which led him to forbid her to see any friends 'behind his back'. Over the years his family learned to anticipate and prepare for his unpredictable moods and his 'overbearing male egoism', so that their every move was conditioned by his likely reaction.[13]

A similar patriarchal presence often loomed behind the surface appearance of companionate harmony in families at the turn of the century. Eleanor Farjeon's literary family, to all intents and purposes joyous, fun-loving and child-centred, dominated, according to her, by a generous, domesticated husband, Ben Farjeon, was increasingly consumed by her unpredictable father's irritability, the 'dominant mood in the family'. Furious outbursts would follow trivial accidents – 'small breakages, forgetfulnesses, a dozen of the minor mistakes we all make every day' – so that the family took the risk of concealing them from him. Outbreaks of temper could at any moment follow 'Mama's failure to lay out his studs for the evening, to pack the blotting paper when going for a holiday, to send the carving knife to the butcher to be ground.'[14] Eleanor Farjeon was later haunted by her childhood memory of lying in bed, listening 'to the tone of the talk in the dining room underneath'. If the quiet murmur continued she slept peacefully, but too often 'the strong voice grew excited, and the gentle voice silent. Then I did not sleep till nearly morning.' Little wonder that her mother became accomplished in the art of avoiding conflict, submitting even to the most absurd commands to keep the peace.[15] Men have never had a constitutional monopoly on irritability and temper, but the deference accorded by their families to the 'nerves' of men like Brenan and Farjeon betrayed shared assumptions that their needs and demands should take priority, regardless of the costs to others.

Yet, for most of these writers, the dominant memory of their families was one of companionship, with fathers often at home and parents deeply devoted to each other. Companionate harmony was a common ideal to which both partners aspired; in some cases there might even be a shared goal of marital equality and friendship. In the lower middle class the stereotype of the mid-Victorian husband, indifferent to domestic concerns and his wife's anxieties, a 'structured absence' in the home, portrayed in H. G. Wells's account of his shopkeeper family, almost imperceptibly gave way to a more sympathetic model, akin to Helen Corke's grocer father, close to his children and frequently solicitous to his wife, tolerant of her own disapproving outbursts against him.[16] But the variations were endless. Roger Ackerley, a successful businessman, was in one sense a stereotypical Victorian husband, for years keeping a clandestine mistress and mostly remaining remote from his family. To his children he was at once a figure of disciplinary retribution and fun. Yet he invariably avoided conflict at home, leaving a 'vacuum of authority' which his son, J. R. Ackerley, thought was never filled by his mother.[17] Mary MacCarthy's account of her upper middle-class family at Eton, where her father was warden, allowed little scope for male dictation. Her 'indulgent and generous' father's perpetual financial anxieties were argued out in regular family 'conferences', where every extravagance and every possible saving would be scrutinized, only to be proved indispensable by her mother. The short period of austerity which followed such conferences quickly gave way to renewed family extravagance, which never seems to have produced the characteristic intervention of husbands' economic control.[18]

In upper-class households, where children traditionally saw little of their parents, many still recollected long hours of play and discussion with their fathers. But this did not necessarily result in a more visible and intrusive patriarchal domestic presence. Beryl Lee Booker thought her father's stomach trouble prompted him to prevent worry and distress by avoiding conflict at home. He 'was no longer master, if he ever had been, in his own house. He adored Mother, but both went their own gay way and lived the lives which suited them best.'[19] In a similar household, Enid Starkie's father, a more dominant man with a much younger, more deferential wife, nevertheless consistently supported his wife's authority over the children, despite deep disapproval of her severe system of management and discipline. His superior power, acknowledged by his wife, counted for little in their most basic difference.[20] In rare cases the appearance of domestic harmony stemmed less from such restraint and forbearance than from ideology. J. Lionel Tayler's father, a Unitarian preacher, shared with his wife a commitment to John Stuart Mill's feminism, and especially to friendship and equality in marriage. According to their son their marriage was mutually satisfying, although his cryptic comment that each 'faced the difficulties of their temperaments in probably the best way they could' leaves rather too much to the imagination. Ironically, their son, together with his own wife, came to repudiate the Millite feminism of his late-Victorian parents.[21]

Rare ideologues like the Taylers no doubt continued to be outnumbered by those committed to the more conventional doctrine of separate spheres. Katherine Chorley's father, Edward Hopkinson, a managing director of a large Manchester engineering firm, founded his ideal of womanhood on Ruskin's *Sesame and Lilies*, and both he and his wife consistently lived out Ruskinian ideology to the letter. For her father their suburban home at Alderley Edge was a retreat from the 'rough outside world', the man's lot, where he came for 'comfort and inspiration and cleansing and rest'. Masterful at home, as at work, 'he expected to be waited on and obeyed', and his wife responded as demanded. She conceived her first 'plain duty' to be to carry him 'through his troubles and difficulties', placing all her energy, judgement and intelligence at his service, and sacrificing any interests of her own which might conflict. To Chorley's knowledge she never nagged, only offered advice, and if she was to get her way in the face of opposition it was effected according to the subtle prescriptions of Mrs Ellis, 'by a tactful use of the strategy of the indirect approach, a use so unobtrusive that even I imagined for long enough that it was invariably what father said or thought that "went" at Ferns'.[22] Domestic ideology continued to serve the industrial bourgeoisie of Edwardian England, just as it had served their early-nineteenth-century grandparents.[23]

The sharpest contrast to this conventional pattern is to be found among the lower middle class, where the separation of spheres, power and authority was more nuanced, and at times more contested. Richard Church remembered his Battersea childhood at the turn of the century as one dominated by his mother, Lavinia, whose wage as a London School Board teacher supplemented her husband's as a mail-sorter, and enabled them, with her obsessive thrift and paring economy, to buy their own home. Lavinia took charge of household finances and negotiated the purchase of the house. She also performed a relentless dual role, in which the daily burdens of teacher and housewife 'were paralleled by her double responsibility in bringing up her sons'. But in this close, lower middle-class 'hugger-mugger home atmosphere', with fierce intimacies and loyalties, it was Tom Church, the husband, who avoided all conflict and argument, and who left the decision-making to his wife. His personal lack of ambition, deeply frustrating to Lavinia, extended to his children, leaving her, obsessively concerned for their future, to take full responsibility for their education. On the surface this 'matriarch-ridden' household, as Church described it, betrayed no signs of patriarchal influence or authority.[24]

Yet at a deeper level this companionate family was dominated profoundly by Tom Church's priorities and interests. Partly because of his fear of conflict and violence, and his avoidance of responsibility, the Church home was 'serene and equable in its domestic atmosphere'. But at the same time it was ruled either by his stubborn sulkiness or expansive enthusiasm for his own favourite family recreations. Musical evenings were common at home, when the family would gather round the old 'Broadwood-White' piano, accompanied by Richard's flute, to play his 'old favourites'. But when Richard's older brother, Jack, showed some musical talent, and his mother supported his wish for a new piano, Tom resisted, and his own plans for two tandem bicycles to get his family 'on the road' took natural priority. A small inheritance allowed the new instrument, a Klingmann, to be bought, but, at Tom's insistence, the old piano was kept in the back room and used for family *soirées*. His hostile attitude was 'a criticism, only half concealed, of all that the new instrument stood for: a too serious interest in music, Jack's precocity, and Mother's encouragement of it.' Jack's attempts to practise invariably were met by his father's sullen withdrawal, only appeased by the family eventually joining him on the 'Broadwood-White' in enforced family togetherness, an exercise in collective humouring.[25]

But it was Tom Church's bicycle mania which most dominated his family. Lavinia could only resist his extravagant tandem purchase temporarily, and, like her sons, grimly acquiesced in his determination to have them all on the open road, exploring the far corners of Britain. Soon after the tandems were obtained, Tom planned a Boxing Day family outing, but became morose when Lavinia refused to go out in the early fog and frost. A silent, tense lunch brought a rare caution from Lavinia:

'Tom!' said Mother, suddenly, at the end of the meal. Both Jack and I detected the note of warning in her voice, and we looked at each other apprehensively. It made us shy and miserable to see Father rolled over and bounced in the flood, as though he were no older than ourselves, though we knew that in the end, as the clouds rolled away, Mother would contrive to restore his dignity and set him up again as the head of the house who could do no wrong and whose word was law.[26]

The weather did, indeed, brighten, and, to Tom's delight, the much-vaunted expedition began, but with fateful and revealing consequences. As the family company proceeded from Battersea to Chelsea, Tom, gaily providing a commentary on historic sites, remained oblivious to the cold, and the fact that the steel tandem was far too heavy for both children, each of whom soon reached exhaustion. Finally, provoked by Tom's wish to prolong the epic journey even further, Lavinia insisted on dismounting at Chelsea embankment, where the two benumbed children collapsed under the weight of their vehicle. On the deserted pavement there followed 'one of those scenes when mother broke through her usual policy of government by seeming acquiescence, and staged an open revolt'. After brushing the children down and, 'in search of evidence', feeling their hands,

> she opened her attack. She cursed the tandems, their weight, their length, their manoeuvrability. She referred to the disabilities of the female body and particularly of mothers of children, she pointed out the singular delicacy of her own children and enumerated several reasons for it, all connected with Father's heredity, personal stupidity and callousness. She called upon God to witness the universal unfairness between the sexes, with woman as the eternal victim and slave.

Throughout all this, Tom 'stood quietly waiting as though being photographed beside the new machine'. When Lavinia stopped, and drew Richard to her, as if 'to face the spears of a hostile tribe, or the rifles of a firing party', his response was infuriatingly disarming: '"That's all right old girl," said Father. 'We'll take a short cut home over Battersea Bridge."' For some years afterwards, though, these cycling expeditions continued, under Tom's influence, to monopolize the family's leisure and holiday time, terminated only by Lavinia's serious illness.[27]

The subtle nuances of dominance and submission in this relationship demand careful reading. For all the see-sawing of influence between Tom and Lavinia, for all Lavinia's sensitivity to Tom's dignity and her awareness of the 'unfairness' of gender difference, it was Tom who most dominated and controlled the Church family. Despite Lavinia's fierce ambitions for her sons' education, for them to follow their creative instincts, ultimately Jack turned to teaching and Richard took up Tom's safer, more circumscribed goal of the civil service, which had been 'good enough for him'.[28] Lavinia was the ultimate victim of her double burden, worn into exhaustion and bronchial asthma, from which Tom fled in fear and incomprehension, leaving their younger son, Richard, before his seventeenth birthday, to nurse her until death.[29] But Tom's use of shared recreation to control his family offers a novel perspective on the potential meaning of conjugal companionship and family leisure. Companionate marriage, complete with domesticated husbands, close family intimacy and shared recreation, could provide another sphere for the more subtle domination of husband and father, whose authority, no longer so blatantly exercised, continued to be sustained by a perceptive wife and her children.

A range of middle-class writers seem to have lived through similar experiences. There were various ways in which husbands' greater involvement in domestic life could simply provide increased opportunities for a less overt form of patriarchal domination. Victor Pritchett's father, in early Edwardian years a small but upwardly mobile businessman, nevertheless spent much time at home, where he showed a possessive interest in his children's welfare. Parental quarrels, whether over money or his mother's jealousy of another woman, to the point of violence, dominated Pritchett's childhood memories. But despite his mother's assertiveness, she and her children were dominated by her husband in both new and conventional ways. The conventional ways were often ritualized personal services, such as kneeling to unbutton his boots or brushing his coat on command. On the surface, Pritchett thought his father could be seen, too simply, as 'the late-Victorian dominant male without whose orders no one could think or move'. Hence he treated his family at home just as he treated his 'hands' at work. But his other, more 'female' side, Pritchett thought, was his primitive jealous urge to keep his children to himself, and this provided an equally powerful motive for control, whether through familiar male territorial hostility to outside visitors or manipulation through his religious infatuation with Christian Science.[30]

Men's religious obsessions, in fact, seem to have provided a common vehicle for family control, capable of imposing a blend of Evangelical fervour and rigid Calvinistic discipline on a reluctant captive audience. Eric Bligh's father, a doctor in Tooting and a strict Congregationalist, combined his practice with a punishing regime of Bible classes, Sunday schools and family prayers. The Blighs' family life gives every appearance of having realized the companionate ideal: there was little evidence of overt conflict, parents were openly affectionate, and Dr Bligh was the model of a sensitive and gentle husband and father. Life at the doctor's house was an uncharacteristic blend of informality and egalitarianism, as the surgery spilled over into the home, servants, children, patients and adults mingled at all hours, and mealtimes became an anarchic hubbub, punctuated by irregular comings and goings. Yet Dr Bligh increasingly oppressed his family with the 'real tyranny of his religious obsession'.

His harsh, literal, religion was not shared by his wife, and she disapproved both of his charitable ways of undercharging his patients and his regular neglect of the practice to conduct his Bible classes. At such times she was left to deal with the patients. But throughout her life, as his piety heightened into obsession, she 'supported him loyally, and battled with the patients (the phrase is hers) when he was out on some approach to his Maker. She thought he had a right to . . . well, to his recreations.'[31]

By the turn of the century, though, there was an increasing possibility that a reluctant family would resist these subtle patriarchal pressures. The devoted and loyal doctor's wife still refused to have anything to do with his Sunday schools, and attempted, with her lighter, more humorous and tolerant manner, to neutralize the 'mild uneasiness' he spread through the house.[32] Bligh records his father's ultimate failure to impose his religion on his children (although he succeeded with his Bible classes), and his description of the farce of nightly family prayers provides a hilarious antidote to our image of the strict Victorian ritual dominated by a feared and respected patriarch. The occasion took place during the evening meal, when father and family 'would use separate tactics of evasion or postponement'. He would emerge from the surgery, seat himself in a corner with the Old Testament, and await a pause in the general chatter, which only encouraged further pre-emptive activity. Eventually, he announced that 'if we had all done supper we would have . . . prayers'. After more disruptions he began, but remained oblivious to the absurd comedy unfolding around him.

> It was curious that he never seemed to be aware of the considerable mockery of these devotions, and that if he himself felt the urge of supplication, we did not. He could not see my brother Allan making faces at my sister as they knelt at their chairs, nor the flying pellets, nor could he see the cat springing gracefully to my mother's back. It was annoying and humiliating to have to explain these proceedings to visitors.[33]

Dr Bligh continued to impose these ritual 'recreations' on his family, but their derision of the proceedings signifies some of the less sensational ways in which the patriarch had developed feet of clay. Even the delicate manipulations of a companionate father might now be called into question, and humorous contempt was every bit as effective as hostile defiance.

Among all these nuances of both the defiance and survival of patriarchal power within companionate marriage, it is difficult to detect any particular stage where unequivocal change might have begun to develop. These late-Victorian and Edwardian marriages echo, in a more subtle, less drastic form, some of the themes we have seen in mid-Victorian marriages which reached the Divorce Court. For some who lived through the 1880s, though, those years later came to be seen as a vital turning point, when the old unquestioned verities began to lose their hold in the conduct of family relationships. Charles Robert Ashbee, the well-known architect, designer and romantic socialist, writing in 1939 about his parents' deteriorating marriage in the 1880s, recalled that it was at this time that 'we of the younger generation first became aware of a cleavage, a parting of the ways'. In his family, while his mother moved on, searching for fundamentals, he claimed, his father's vision was still framed by 'the conventional and superficial machinery of life'. In his mother's case the changing climate and her own tenacity impelled her

> to win a wider scope and freedom in thought for herself and her children. The eighties saw a weakening of the *patria potestas* in the home; a passing of 'the Governor', as Leech drew him; of Mr Pontifex, Samuel Butler's 'will shaker'. We begin to see a little more clearly now what that age was doing with us.[34]

Charles Ashbee's account of his mother, written expressly for his own children, is known to be heavily romanticized, influenced as much by his close relationship with her as by his own embittered rupture with his father in the eighties.[35] But the experience of his parents does offer an instructive glimpse into the accumulating tensions of a companionate, upper middle-class marriage, and warrants fuller analysis.

Henry Spencer Ashbee is best known as the obsessive collector and bibliophile of Victorian pornography, whose huge collection he bequeathed to the British Museum.[36] His interests in erotica, which he insisted were purely scholarly, have led some writers to identify him, probably incorrectly, as 'Walter', the author of the pornographic volume *My Secret Life*.[37] But these interests tell us little of the Ashbees' early family life. When he married Elisabeth Lavy in 1862 Henry was a hard-working businessman, but his marriage brought a bonus of instant prosperity. The Lavys, a Jewish-German, and Anglophile, merchant family in Hamburg, established Henry as the senior partner of an independent exporting company in London. It was sufficient to ensure Elisabeth's future and to guarantee Henry the life of an increasingly prosperous, well-travelled and mostly leisured gentleman.[38]

All the sources point to a contented, companionate early family life among the Ashbees, as first Charley, the only son, was born, followed by three daughters. Henry's diary entries are regularly punctuated with descriptions of typical Victorian family scenes, in which all of them delighted. In spring he would drive the family landau from their Bloomsbury home to Bushy Park and Hampton Court, where they would picnic under the chestnut trees.[39] He was closely involved with domestic rearrangements during the children's illnesses and proudly showed off his children's precocity for the benefit of dinner guests.[40] The dinner guests appeared regularly on Tuesday nights, when Henry and Elisabeth enjoyed the company of the likes of Richard Monckton-Milnes, Richard Burton, George Cruikshank and Elisabeth's close friend, Frances Mary Buss.[41] In 1875 Henry wrote in his diary:

> My wedding day, thirteen years married, do not think it possible for any man to have a better wife, or nicer children, am perfectly happy. Drove my dear wife and children to Bushy Park where we picnicked. Glorious weather, spent a most pleasant and enjoyable day, were quite alone.[42]

Ashbee's friend, Ralph Thomas, later described him as a man of admirable and even temper, a 'devoted and indulgent father' with the 'keenest interest in the progress of his children's studies'.[43]

There is little in these idyllic recollections of domestic contentment to make of Henry Ashbee the aloof, dictatorial Victorian patriarch. His views of the proper way for a husband to treat his wife accorded with many of the companionate imperatives so evident at the time. Mrs Dickens, for example, he considered to have been 'undoubtedly badly treated by her husband', Charles.[44] According to Charles's wife, Janet, the systematic three-year spacing between each child was Henry's doing, for he 'was before his times, and arranged these things carefully'.[45] This needs to be seen together with the mostly rigid separation between Henry's domestic life and his other activities. Apart from his business there were his varied scholarly interests, the pornography especially, most of which he seems to have pursued in his private rooms at Gray's Inn.[46] He also travelled abroad frequently, and there is an unsubstantiated family tradition that he had a mistress and another child in Paris.[47] What is certain is that as the children grew older, the domestic bliss turned to rancour and bitterness, provoked, it seems, by Henry's inflexible will and vindictiveness when his family defied him. The reasons for this are obscure, but Charles Ashbee's later inability to write or speak of his father with any frankness suggests that the son was intimately involved in the eventual breakdown of the marriage.[48]

Charles himself later attributed the break to a growing difference in his parents' aesthetic tastes. Elisabeth, he recalled, was receptive to all the new influences in music, architecture, poetry and painting, while Henry scorned them. To him the pre-Raphaelites and Swinburne brought no message, Wagner brought mere noise and in William Morris, he 'could not see the poet in the craftsman', but only a Philistine 'craftsman in the blue shirt'. By contrast his wife 'caught the meaning of the new message, she sprang to it and made it her own'. There is no doubt too much in this of Charles's own artistic prejudices to take literally, but he was probably correct to identify it as one growing difference among many. Such differences, he added, are not the cause of quarrels, simply 'the banners under which contending forces gather'. His mother he described as a Victorian rebel in refusing, in this way, to take the 'worse' side of the marriage service injunction seriously.[49]

By the time Elisabeth left Henry, in 1893, other differences probably loomed larger than these. Particularly aggravating was Henry's attitude to Elisabeth's favourite child, Charles. The son recorded bitterly his father's humiliating treatment of him when he visited his city office wearing forbidden costume, a straw hat and flannels, and was forced to make an abject public apology.[50] A more enduring difference stemmed from Charles's refusal to follow his father's footsteps in the family company. Elisabeth supported her son's decision to go to Cambridge in 1882, while Henry, perhaps hoping the errant son would come round, grudgingly acknowledged it by giving him £1,000 and insisting he make his own way for the next three years.[51] But the rift widened. In 1884 father and son were still on speaking terms, planning European trips together,[52] but in 1885 Charles entered a 'solemn protest' in his journal about 'future indifference which papas of certain creeds tend to fall into';[53] in 1886 Elisabeth was writing to her son, regretting 'to have lost you out of my home circle, but if truth be said, you have done rightly'.[54] As Charles's determination to avoid a business career became more certain, Henry's annoyance increased, and by 1887 the domestic atmosphere at the Bedford Square home reflected a crisis. On 10 July, 1887, Henry recorded in his dairy: 'My Silver Wedding, one of the most unhappy days I ever spent; let me forget it.'[55]

One cannot know how far other issues may have combined with these to contribute to the Ashbees' alienation. It is tempting to speculate about the impact of Charles's homosexuality, which seems to have developed at Cambridge at this time, but there is no evidence that either Elisabeth or Henry were aware of it, and more likely Henry simply disapproved of his son's friendships with the likes of Edward Carpenter, Roger Fry and Goldsworthy Lowes Dickinson.[56] There is no evidence, either, to indicate the extent to which Henry's interests in pornography may have worked as an irritant. What is clear is that the split was between Henry and the rest of the family, and that it developed over many years. Charles thought 'things . . . went more serenely' when Henry was away on his travels,[57] and in 1890 his sister, Agnes, spoke of the 'dread' she had come to feel for the newly married, convinced that their happiness must be only temporary.[58]

The family papers do not reveal how much of the increasingly rigid Victorian patriarch in Henry, as depicted by his son, made itself felt in the Ashbees' daily life. But Charles was probably right to stress his father's inability to adapt to Elisabeth's widening interests. These were reflected not only in artistic tastes but in her friendship with Frances Mary Buss. Buss was a regular visitor at the house, and Elisabeth sent all three daughters to her reformed school for girls, North London Collegiate. To Henry, Frances Buss simply provided another opportunity to belittle her 'feminine vanities' after a heated discussion on women's education.[59] The patronizing note may have been taken for granted in most Victorian households, but it clearly jarred with Elisabeth's heightened expectations.

If the Ashbee patriarch seems to us shrouded from view prior to the separation in 1893, it became dramatically obvious in the aftermath. The eldest daughter, Frances, had already quietly 'escaped' the household in 1890 to marry 'Teddy' Langham, but her two unmarried daughters left with Elisabeth, and, along with Charles, ensured Henry's lasting enmity.[60] There was no resort to the Divorce Court, simply a deed of separation, in which Henry made a lifetime settlement upon Elisabeth of £500 a year. With other assets, her finances were sufficient to purchase a plot in Cheyne Walk, Chelsea, where her son built her a substantial residence, and established an office of his own.[61] Here the remnants of the Ashbee family lived a more adventurous life free from the restraining hand of Henry, hosting a wide range of their own artistic and bohemian friends and putting on elaborate entertainments like Charles's 'Modern Morality Play' which included a sketch on 'The New Woman'.[62] But in his will, which was read after his death, in 1990, Henry, in the words of an old friend, ensured that his 'dead hand will . . . rule the land for 70 years to come'.[63] Elisabeth's earlier settlement was simply confirmed, if any of his daughters were ill or indigent they could, upon application, receive an allowance of £2 a week provided they were not living with their brother, otherwise his children received nothing. Most of the income from his estate, of nearly £63,000, went to his cousin, Maud Ashbee, and his business partner, Arthur Petersen; the capital was only to return to the family after their death, when it was to go to the children of Henry's eldest daughter, Frances Langham.[64]

How far all this reflected Henry's bitterness at the separation itself, how far it sprang from much earlier family tensions, is impossible to know. But the will is a striking illustration of the manipulative power of the provoked Victorian paterfamilias, even from beyond the grave. For all the affectionate companionship of the Ashbees' marriage, Henry's knowledge of his power was omnipresent, and made itself felt powerfully in the years leading up to the separation. Ironically, by 1900 his family were mostly impervious to his final manipulations.

For Elisabeth the separation had opened up new interests and opportunities, and it is tempting to see her after 1893 pioneering wider feminist horizons with all the enthusiasm of an elderly, newly liberated 'new woman'. It is undoubtedly true that her relative wealth enabled her to make the best of her separated status compared to many other middle-class women. But her action was also a pointer to ways in which the options for discontented wives were widening by the later nineteenth century; such women were increasingly reluctant to tolerate unhappy marriages, and the notorious stigma surrounding separated wives was losing at least some of its power as a deterrent against leaving a difficult husband. Taking the initiative, though, remained a painful process, and Elisabeth's correspondence with Charles testifies to some lingering regrets about her action. In one letter in 1905 she reflected that if she had read some words from Havelock Ellis on patience and forbearance twenty-five years earlier she would probably have been more cautious and stayed with her husband.[65] Much of what Charles Ashbee wrote about his mother was idealized to the point of mystification, but in making her action a metaphor for contemporary social change he put his finger on one way in which ideology was influencing marital relationships:

> In the eighties it was much harder than it is now for a woman to act as 'Grannie' acted. Women were looked upon as men's property, and the wife's property – often including the wife, was the husband's to do with as he willed. . . . Even after the law of England had been altered men still could not believe that the change had come in their own homes. They could not believe that a woman might have a life and soul of her own. Where love and unity between husband and wife are continuous, there is one life and soul, but where husband and wife grow apart instead of together, perhaps it is better to face bravely the tremendous consequences that follow. It is not a thing to be lightly done. Life can only be lived once.[66]

Henry Ashbee was aware that a harmonious marriage and contented family life required effort and forbearance in the domestic setting, from himself as well as his wife. But he was also aware, like James Kelly, that the final power remained in his own hands, and that his authority was, ultimately, supreme in his own household. Charles's hint of male incredulity in the face of challenges to this domestic sovereignty is in tune with much of the behaviour of those husbands who resisted their wives' divorce petitions, and with the intense anti-feminist backlash that greeted explicit criticisms of male supremacy in marriage. It also echoes the more subtle male domination of their families described by many of the autobiographers.

It is hardly surprising that the late-Victorian and Edwardian marriages we have examined reveal a wide diversity of relationships and conduct; it is unlikely ever to be otherwise, and is necessarily reinforced by the random nature of picaresque anecdote. But the diversity was mediated by popular ideals of companionate marriage, and by the egalitarian ethos in such contemporary legislation as the 1882 Married

Women's Property Act. Few husbands could have been unaware of some of these pressures and changes, and few wives uninspired by them, even those who took care, like Lavinia Church, to prop up the dignity and authority of their husbands at the crucial moment. But for many such families the new companionship and domestication of husbands simply offered a further sphere for the exercise of patriarchal power, which was etched deeply in the childhood memories of most writers. Marriage had, increasingly, been contested territory in this sense throughout the nineteenth century, and the Divorce Act had begun to offer women some wider solutions in the 1850s. But it was only in the last Victorian decades that separations like Elisabeth Ashbee's became conceivable without risking dire social consequences, or that a family could challenge a father's authority without provoking the violent reactions we saw in the Divorce Court. Men's authority had become an issue, and the experiences of these families mirrored a discourse which was carried on in marital advice to men, in fiction, and in feminism, to which we will now turn.

MASCULINITY AND THE LIMITS OF COMPANIONATE MARRIAGE

The struggles over authority which marked many of the marriages we have examined reflected an increasing public preoccupation with standards of manliness and men's marital conduct. We have seen how prescriptive literature before the 1857 Divorce Act had already begun to subject men's behaviour in marriage to critical scrutiny, although at this stage it was women's conduct which continued to attract most attention.[67] Despite persistent criticism of lapsed femininity from conservatives like Eliza Lynn Linton in the late nineteenth century, the critical focus tended to shift increasingly to abuse of authority by husbands rather than women's defiance.[68] Even early-Victorian satire, so consumed with the inverted images of nagging wives and hen-pecked husbands, could, with some profit, poke fun at tyrannical husbands, with an implication of serious criticism. Douglas Jerrold's biting caricature of the scolding wife in 'Mrs Caudle's Curtain Lectures', for example, was succeeded by an equally barbed image of an oppressed second wife in 'Mr Caudle's Breakfast Talk', harassed and victimized by Job Caudle, now transformed into a brutally inconsiderate husband.[69]

In court reports after 1857 the increased exposure of unreasonable male behaviour, with or without violence, but usually described simply as 'cruelty', coincided with heightened public interest and criticism, culminating in the marriage debate of the 1880s and 1890s. In the Divorce Court men like John Curtis and James Kelly provided graphic examples of the worst autocrats, while husbands like Tom Church and Dr Bligh managed to exert authority in far more subtle and understated ways. Such relationships suggest that men responded only hesitantly to the various exposures and pressures to modify their behaviour, as Charles Ashbee had claimed, although responses varied, and were mediated by socio-economic background. But the pressures and contradictions undoubtedly increased in late-Victorian years, and in many respects the intensifying debate on marriage masked a controversy about standards of masculinity.

Recent work has given us a clearer understanding of ideas of masculinity in the early nineteenth century compared to later-Victorian years. Contemporaries were certainly conscious of change. In a memoir written for her daughter in 1851, Sara Coleridge reflected on the 'grave and earnest discussions' that her father, Samuel Coleridge, used to have at Grasmere with William Wordsworth and Robert Southey. They would discuss

> the affairs of the nation, as if it all came home to their business and bosoms, as if it were their private concern! Men do not canvass these matters now-adays, I think, quite in the same tone. Domestic concerns absorb their deeper feelings, national ones are treated more as things aloof, the speculative rather than the practical.[70]

Sara Coleridge's impression of the progress of the domestication of middle-class man by the mid-nineteenth century echoes Davidoff and Hall's recent analysis of the development of a more 'domesticated manliness' during the same period. Under Evangelical stimulus an earlier notion of masculinity, which focused more on military and public power and private pursuits like hunting and drinking, made important concessions to the softening features of domestic virtues. Tenderness, love and care, the protection of the weak, especially women, and the education and cultivation of dependants became the new hallmarks of male virtue.[71] These were vital building blocks in the evolving model of companionate marriage, which flourished in so much early-nineteenth-century writing. The domestic idyll promised a conjugal utopia of mutual forbearance and respect, where husbands' and wives' understanding of each other's separate responsibilities and cares would guarantee marital harmony.[72]

It is central to Davidoff and Hall's analysis, though, that this model of masculinity was bedevilled from the outset by fundamental contradictions, which emerged from internal ideological inconsistencies as well as from material constraints in daily life. Since the model developed alongside that of separate spheres, which emphasized gender segregation and celebrated men's public virtues and women's domestic containment, it is hardly surprising that tensions developed rapidly. Critics were quick to equate manly emotion and tenderness with effeminacy and weakness, and the passionate outbursts associated with

Romanticism gradually fell into disfavour, to be replaced by a more controlled and rational male demeanour. This accorded with men's increasingly exclusive association with work and public affairs and their need for commercial success to sustain and provide for their dependants. In so far as domesticity was consistent with this orientation it stressed the divinely sanctioned moral authority of household heads, whose absolute rights in the home were 'enshrined in law and custom'.[73]

Despite this apparent ideological resolution the issue of men's domestic presence, with all its contradictions, continued to stimulate controversy. Davidoff and Hall noted a concern that domesticity was becoming 'too important to be left to weak subordinates' – women.[74] Similar concerns continued to dominate discussion till the end of the century, but were affected profoundly by the accumulating evidence of unacceptable male behaviour in marriage. Observations like those of Sara Coleridge, above, suggest the importance of changing notions of masculinity in this later period, particularly as it was played out in the domestic sphere. Some novelists came to focus in increasing detail on the qualities most suitable in a husband, prescriptive literature continued to dilate upon proper domestic behaviour for men, and by the 1880s feminist criticism was publicizing glaring flaws and inequities in marriage. All these analyses dwelt on the contradictions inherent in the coexistence of domesticated manliness with untrammelled patriarchal power in the domestic sphere, contradictions which paralleled similar tensions between 'Muscular Christian' manliness, incorporating a chivalrous ideal, and some of the aggressive realities of boys' public schools and literature.[75] The simultaneous growth of a contrasting discourse of aggressive heterosexual manliness which rejected 'feminine' qualities and close male friendships only increased the tensions.[76]

The discourse of religious prescription, from mid-century, as in the earlier period, continued to offer the most earnest and frequent advice to men on their marital conduct. The issue of men's domestic presence and family involvement remained one of symbolic importance for the health of companionate marriage, but if companionate partnership continued to be promoted as the ideal of marriage, husbands' authority increasingly preoccupied writers of marriage advice manuals. Palpable evidence of defiant wives in daily press reports from the Divorce Court, feminist critiques of marital inequality and fictional preoccupations with tyrannical husbands forced the issue into prominence and prompted much of the advice to adopt a defensive tone.

Equally important were the contradictions inherent in the model of domesticated manliness. If husbands were to spend more time at home and to take more interest in household matters, then domestic relations assumed even greater importance. If wives were not simply to 'manage'

and manipulate their husbands, a habit long deplored by writers spanning the ideological spectrum from Sarah Ellis to Frances Power Cobbe,[77]
then some way had to be found which would prevent a husband's
sovereign authority from becoming an invitation to domestic discord
and contestation.

For feminist writers like Frances Power Cobbe, the difficulty was
resolved by rejecting the whole notion of 'wifely subjection'. Command
and control were inimical to love, subjection inspired husbands to the
worst faults of selfishness, despotism and abuse, and the only effective
model for a loving marriage was a miniature republic, where voluntary
yielding would take the place of arbitrary command.[78] Most of the
popular marriage guides, operating within a more explicitly Christian
framework, took a more cautious line, but the adaptation of Pauline
injunctions on wifely submission to changing conditions produced
some elaborate doctrinal contortions, especially in determined attempts
to refute feminist arguments. Central to the advice was the language of
forbearance, urged upon both husbands and wives, requiring sympathetic understanding of each other's difficulties and anticipation and
avoidance of conflict before it could erupt openly. According to the
popular Baptist writer, William Landels, the 'subjection which is considered so galling' would never be felt by a well-matched couple, because
'the authority that requires it will never be exercised'. In a genuinely
companionate and loving relationship, each

> would understand the other so well, and be each so ready not only to
> comply with, but to anticipate the other's wishes, that their life
> would flow on like an unbroken stream, unruffled or undisturbed
> by any cross current or obstructing obstacle. And if, unhappily,
> there should occasionally arise a difference of view, their mutual
> love would so gently lead to an adjustment that probably neither
> would know which had yielded to the other; and if the husband's
> will prevailed (as it ought to prevail, if it be merely a question of will,
> and not of persuasion), it would yet be so gently asserted, and so
> readily yielded to, that the thought of being oppressed would never
> enter the wife's mind.[79]

But for all the recommendations to wives and husbands to exercise tact
and forbearance, for husbands to 'honour' and respect their wives, while
showing a greater interest in their domestic concerns, the scriptural
injunction to wifely obedience remained. Except in the case of violation
of a wife's religious conscience, 'it is the right of the husband to rule, and
the duty of the wife to obey'. All that remained for debate was the
character of the husband's rule. No rebuke should be harshly administered, and nothing justified the exercise of a husband's authority in 'an
unreasonable or ostentatious or tyrannical manner'.[80] This benevolent

sovereignty was to be inspired by dutiful and domestic wives, who would naturally attract their husbands to gentleness, while bringing them to share 'their endeavours to make home happy, and gladden them by the presence which they seek to attract'.[81]

The preoccupation with these themes in so much late-Victorian advice literature marked a heightened concern with the problematical nature of authority in companionate marriage. There was still criticism of 'unfeminine' wives who usurped the natural authority of husbands, but 'unmanly' husbands who exercised a 'harsh tyranny' over wives they should cherish came in for increasing criticism.[82] In part, as already noted, this was a response to the wider popularization of feminist critiques of marriage, and some writers went out of their way to acknowledge and refute arguments on marital equality, women's suffrage and women's education.[83] But the focus on 'unmanly' behaviour in marriage embroiled itself in those very contradictions that emerged inescapably from urging greater domestic presence on men together with authority tempered by nothing more than discretionary forbearance. Those who read sensation novels and reports of divorce cases in the press knew only too well that the forbearance could be a shibboleth, and that some men might require more than religious urging to reform their marital behaviour.

During the 1860s, in the shadow of the Divorce Act, and in tune with so many of the press reports of the new court's proceedings, novelists devoted an increasing amount of attention to errant husbands like James Kelly.[84] The fictional characters invariably offended against the norms of companionate marriage by carrying their desire for mastery over their wives to extremes. The sensation novels of the 1860s mostly depicted husbands whose faults stemmed from selfishness and insensitivity to their wives' needs, contrasted with more attractive men whose manliness consisted in their sympathy and flexibility.[85] George Eliot's portrayal of the grievous mismatch between Dorothea and Casaubon in *Middlemarch*, written at the time of the Kelly case, comes to mind immediately as a famous instance of art following nature.[86] But it was in Trollope's *He Knew He Was Right*, published, uncannily, barely a year before the Kelly case was heard, that these themes were played out in most detail for a popular audience.[87] The novel's central plot follows the breakdown of a marriage caused by dissension over the extent to which a wife could reasonably be expected to submit to her husband's demands. Louis Trevelyan, drawn as a modern Othello, is driven by blind jealousy and desire for mastery to the point of madness. His obsession is highlighted by contrast with a range of other characters, all of whom, in varying degrees, 'knew they were right', but whose stubbornness was mitigated at some point by an ability to adapt to disagreement.[88]

The story opens with Louis and Emily Trevelyan apparently happily married with a young child. Louis' jealousy is aroused by visits from an elderly family friend, Colonel Osborne, a man with some reputation for disrupting marital harmony. His clumsy attempts to warn Emily about Osborne, and to insist that she discourage his visits, only provoke her anger. She interprets his demands as an insulting lack of trust, and although she initially responds with grudging obedience, to Louis she is 'hard, dignified, obedient and resentful'.[89] Trollope was at pains to portray the decline of the marriage as a product of two conflicting stubborn wills. Louis' insistence on passive submission is matched by Emily's brooding obstinacy and neither is capable of practising such companionate virtues as forbearance and compromise. But it is Louis' obsession with jealousy and power that dominates the action, and highlights Emily's powerlessness. After their separation she is unable to regain custody of her son when he is kidnapped by Louis; sent off to live in Exeter with her sister, she is dependent on Louis' generosity for an income, and her reputation rapidly becomes the focus of local gossip. At first convinced that Emily was guilty of nothing more than disobedience and refusal to relent, Louis, under the influence of Bozzle, an unsavoury private detective, later comes to believe in her infidelity, and becomes progressively more deranged.

Trollope's portrayal of Louis' path from obsession to madness, and ultimately death, skirts the boundaries of plausibility in its relentless, unbending self-righteousness. But for a Victorian audience familiar with a discourse of marital relationships which dwelt on the contradictory themes of authority, submission, forbearance and restraint, the story was compelling and credible. Even a predominantly critical press, tired of 'stories turning upon conjugal infidelity',[90] acknowledged the realistic nature of Trollope's characterization.[91] At the outset Louis is depicted as a man acutely conscious of companionate prescriptions, but unable, in his quest for mastery against his better judgement, to yield to them. Pondering his inability to enforce Emily's subjection, he reflects: 'Let a man be ever so much his wife's master, he cannot maintain his masterdom by any power which the law places in his hands.' He contemplated restricting her visitors, but unlike James Kelly, felt he could never 'call in the aid of a servant to guard the conduct of his wife'. If she would only yield to him 'then his tenderness would begin, and there should be no limit to it'. Without yielding, there must be separation, but still he reflected upon his own duty of gentleness; his undoubted 'privilege of receiving obedience' could only be maintained 'by certain wise practices on his part in which gentleness must predominate'. Wives were bound to obey their husbands,

> but obedience cannot be exacted from wives, as it may from servants, by aid of law and with penalties, or as from a horse, by

punishments and manger curtailments. A man should be master in his own house, but he should make his mastery palatable, equitable, smooth, soft to the touch, a thing almost unfelt.[92]

Trollope makes Louis' inability to exercise that companionate forbearance his tragedy. Much later in the novel, when even he is half persuaded of his madness, he reflects that if he should yield to Emily he might be incarcerated 'in dark rooms', robbed of his liberty, 'robbed of what he loved better than his liberty, – his power as man'.[93]

Louis' unreasonable exercise of his 'power as a man' is the source of his destruction. To his listeners his demeanour in making speeches on obedience and submission becomes ridiculous. Like James Kelly, who complained of the 'obloquy and ridicule' he encountered, Louis comes to appear 'pompous, unreasonable, and absurd'.[94] Yet for Trollope none of this is meant as a serious critique of inequalities in marriage, and other successful marriages in the book work to legitimate the values of companionate marriage where male power is retained but not abused. Louis' obsession with power is aggravated by Emily's stubbornness, so that shared personal failings, like inability to exercise forbearance, are responsible for the ultimate tragedy. In his autobiography of 1883 Trollope confessed that he felt the novel was 'altogether bad' and failed in its intention, because it had been

> my purpose to create sympathy for the unfortunate man who, while endeavouring to do his duty to all around him, should be led constantly astray by his unwillingness to submit his own judgement to the opinion of others. The man is made unfortunate enough, and the evil which he does is apparent. So far I did not fail, but the sympathy has not been created yet.[95]

With cases like those of the Kellys appearing in the press, it is hardly surprising that Louis Trevelyan failed to attract a sympathetic readership. The 'unreasonableness' of such husbands, real or fictional, attracted increasing interest, but by the 1880s some were making the more explicit connection to sexual inequalities inside and outside marriage as well as men's discretionary forbearance. We have already seen Frances Power Cobbe's rejection of any hint of patriarchal controls in marriage.[96] The public debate on marriage, which intensified during the eighties and nineties, stimulated more explicit feminist rejection of the notion that companionate forbearance alone would mitigate the evils of unrestrained male power. Trollope's behavioural solution, which echoed prescriptive advice, continued to be aired during these debates, but it was met by feminist doubts that marriage could ever be reformed without more fundamental equality between the sexes.

The issue of men's power in marriage, and of standards of masculinity generally, was a central feature in the development of feminist discourse during the second half of the nineteenth century. Simultaneously it drew on and influenced the debate on marriage and divorce that had been growing in intensity since the 1857 Divorce Act. This aspect of feminism has mostly been overshadowed in recent work, which has concentrated more exclusively on campaigns centring on the issues of married women's property and sexuality.[97] The demand for women's property rights, the struggle against legalized prostitution, against the sexual double standard, and against predatory male sexual culture generally, were basic elements in feminist ideology by the turn of the nineteenth century. Their vital role in creating much of the force behind the movement which coalesced into the formidable suffrage campaign of Edwardian years can hardly be overestimated.

The importance of these issues should not blind us to equally important, though less sensational, feminist concerns with more mundane aspects of marital relationships and men's behaviour. Feminists engaged with the same behavioural issues which preoccupied prescriptive writers and novelists. They were also sensitive to the pleas of the women we saw who charged their husbands with cruelty, and who resisted men's attempts to control even their domestic management. We have already seen elements of this in the feminist campaign against working-class domestic violence. If middle-class men were to challenge every aspect of their wives' autonomy, from household budgeting to friendships and management of servants, and to exact to the letter the obedience enjoined by the marriage service, then feminist ideals of marital equality and companionship were doomed. For these reasons the reform of male behaviour was central to feminist objectives.

It would, no doubt, be misleading to compartmentalize unduly the debate about men's conduct in marriage. As early as 1869, for example, John Stuart Mill's *The Subjection of Women* ranged over a wide spectrum of legal and social inequalities inside and outside marriage. His exposure of the wife's position as 'the personal body-servant of a despot', focused particularly on wives' sexual vulnerability to their husbands, especially to marital rape, without legal recourse. Like a slave, the wife was unable to refuse her master 'the last familiarity', and could be made the instrument of 'an animal function contrary to her inclination'.[98] His analysis gave equal weight to women's occupational and property disabilities as impediments to marital equality. But central to his argument, and to most later feminist critiques of marriage, was an ideal of marital friendship which was inconsistent with legal and economic inequality, and which drew attention to the day-to-day need for mutual tolerance and forbearance. Here the problem remained men's unwillingness to grant women legal equality 'because the generality of the male sex cannot yet tolerate the idea of living with an equal'.[99] Mill's claim vividly recalls James Kelly's objections in the same year to his wife's 'indecent clamour about her rights'[100] as well as Charles Ashbee's later reflection that men would not believe that elements of legal equality already granted to women could have any impact on their own domestic relationships. It also underlines the feminist emphasis on companionate marriage which survived into Edwardian years.

The importance of spousal friendship to feminist aims has been elaborated recently by Mary L. Shanley, who rightly stresses the influence of John Stuart Mill's and Harriet Taylor's arguments.[101] Particularly important is her identification of marital equality for Victorian feminists as a commitment of 'a different and higher theoretical order than their acceptance of a continued sexual division of labor in the family'.[102] It is true that Mill, although not Taylor, clung to traditional notions of the sexual division of labour in the home, apparently with little understanding of its implications for domestic relationships. It is also true that Mill's ideals of marital friendship were inseparable from his exaggerated assessment of his own relationship with Harriet Taylor, which he praised not only for its lack of hierarchy, but for its intellectual basis, far above commonplace base animal instincts.[103] But Mill's *Subjection* of 1869 certainly set the tone for subsequent feminist writings in its insistence that legal equality would assist in the reformation of men's conduct, enabling companionate marriage and true partnership to flourish.[104]

Mill agreed with many of his contemporaries that by the 1860s 'Men's life is more domestic', that men spent less time in male company, more in female, and that 'the improved tone of modern feeling as to the reciprocity of duty which binds the husband towards the wife – have thrown the man very much more upon home and its inmates, for his personal and social pleasures.' But without full equality men's domestication brought no direct benefits and increased women's vulnerability; there could be no equality of intellectual interests, and more frequent association brought increased risks of the abuse of unlimited power and command.[105] Mill clearly had the middle class in mind at this point, and his discussion of 'brutes' who assaulted their wives[106] was followed by a description of other infinite gradations of abuse of domestic power,

> often under an outward varnish of civilization and even cultivation, living at peace with the law, maintaining a creditable appearance to all who are not under their power, yet sufficient often to make the lives of all who are so, a torment and a burthen to them![107]

Male selfishness of this order, Mill argued, was a product of wielding absolute power, and its abuse corrupted men and women alike. It gave men the licence to indulge their worst characteristics, which elsewhere they were forced to suppress, and made women narrow and selfish, often

157

surreptitiously manipulating husbands to exercise some form of influence or power, which, nevertheless, was no compensation for their loss of
freedom.[108]

Mill's prescription for elimination of these conjugal infelicities was
legal equality, the essential prerequisite to marital justice. Women's
equal rights to divorce and property, to education and employment, were
not only the sole means of reforming marriage 'consistent with justice to
both sides, and conducive to the happiness of both', but they were also
the only way 'of rendering the daily life of mankind, in any high sense, a
school of moral cultivation'. This involved an act of faith on Mill's part
that equality would reform both men's and women's characters; men, no
longer worshipping their own will, would become more unselfish and
self-sacrificing, while women would shed their 'artificial ideal' of 'exaggerated self-abnegation'.[109] Others have pointed to Mill's inconsistency
in assuming that men's behaviour, particularly, might be transformed so
easily through legal reform, when he gave so little attention to the
implications of traditional assumptions about separate spheres.[110] His
discussion of the need for husband and wife to share and exchange
power, so that leading and following would be 'alternate and reciprocal',
rested on a similar act of faith in men's willingness to relinquish advantages accruing from separate roles and responsibilities, which he either
failed to understand or regarded as unimportant.[111] Without sweeping
changes here, even some legal reforms, such as freedom of divorce, as
Susan Mendus has argued, would positively disadvantage women.[112]

For all its naïvety in anticipating the reform of men's behaviour simply
through legal change, Mill's ideal of marital friendship went much
further than the simple recommendation to discretionary forbearance
which was explicit in prescriptive texts and implicit in much contemporary fiction. But common to all these writers was a continued
commitment to marriage as a chief source of happiness for men and
women, and confidence that men's conduct could be reformed. The first
generation of feminists mostly shared these beliefs, but by the turn of the
century some of their successors, disillusioned with the progress of
reform, and more preoccupied with sexual exploitation, began to take a
harder line and reject marriage altogether.[113]

Frances Power Cobbe, who, as we saw earlier, inspired the 1878
campaign against wife-assault, was characteristic of the early generation
of feminists who mostly remained committed to ideas of the harmony of
natural sexual difference. Equality in the home for her did not mean the
abdication of women's natural domestic functions. Making a 'true home'
was women's 'inalienable right', a right which 'no man can take from us,
for a Man can no more make a Home than a drone can make a hive'.
Women, the true 'Home Rulers', remained the guardians of morality and
justice in the family. Thus far the similarity to prescriptive writers like

Ellis was obvious; the difference emerged in her criticism of legal and customary inequalities in marriage and their effect on men's conduct. Particularly odious was the vow of obedience, which could not fail to encourage men's worst faults of selfishness and despotism, inspiring 'contemptuous ideas of the very woman and *elevation* of their souls to honour'. Physical outrages on wives, and tyrannical behaviour generally, could all be traced to this source, and would only cease when men were no longer taught by law and custom to regard their wives as servants and property, until 'the whole notion of wifely subjection be radically changed'. Like Mill, Cobbe anticipated reform of men's behaviour without confronting the problem of separate spheres; a husband's greater knowledge of business and economics, for example, would make him the more suitable decision-maker on financial matters. Any potential conflict here was to be avoided, again, by appeals to forbearance inspired by love. The husband's arbitrary right to command would be replaced by a willingness of both to 'yield'. It remained unclear, and unexplored, how the reform of men's conduct could be so complete while such a sharp separation of responsibilities continued.[114]

Most feminist reformers up to the 1880s shared this confidence in the efficacy of legal change and mutual goodwill to reform marital behaviour. Annie Besant, whose writing on marriage has attracted less attention than her contemporaries', drew heavily on the earlier more radical views of Harriet Taylor, but still confined her criticism to legal inequalities, especially in married women's property.[115] Men's tendency to tyrannize was generated by legally sanctioned authority, women's tendency to rebel by enforced submission, and the law remained the cause and the potential remedy for both.[116] Towards the end of the 1880s, though, there were signs of a more radical and fundamental critique of marriage, which culminated in its outright rejection by some writers during the suffrage campaign. Again, the capacity of men to change their behaviour towards women was central to this transition.

It is surely significant that just as feminist views on these questions were in flux, public interest in marriage, and men's behaviour, constituted as a problem, reached its peak. This is best exemplified by the popular and well-known 'debate on marriage' of the late 1880s, and particularly by the press debate in the *Daily Telegraph* of 1888. It is no coincidence that this debate, which provoked some 27,000 letters to the editor, was stimulated by a radical attack on marriage by a feminist writer, Mona Caird. Her article in the *Westminster Review*, entitled simply 'Marriage', concluded that marriage was a vexatious failure. The editor of the *Telegraph* invited readers to comment, and the correspondence which followed, as well as Harry Quilter's later condensed selection for publication, was dubbed *Is Marriage a Failure?*[117] Even more intriguing is the fact that Caird's public reflections on marriage had been stimulated by the initiative of a mixed private gathering of intellectuals, led by Karl Pearson and Maria Sharpe, in the 'Men and Women's Club', earnestly discussing marriage and sexual relationships. Their rejection of Mona Caird for membership probably encouraged her to publicize her views more widely in the *Westminster*.[118] Feminist discourse in this way intersected with public preoccupations, as it did in the debate on domestic violence,[119] and reflected the profound discontents that we have seen in accounts of married life.

Mona Caird's critique of marriage was as radical and far-reaching as her proposed remedies. Since it was written after the 1882 Married Women's Property Act, it is likely that it drew on growing feminist disillusion with purely legislative changes. Originating in an ancient form of 'woman-purchase', modern marriage, she argued, remained no different in principle from prostitution, and for women was akin to slavery. There was no attractive alternative for a woman to sexual and household servitude to a man in exchange for a livelihood. Cloaked in respectability, the system nevertheless generated a 'tyrannical spirit' in men and women alike, but gave men very much the advantage. Such tyranny took various forms, some even based on pleas of love:

> Often the tyranny expresses itself profitably by appeals to the pity and the conscience of the victims, by threats of the suffering that will ensue to the despot, if his wishes are heartlessly disregarded. Should these measures fail, more drastic methods are adopted. There are stern or pathetic reminders of indisputable claims, accusations of selfishness, of failing duty, and so forth. Between married people, this system is carried to its extreme, and derives much of its power from the support of popular sentiment.[120]

Even in apparently happy marriages the process of mutual self-sacrifice stunted the development of each partner, so that 'every estimable person is acting vicariously on the motives of somebody else'.[121]

For Caird this system would never be changed simply by piecemeal reforms or appeals to male gentleness. Not marriage *per se* but the 'whole social drift' required radical reordering, and central to that goal was fundamental equality for women inside and outside marriage. A complete end to the 'tyranny of surviving superstitions' which maintained the 'patriarchal ideal', as well as equal rights with men to employment and education, equal rights to private contract, to property and to the franchise were essential preconditions to bring domestic life 'into harmony with civilization'.[122] She admitted that the state had a deep concern in the marriage contract, just as it did 'when men grow absorbed in the business of money-making, and have no time or ability to assist in the development of a higher type of manhood'. But those concerns gave the state no right to interfere with individuals and private contracts. A

160

gradual extension of individual freedom and freeing of the limits on private contracts was the key to the rise in moral standards which she sought for both men and women.[123] This 'moral renaissance' would leave independent individuals free to choose their own partners without social and legal coercion, recognizing that 'so long as affection and friendship remain between a married couple, no bonds are necessary to hold them united; but that when these cease, the tie becomes intolerable and no law ought to have power to enforce it.'[124] In this way, while she rejected the legal institution of marriage as currently understood, Caird, like her feminist forebears, carefully built the 'monogamic ideal', or marital friendship, into her utopian vision.

It should be noted that Caird's more radical analysis shifted attention away from men's tyrannical behaviour *per se* to fundamental social beliefs and values as the cause of the problem. It was a 'startling' fact that 'the tacit beliefs on which the best of English homes are founded . . . are those which render possible and law-protected, the outrages suffered by women in the very worst'.[125] These 'outrages' pointed most obviously to sexual abuse, particularly marital rape, and much of Caird's writing focused on male sexual excesses sanctioned by patriarchal power in the family. But these were inseparable from other forms of male 'tyranny' which we have seen throughout this book. It was for this reason that Caird extended her criticism even to apparently happy marriages which were based on inequality and separate spheres.

This point is important because of the substantial emphasis already noted in recent writing on some feminists' preoccupations with men's sexual exploitation of women.[126] It is undoubtedly true that Edwardian suffrage campaigners launched a radical attack on male sexual culture, targeting such evils as child prostitution, the 'white slave trade', men's wanton infection of their wives with venereal disease, and marital rape. The campaign was climaxed by Christabel Pankhurst's attack on male sexual excess and presumed high rate of venereal disease, and her call to women to withdraw from sexual relations with men. All this epitomized the feminist attack on the double standard and the belief in women's higher moral qualities, which, under an equal electoral system, would civilize and purify men's morality – hence Pankhurst's slogan: 'Votes for women, chastity for men.'[127] At the same time, some feminists, especially 'new woman' novelists, cautiously explored alternatives to marriage such as 'free unions'.[128] But while this was central to the suffrage movement, and at least implicit in most feminist arguments by the turn of the century, it was not the whole story of feminist criticisms of marriage. Indeed, as Caird insisted, abuses stemming from marital inequality were not confined to those sensational cases of 'outrage', but occurred as well in far more subtle ways where the outward forms of conjugal harmony were observed.

161

The press debate provoked by Caird's criticism encompassed the full range of current opinions for and against marriage, mostly based on personal experience. Enthusiastic accounts of contented partnerships were countered by tales of misery, in which the chief villain featured variously as the husband, the wife, a mother-in-law, men's clubs, bar-maids, or more fundamental weaknesses in marital law or the social system. But Caird's views received a consistent airing, and much support from aggrieved wives. Some of the complaints were clearly sexual, like that of the 'widow', who described the errant husband 'whose marriage oath lies lightly on his conscience as he calmly enters with his latch-key about two in the morning'.[129] Others lamented men's preference for their 'recreations', from clubs to cricket and operatic singing, rather than their wives' company.[130] As in the advice books, a persistent theme was men's selfish indulgence and temper. A middle-aged 'victim to bad temper', who endorsed Caird's pleas for equality, had found that all her attempts to submit to her husband and practise the 'soft answer' in 'reasonable things' had been met only by 'the demon of bad temper'. She had seen the same pattern repeated in countless households; how many women, she asked, could unfold a tale

> of petty persecution, vile language and bad usage. I have noticed that it is more often the agreeable man in society, the 'generous good fellow' amongst his chums, the man who smokes the best cigars and drinks the best wines, who is the greatest brute at home, making wife, children and servants scurry about with white faces as they listen to his violent language. Of course there are bad-tempered and selfish women; but there are not so many of them in a position to make their idiosyncrasies felt and to be the tyrants of their households.[131]

A 'plain man's' answer to this was the familiar appeal 'to bear and forbear', and to exercise 'self-restraint, tact and fortitude'.[132] But Caird and her supporters had abandoned such appeals with their insistence that the abusive indulgence of 'temper' was a prime symptom of deep-seated inequalities.

The popular debate was accompanied and sustained by a more serious set of polemics by feminists and their critics throughout the 1880s and 1890s, especially in the outpouring of controversial opinions on relations between the sexes in the *Westminster Review*. The *Westminster* made space for a broad range of views, many of which referred explicitly to the 1888 debate provoked by Caird. Emma Hewitt, for example, thought that higher expectations of husbandly behaviour had frightened 'new men' away from traditional conjugal responsibilities, so that the trend to wider female employment seemingly opened the way to a masculine flight from commitment.[133] The most commonly expressed view was that in its present state the appeal of marriage was wearing thin. Husbands and wives, 'Eugenius' argued, might be reluctant to proclaim their matrimonial failures in public, but increased education and culture were inducing greater scepticism about the rewards of married life. If the number of those who, if they could, would conveniently 'sever their inauspicious marriage knots' were to be added to those who 'chiefly for cultural reasons are content to remain in single blessedness, the small residuum of really happy marriages would strike the enthusiastic advocates of the institution with dismay.'[134] Far from stimulating forbearance and friendship, education, it seemed, was exposing the seamy side of marriage, and the higher development of individual culture made compatible unions less likely. This was a long way from the optimism of Mill's visions of marital friendship.

Public interest in failed marriages was by no means new, and was certainly not confined to the late nineteenth century. What was new about this debate was the more intense focus on patriarchal power in marriage and standards of masculine behaviour. In a short space of time, masculinity had come to be defined as a crucial ingredient in marital fortunes, and, regardless of the recipes for reform, proper standards of manliness were repeatedly defined as the problem. It seems remarkable that by the 1880s the middle-class family, which had only recently come to be constructed as a fortress of individual privacy free from outside interference, and especially political interference, was coming under increasing public scrutiny, a major element of the scrutiny being men's behaviour. The most intensely private element of the most private Victorian institution had entered the sphere of public discourse, not simply with a view to debate and dramatize, but to investigate, judge and regulate. Public scrutiny implied, as Jeffrey Minson has argued, that the family had been reconstructed, not as 'an essentially companionate space . . . but as a space of conflicting desires and responsibilities'.[135] Most crucially, it was a space where power was contested, often successfully, and increasingly with good reason.

The exposure of domestic conflict simultaneously created and fed a social need, not only for public scrutiny, but for management of the most obvious sites where orderly relations were seen to have broken down. Paradoxically, patriarchal power, which was identified as the source of the trouble, continued to be invoked by prescriptive writers and some novelists as the solution, or regulative mechanism. But the preoccupation with patriarchy also encouraged women's resistance and enabled alternative visions of conjugal relationships, from Cobbe's 'miniature republic' to Caird's 'vigorous moral Renaissance', to gain a wider hearing. In that sense the intense preoccupation with patriarchal marriage, where personal experience and ideology intersected, marked an historically decisive turning-point.

CONCLUSION

The erosion of patriarchal power in marriage charted in this book was riddled with contradictions and far from complete. Perhaps the most ironic feature of the process was the frequent prescription, by so many observant critics, of a cure for its excesses by male domestication and greater companionate forbearance within an unaltered framework of patriarchal authority and female submission. This seems tantamount to the practice of homoeopathic medicine, by dosing the patient with a concentrate of the toxin that is already causing the damage. The inherent paradox need not be belaboured, since so many critics, and not least judges of the Divorce Court, deliberately framed their remedies to ensure the survival of patriarchal power rather than its weakening. Moreover, the strategy of preserving authority by making it more palatable was a familial extension of the eighteenth-century 'Lockean paradigm' on parent–child relations, which, according to Jay Fliegelman, sought 'to make authority and liberty compatible, to find a surer ground for obligation and obedience than "fear of the rod"'.[1] By the end of the nineteenth century the same ambiguous approach to husbands' power remained dominant, but the scepticism and radical alternative proposals which had surfaced in the 1850s posed a more intense and public challenge. The routine exposure of men's marital behaviour to public scrutiny and regulation in itself constituted a check on their power over their wives, but still remained subject to challenge and ideological backlash against women's assertion of rights, in public or private. For all its profound importance, the change embodied in this increasingly critical discourse, like most change hingeing on tentative shifts in mentalities and deeply embedded ideologies, was intermittent and subject to reversal.

Still, this should not obscure the dramatic nature of the process by which a critical discourse was driven largely by women's resistance to their husbands' treatment, and their willingness to take their private complaints into the public arena. Women had undoubted allies in this process: judges, journalists, politicians, feminists and even paternalistic moralists all assisted in the progressive definition and refinement of what came to be agreed upon as 'unreasonable' behaviour in marriage. The ideologically

164

diverse origins of the critics is a mark of the wide currency of their views. Mainstream commentary, which selectively drew on feminist analysis, or pursued the same demons independently, enabled feminist arguments to be heard more effectively. Where feminist discourse was closely related to similar themes pursued by non-feminists in a wider forum, each might intermittently support or oppose the other, but ultimately they gave each other a wider hearing on select issues, and, as with Frances Power Cobbe and Henry Labouchere in 1878, increased the chances of legislative success. Moreover, in promoting popular controversies like the 'marriage debate' of the 1880s, orthodox critics lent some respectability to feminist arguments about marriage.

Crucial changes in matrimonial law, though, as well as public opinion, ultimately owed more to the willingness of ordinary women to declare the limits of their submission than to the great names, such as Caroline Norton and her parliamentary allies, who are usually credited with responsibility for the legal landmarks. As well as stimulating shifts in judge-made law, the actions of these lesser known women helped to shape the agendas of feminists and parliamentary reformers. It is a vivid illustration of the translation of processes of subjectivity into the public realm. It also suggests some areas where the origins and trajectory of Victorian feminism might fruitfully be reassessed. The part played by ordinary 'inarticulate' women's publicly advertised grievances in influencing the nature and timing of feminist reform agendas could be much greater than we have allowed.

The causes of women's better powers of resistance in the later nineteenth century, if indeed that is what we are seeing, may have been connected in some ways to broader demographic changes, though the relationship is certainly no more than suggestive. The declining birth-rate from the 1870s may have eased some of the pressures for adult male authority to be so ubiquitous among a youthful urban population; with some of the burdens of child-bearing and rearing lifted for women, their opportunities to challenge what they readily defined as 'unreasonable' authority may have improved. The connection should not be overdrawn, especially in the short-term, since women with large families, like Charlotte Bostock, were no less likely to learn to contest their husbands' power over time.

But in more general cultural terms the link between marital conflict and family size and structure may be much more persuasive. Demographic historians largely accept that the late-nineteenth-century decline in the birth-rate is not explicable simply on economic or technological grounds, but their efforts to seek cultural explanations have had limited success. Women's increasing participation in the labour force, in itself, is only a partial explanation, and may have been more of an effect of the change than a cause.[2] Judith Allen has pointed, more generally, to the crucial role of 'altered negotiations between men and women across the past century and a half', and it is here that the more potent influence of contested marital authority may be found.[3] Rising standards of expectations and self-respect for women, which had spread to most classes by Edwardian years, required more autonomy in domestic life, in sexual relationships and in control of fertility. Contested authority only infrequently entered the public forum of the Divorce Court, but when it did it reflected a deeper process of negotiation which was producing far-reaching change.

Marriage, then, despite its persistent idealization as a site of harmonious separate spheres, was increasingly seen to be contested territory throughout the nineteenth century. But between the middle and the end of the century there was a progressive shift in the main direction of criticism of those responsible for marital breakdown. Before the 1857 Divorce Act, when Mrs Ellis's prescriptive works and others of the genre were at their height of popularity, the spotlight was on women's domestic failures. Working-class women's inadequate household skills and shrewish tempers, middle-class women's failure to practise submissive forbearance, were identified as the deeper causes of conjugal unhappiness, with men's failings viewed as subsidiary and often the consequence of women's fractiousness.

This critique persisted throughout the century and, to the extent that it drew on actual observation, testified to women's capacity to resist the subordinate role prescribed for them. But it was increasingly overshadowed by a parallel critique of men's conduct in marriage. Among the working class this arose from the campaign against domestic violence, among the middle class from mounting criticisms of men's tyrannical dictation, insistence on literal obedience and lack of sympathy with women's burdens in the domestic sphere. Despite the fact that the critique of domestic violence mostly contained it within an attack on the 'rough' culture of the poor, and ignored persistent evidence that it occurred more widely, the two veins of criticism came together, and by the late nineteenth century men's unreasonable and selfish behaviour was being identified and debated as the chief cause of failing marriages.

This development, by which men's marital performance, judged by companionate and domestic standards, was subjected to surveillance and regulation, had long-term and far-reaching significance. At the very least it constituted a chipping away at the edges of patriarchy, making it more difficult for men to indulge freely in gross abuse of their power over others, though much of the power remained firmly in their hands. For all the well-known ways in which men continued to dominate their wives and families, in which the behaviour of the 'old men' failed to match the challenging visions of 'new women',[4] the modification of patriarchal marriage which was implicit in the new discourse signified genuine change.

The evidence of how men actually responded to this process is ambiguous and problematic. The sources explored here suggest that the criticism developed alongside an increasing responsiveness of many men to the pleasures and responsibilities of domesticity, although the trend was uneven and many used the new opportunity to practise ever more intrusive means of control over their families. Some of the more subtle means of manipulation noted in chapter 5, like that of Tom Church, convey a distinctly twentieth-century resonance. All these subtle changes may best be understood in generational terms, and still await thorough historical investigation. There is also suggestive evidence, at least, that for working-class men respectability signified more companionate and protective relations with their wives, but that the simmering issue of domestic violence could produce anxiety and guilt about failure to live up to the higher standards.

Similarly, middle-class men like James Kelly betrayed nervousness over the new standards as well as women's developing assertiveness when they condemned their wives' 'indecent clamour' about their rights; Kelly's persistence in confident declarations that all his persecution of his wife was warranted by his natural authority helped to undermine his own case. A similar stubborn confidence led Charles Dickens to attempt to justify his own shabby treatment of his wife in public. But instead of gaining him sympathy, his actions became a common metaphor for husbands' abuse and neglect of their wives, even for men like Henry Ashbee, who himself had no spotless conjugal record.[5] Charles Ashbee's suggestion, that men might accept legal equality for women in theory, but refuse to believe that it could apply to their own relationships, provides one persuasive explanation for the ambiguities, but we still need to know much more about these contradictions and nuances, which are at the heart of changing notions of masculinity in marriage. The fact that the campaign against domestic violence among the poor was joined by many middle-class men just as their own behaviour was coming under scrutiny reinforces the ambiguity. How far this was a deeply felt defence of Victorian values of honourable manliness, or how far it reflected displaced fears about their own behaviour, is impossible to say, but both patterns are equally plausible.

If domesticity was the vehicle for promoting a more companionate vision of family life for men in the late nineteenth century, it is evident that this was no new discovery of the Victorians. These ideals echo the gradual turn to domesticity by the eighteenth-century aristocracy outlined by Randolph Trumbach, and might be seen simply as a more intense development of the early-nineteenth-century middle-class domestic idyll for men highlighted by Davidoff and Hall.[6] What was new was the late-Victorian willingness to scrutinize and vilify men's failure to live up to popular standards of domestic harmony, which has more in common with our own time than with earlier periods. Feminists like Mona Caird developed radical visions of monogamy well ahead of their time, but Victorian criticism stopped short of the more far-reaching attempts to reconstruct masculinity so common in the late twentieth century.[7] Still, far from being unprecedented, our own critique should be seen rather as a logical extension of the critical discourse developed by the Victorians, who first placed men's marital behaviour on the agenda as a subject of major public concern. Each critique fostered new ways of thinking about masculinity and gender relations, just as each provoked an extensive male backlash, whether in the form of antifeminism in public or abuse of power in private. By the late nineteenth century there was even some evidence that men might be becoming increasingly reluctant to enter into marriage and accept its new legal constraints, possibly foreshadowing today's male 'flight from commitment', detected by Barbara Ehrenreich in modern America.[8]

These parallels should be less puzzling than the apparent decline of critical interest in marital behaviour in the early twentieth century. After the war the issue of domestic violence receded as the labour movement promoted a more dignified identity for working-class men, and shifted attention away from individual failures to the role of more general environmental factors and low wages.[9] Feminist attention in this area turned increasingly to economic dimensions of the welfare of mothers and children, and fought for family allowances and access to birth-control information.[10] More firmly than before, it seems, the stigma of wife-abuse was consigned to the exclusive territory of the very poor, where it could safely be ignored or more intensely pathologized. Similarly, issues of middle-class women's employment and education consumed the time of feminists and others, and the intense interest in marital behaviour and ideals which flowered in the 1880s and 1890s was not sustained. By the 1920s interest in marriage tended to focus increasingly on the quality of the sexual relationship rather than on more generalized companionate ideals, which survived mostly in the specialized literature of marriage guidance from psychologists.[11] The abolition of the double standard in the 1923 divorce legislation, easier access and increasing resort to divorce by women, may all have contributed to this trend. The need for women to allege cruelty charges, for example, was diminished substantially once they could obtain a divorce simply by proving a husband's adultery. Thus the opportunity for the kind of publicity advertising cruel behaviour which had characterized earlier years declined. But none of this proves that men's behaviour had actually changed, which the revived criticism of the later twentieth century would question in any case.

It should be apparent that the broad outlines of change indicated here are largely inconsistent with contentious claims for long-term transitions from patriarchal to companionate models of marriage argued by Lawrence Stone and other historians. The problems apply as much to simple linear models of change over time as to more complex, fluctuating models, such as Stone's 'revival of patriarchy' in the Victorian period.[12] It is no doubt easy to see how the longer-term development of companionate ideals was reflected in the increasing idealization of separate spheres and the construction of women as domestic and sentimental.[13] But, once these ideals are viewed alongside evidence of actual behaviour and the resulting critical discourse, any notion of a revival of patriarchy among the Victorians breaks down. Eileen Spring has pointed to the inconsistency of this notion with successive Victorian legislation in the direction of marital equality.[14] It is even more at odds with the evidence of contested power in marriage and public scrutiny of men's behaviour which dominates this book. In all the turbulence of discordant marriages and public responses to them, we can find abundant evidence of both companionate and patriarchal ideals, each, seemingly, at their most forceful. But the source of the ideal was invariably determined by gender; women appealed to companionate models to justify their own behaviour and condemn their husbands'; men, with apparently decreasing confidence, maintained patriarchal principles, even as these were being modified by the courts and legislature and lampooned by sections of the press.

These trends reinforce the impression that any interpretation, like Stone's, which defines patriarchal and companionate marriage as opposites is fundamentally misconceived. Each ideal embodied elements of the other, whether it was expressed as prescription, reconstructed to encourage reform, or appealed to by spouses to justify their marital conduct. The complexities run too deep to warrant a simple dichotomy, but rather highlight the ways in which thinking about gender relationships always remained a dialogue and a matter of negotiation, at both experiential and theoretical levels. This suggests that we will more readily understand the complexities of marriage in the past by focusing on that dialogue, and on the varying links between behaviour and discourse, rather than on the simple rise and fall of predominant models of marriage over the *longue durée*, which never tell more than a partial, often misleading, story.

Heightened criticism did not signify the end of patriarchal power in marriage, as its decline in the early twentieth century suggests. Rather, patriarchy in the home made further adaptations to the increasing pressures, remaining subject to others in the future. The critical discourse which targeted masculinity produced no revolution in marital relationships, but, in opening up male behaviour in marriage to public gaze and censure, it laid the groundwork for deeper questioning of conjugal performance, which, in the late twentieth century, has finally been taken up again.

APPENDIX 1

A note on sources: court records and family history

Family history, as a specialized offshoot of social history, shares the risks and benefits of all specializations. At worst, if detached from the intricate contexts of community, culture and society, it can wallow, with anti-quarian fascination, in the idiosyncrasies of individual family life and hagiography. At best, when it explores the relatedness of family experience to prevailing ideologies and the constraints of dominant discourses and cultural norms, it can contribute to a deeper understanding of the wider society.

Obviously a key determinant of the value of family history in this sense is the nature and breadth of sources used to reconstruct family life, and to understand how different members of families perceived their experience. But if it is to venture beyond the narrower focus of family biography and anecdote, direct sources of family experience must be viewed alongside a range of more conventional evidence. This study has attempted to integrate evidence of family experience with wider material drawn from press opinion, community responses, imaginative literature, political and judicial action and public commentary ranging from the most radical feminist activists to the most socially conservative critics. All these are central to a holistic understanding of family and society, which here attempts to illustrate the close relationship of family experience to a discourse which increasingly acknowledged the conjugal home as a locus of conflict and simultaneously pressed for change and regulation, alongside the retention of traditional power relationships. But the nature of our understanding of experience in individual families remains over-whelmingly reliant upon the quality of sources drawn from family life. Since none of these sources come without their difficulties, some discussion of their strengths and weaknesses may be profitable.

The most commonly used testimony of family experience, of course, is the private family archive, normally extending from letters, diaries, and journals to the private memoir. Others have noted the dangers with all such private sources of mistaking the exception for the rule, the regional for the general, and the need to read widely to gain a sense of context and deeper trends among the infinite range of family experience.[1] But these are not the only difficulties. Undoubtedly, at their most frank, such sources are essential to a grasp of the subtle dynamics of family relationships, and they have provided the vital raw material of fine family histories like Davidoff and Hall's *Family Fortunes*, Barbara Caine's *Destined to be Wives* and Pat Jalland's *Women, Marriage and Politics*.[2] It is hardly accidental, though, that the emphasis in many such texts is on marital harmony rather than conflict. Jalland's work, based on the archives of political families, conveys only subtle hints of the resentments and discords often seething behind the impressions of companionate partnership.[3] Jeanne Peterson's study of Victorian gentlewomen, again based largely on family archives, gives a mostly unrelieved impression of conjugal harmony, where strained relations were the exception, which, she argues, was even empowering to women.[4] A less common picture, and an historiographical exception, emerges in Caine's feminist analysis of the marriages of Beatrice Webb's eight sisters, which pays special attention to some of their lifelong frustrations and marital failures.[5]

None of this should be surprising. Private diaries and letters between spouses and other family members can certainly betray important family tensions, in rare cases, where the disputes became public, even sensational ones.[6] But for the most part intense conflict is either nuanced or suppressed in such sources. Possibly the Victorians were not so unique in their reticence when they shrank from committing the darker side of their most intimate relationships to paper, but for them, conflict, like sexuality, was not a subject for close written reflection. Where it did make its appearance it might also be subject to the censorship of family hagiographers or executors anxious to conceal the worst skeletons in the family closet. The emotional struggles of the Ashbee family, discussed in chapter 5, emerge plainly enough from letters and journals, although they leave much of the causes of the conflict shrouded in mystery, largely because Charles Ashbee could not bring himself to speak frankly about it. Even the more explicit autobiographers of the twentieth century, fascinated by the troubles of their parents' marriages, convey a relatively subtle impression of marital discord compared to that which emerged from the more direct sources of the Divorce Court.

Given these difficulties, any attempt to place marital conflict in a clearer perspective, alongside expectations of harmony and companionship, has much to gain from the kind of court records which have been used here. Conflict was the business of courts of marital jurisdiction, so we would naturally expect it to be explored there in most detail; unfortunately, we might also expect it to distort experience, as each party not only detailed its grievances but, often with the connivance of legal counsel, sought to exaggerate them to win a case. The weakness is one shared with all legal records from courts based on an adversarial system, and acutely apparent in the records of the Divorce Court. The problem has led one historian of divorce to characterize marital litigation as no more than a 'theatrical display', designed to produce dissolution rather than to reveal the truth about marital breakdown.[7] But the force of this is mitigated by the fact that in most cases a defendant was intent on presenting an alternative version of essentially similar facts, which led to closer, often more revealing, investigation.

The system of marital fault, which formed the basis of the divorce law, made an adversarial system inevitable. Its most glaring defects were exposed in the twentieth century in A. P. Herbert's biting satire of fictional 'hotel room' adulteries which made a mockery of the rigidity of the law.[8] Less sensational, but equally problematical for historians, was the interest of petitioners and lawyers in inflating and exaggerating, occasionally even inventing, charges of cruelty. Because of the double standard of the 1857 law, which required women to prove an additional offence to adultery to gain a decree, it was they who were most often placed in this situation. Also husbands, anxious to prove that any cruelty had been incited by their wives' unwarranted 'provocation', had an interest in exaggerating women's assertiveness, or even justifying their own violence as acts of self-defence against violent wives. The court's role, of course, was to sift through such accusations to arrive at its own version of the 'truth', but even without relying on its conclusions, historians are able to make some profitable headway through this minefield of conflicting allegations.

There are three main sources of Divorce Court cases. The most commonly used and most accessible are the routine court reports in the national daily press, with the fullest accounts usually published in *The Times*. For some cases these provide the most thorough surviving account. They might give the only record of actual court proceedings, particularly details from cross examination of witnesses and the judge's analysis and summing-up. Cases which were complex and drawn-out, as in criminal trials, could be reported over long periods, and clearly attracted public interest. On the other hand, both the cases and details reported were highly selective, often chosen with an eye to sensational interest, which was most likely to stem from adultery in high places. But despite the arbitrary basis of selection many routine and revealing cases were reported, especially in the early years of the court, often providing important evidence that is otherwise unavailable.

For a minority of cases a further source is easily accessible in the published law reports of select cases, chosen by lawyers for their legal significance. These cases were not printed for their sensational public interest but for their importance to the legal profession in forming a body of case law based on precedent. While for lawyers their importance lies in the judges' rulings, conveniently summarized at the beginning of each report, their historical value consists more in the often copious evidence cited by the judge in support of his decision. Letters cited by Cresswell in *Curtis* v. *Curtis* (1858), for example, provide insights into that marriage which are simply unavailable elsewhere.[9] A valuable by-product of these sources is the history of judges' rulings themselves, particularly the evolution of their own ideological assumptions about marriage and their responses to the kind of grievances brought to the court, which is explored in chapter 4. Many cases were reported in so brief a fashion as to convey little more than the ruling itself, although if a judge felt that his judgement would have a profound bearing on future cases he would be likely to go into great detail, with a report often extending to over twenty closely written pages.[10] In such cases the greatest value of the report is undoubtedly the often unique evidence of marital relationships and household dynamics which the court often presented to the public gaze.[11]

For historians, though, both the law and press reports are based on an arbitrary system of selection which necessarily excludes the great majority of cases. For a closer insight into the wider experiences of the court it is essential to use the surviving records of each case, retained in the Public Record Office. These records are far from complete. Access to them is restricted by a 75-year exclusion rule,[12] the files do not provide details of the court hearings and it is rare for them to include supporting evidence, like letters, which may have been produced in court. The thinnest files may contain no more than a complainant's petition citing addresses, occupations, numbers of children and allegations in the briefest manner, together with an even briefer register of the progress of the case, although often even the final outcome is not recorded.

Many files, though, contain much more than minimal pro-forma detail. A copy of the marriage certificate is usually included, giving the date and place of the ceremony, husband's occupation and the occupation of both parents. The initial petition is often supported by a further more detailed affidavit, occasionally further affidavits from witnesses, and more often denials and explanations from the respondent in one or more affidavits. Clearly it is those cases which were defended, and which caused intense argument and contest over details, rather than the undefended cases which passed through with little discussion or defence, which offer most to historians of marriage. Other sources barely touch on the intimate themes debated here, and while the texts pose complex problems of interpretation, their information, perversely dismissed by one historian as containing 'rarely anything of earth-shaking importance', is of unique value.[13]

Clearly such a large mass of data lends itself to quantitative as well as qualitative analysis. For historians of divorce the potential for ambitious surveys through large-scale sampling techniques is only just being realized.[14] For historians of marriage the quantitative dimension is perhaps less promising, especially in the nineteenth century when divorces formed such a tiny proportion of marriages in general. Nevertheless the brief survey reported in chapter 4 does establish some suggestive trends, notably the broad class profile of petitioners, the increasing tendency for women to allege cruelty under the influence of the double standard and the kinds of conduct most commonly complained of by both spouses. The size of the samples used for this analysis was small, and the findings might not be so significant if it were not for the fact that most of them coincide with other investigations by contemporaries and recent scholars. But for the history of marriage the real value of these records lies less in the statistical trends they reveal than in the detailed illumination some of them provide into actual relationships.[15]

The most richly documented cases do indeed present a vivid and unique insight into marriages over many years; some of these are discussed at length in chapter 3. Uncovering these cases of necessity involves a search through large numbers of files simply for those with the fullest and most reliable testimony, always with an eye for the most common and the most exceptional cases. But it is here, of course, that the methodological difficulty becomes most apparent. A wife's simple charge that her husband 'beat her cruelly' tells us little more than the fact of the accusation; if unproven or dismissed by the court its value is even more limited. But if supported by further descriptive detail, corroborating witnesses and other similar incidents, its credibility and significance is altogether different. Much more telling, though, is the intense argument, contest, denial and counter-charge which so many couples engaged in once a case was seriously defended. Hence, when Robert Bostock denied his wife's accusations of violence, then admitted he had merely 'boxed her ears', and followed his admission with a long catalogue of complaints about her extravagance and household neglect, which she later challenged, we gain far more insight into that marriage than any simple accusation of violence could afford.[16] Among all the denials there is a common ground of agreement about some of the facts and root causes of conflict that attest to their credibility and reveal far more than the circumstances of one specific assault.

Much the same is true of some rare gems in the records, like James Kelly's lengthy affidavit of self-justification, which, in its self-righteous chronicling of his own and his wife's actions, together with full quotation of letters, revealed far more about his treatment of his wife which helped her to win her separation.[17] More commonly, letters like those written by Frances Curtis to her mother about her husband's behaviour, well before a court case was thought of, provide frank testimony uninfluenced by legal imperatives.[18] These are precisely the kind of letters that rarely seem to appear in carefully preserved family archives. As illustrated in chapter 4, they also probe mundane elements of domestic detail, as opposed to highly publicized sensational discord, which mostly remained shrouded behind the veils of domestic privacy but which so often sowed the seeds of marital breakdown.

Piecing together all the different categories of the available divorce records, then, can begin to open a valuable window on the sexual politics of marriage. Inevitably the resulting picture is a partial one, and potentially one-sided, as it must be from any single source. But it is a picture which is extremely difficult to obtain from the more conventional sources, which in this area mostly remain silent. Moreover, its accuracy and credibility in general can be tested in other texts, such as prescriptive writings, reformist and other public commentary, fiction and auto-biography. Through these sources this book has attempted to illustrate the varied ways in which the experiences reported in the court were more than simply a minority of 'hard cases', and were recognized widely as part of a wider crisis in married life. But the wide range and richness of the records should provide a rare opportunity for more rewarding research to family historians.

One of the clear findings of quantitative analysis of the divorce records is a wide class profile of men and women petitioners which belies persistent notions of upper-class monopoly of the early Divorce Court.[19] There can be no doubt of the significance of working-class and lower middle-class resort to the court, despite its expense. But this still left an enormous pool of discontented spouses without the resources to obtain relief from the Divorce Court. Their only recourse was to the courts of petty sessions, in the towns to the police courts, collectively known as the magistrates' courts. During the second half of the nineteenth century the facilities for marital relief in these courts became more elaborate, and the numbers of those resorting to them, especially women, increased enormously. But their procedures, which remained mostly informal, never paralleled the legal and bureaucratic complexities of the Divorce Court, and thus the records they generated were comparatively sketchy and minimal. Most police courts kept a daily register of cases, a few of which survive in county record offices, but these do not provide detailed descriptions of individual cases.

This paucity of legal records means that the only qualitative evidence of actual cases survives in the court reports in local newspapers. It is a poor substitute for a fuller legal record. Again, as with all court reporting, journalistic criteria determined both the selection of cases and the extent and nature of the accounts. Many of them contain no more than bare details of the charge and sentence, while others delved deeply into social backgrounds of the couple, precipitating events, testimony of witnesses and judicial pronouncements ranging from sentencing to moral homilies and appeals for reconciliation. In those few cases where an assault resulted in death the magistrates' hearing was quickly followed by an inquest and a later trial at the assizes, where much greater detail became available. But any researcher using these records needs to be conscious of their severe limitations.

Despite this the press reports do have some value, as the material in chapter 2 attempts to illustrate. The Preston survey, based on a sample of one year in ten, spanning eight decades, gives some evidence of the responses of working-class wives, as well as magistrates, to the changing facilities for relief that were offered.[20] The more detailed reports are numerous enough to allow a rough impression of the class profile of complainants, which certainly extended further up the social scale than other contemporary estimates suggested. This helps to correct the widespread impression that domestic violence was an exclusive problem of the very poor, where depraved brutes of the lumpenproletariat were demonized as the essence of the problem.

On the other hand, while some cases give valuable evidence of marital conflict and its context in the wider community, very few of the reports provide insights into the dynamics of working-class married life to parallel the detail offered in the Divorce Court. Social investigators, police court missionaries, reformers and other commentators, notwithstanding their social bias, tend to provide far richer accounts of conjugal domestic life, although, with rare exceptions like the Women's Co-operative Guild, most of them concentrated on the very poor where they assumed the problem rested. Local studies of marriage and the family in working-class communities, though, have much to gain from supplementing descriptive commentary with the court records.[21] Moreover, uncertainties noted by one recent historian about how far magistrates genuinely took advantage of legislation enabling them to grant separation and maintenance orders to abused wives can only be answered by systematic local surveys of reported cases.[22] For all their deficiencies the local newspaper reports still offer the only key to resolution of many such unanswered questions.

A few years ago Olwen Hufton suggested that one of the most promising ways forward in family history – one could add social history more generally – lay in the use of legal records.[23] The point is especially pertinent to the history of marriage. Earlier courts of marital jurisdiction are already receiving thorough scrutiny, although more often for historians of divorce than of marriage. For all the methodological difficulties involved in their use, court records serve a valuable purpose in uncovering some aspects of married life simply not available elsewhere. Their potential has only begun to be tapped, but the cautions suggested here should warn against their use without extensive reference to other records, to which they provide both a unique supplement and a vital corrective.

APPENDIX 2

Street ballads celebrating the attack on General Haynau

FIRST BALLAD

There was a chief well known to fame,
General Haynau was his name,
Who a tyrant's favour sought to gain
By causing bitter grief and pain.

When fair Hungary prostrate lay
Beneath a tyrant's despot sway,
And many mourned the fatal day,
   Oh! Barclay and Perkins' draymen.

Her bravest sons he put to death,
Her fairest women by the lash!
Had their flesh cut from living flesh!
While freedom to the earth was dash'd
By this monster man in human shape!
But you shall quickly know his fate,
He got his deserts at any rate,
   From Barclay and Perkins' draymen.

Then out of the gate he did run,
A rotten egg he got from one,
For all did try – yes every one,
To show how we loved such a brute
Who women flogg'd and men did shoot,
For trying tyranny to uproot,
   Oh! Barclay and Perkins' draymen.

Hit him, kick him, up and down,
Box him! Knock him round and round!
Out of his hat break the crown,
   Cried Barclay and Perkins' draymen.

At length he found a place to hide,
All at the George by Bankside,
But not till they'd well tann'd his hyde,
   Barclay and Perkins' draymen.

Then for Barclay's men we'll give a cheer,
May they long live to brew our beer,
And from their masters nothing fear,
Barclay and Perkins' draymen.

      Source: E. Bligh, *Tooting Corner*, London,
      Secker & Warburg, 1946, pp. 13–17.

SECOND BALLAD

Jolly boys who brew porter for Barclay and Perkins,
The prime London stout of our cans and our firkins,
Here's a health, English hearts, what'er may betide,
For the dose you gave Haynau along the Bankside.
   Derry down, down, down, Derry down.

The deeds of this butcher we all have heard tell,
How died Bathanyi, how Leiningen fell;
Gallant Aulich, he hanged like a felon and slave,
Tho' he prayed like a soldier to go to his grave.

And 'twas all in cold blood when the battle was won,
Was won by the Russians – for Austria had run;
When Georgey had o'er to the enemy passed;
But brave English Guyon he fought to the last.

Oh, the cord for the neck, and the lash for the back,
When Haynau commanded, they never were slack;
And women he scourged, till the red blood ran down,
This chief of the armies of Austria's Crown.

Ye lasses of Southwark, a health unto you,
Who aided to give Marshal Haynau his due.
The wretch who flogged women deserves well to meet
Rough welcome like yours, in each fair London street.

Turn him out, turn him out, from our side of the Thames,
Let him go to great Tories and high-titled dames:
He may walk the West End and parade in his pride,
But he'll not come again near the 'George' in Bankside.

    Source: *The Red Republican*, 21 September, 1850, p. 112.

APPENDIX 3

Lancashire dialect poetry on domestic relationships

Domestic themes were common and highly suited to the sentimentality that dominated much Lancashire dialect poetry. The first poem, Laycock's 'Welcome, Bonny Brid', was written during the cotton famine of 1861–5 and celebrates affectionate fatherhood during times of economic depression. The second poem, also by Laycock, 'Uncle Dick's Advoice to Wed Men', typifies those poems which traversed very different territory in raising the issue of violence. The third poem, Sammy Mee's 'Wod Wer th' Good of Bothering', which was published in the 'poet's corner' of the *Preston Herald* in 1913, suggests how far the same themes continued to occupy popular consciousness, largely taken for granted as subjects of entertainment and scrutiny.

WELCOME, BONNY BRID

Tha'rt welcome, little bonny brid,
But shouldn't ha' come just when tha did;
   Toimes are bad.
We're short o' pobbies for eawr Joe,
But that, of course, tha didn't know,
   Did ta, lad?

Aw've often yeard mi Feyther tell,
'At when aw coom i'th world misel'
   Trade wur slack;
And neaw its hard work pooin' throo –
But aw munno fear thee, iv aw do
   Tha'll go back.

Cheer up! these toimes'll awter soon;
Aw'm beawn to beigh another spoon –
   One for thee; –
An' as tha's sich a pratty face
Aw'll let thi have eawr Charley's place
   On mi knee.

179

God bless thi, love! aw'm fain tha'rt come,
Just try and mak' thisel awhoam:
   Here's thi nest;
Tha'rt loike thi mother to a tee,
But tha's thi feyther's nose, aw see,
   Well, aw'm blest!

Come, come, tha needn't look so shy,
Aw am no' blamin' thee, not I;
   Settle deawn,
An' tak' this haupeney for thisel',
Ther's lots of sugar-sticks to sell
   Deawn i'th teawn.

Aw know when first aw coom to th' leet,
Aw're fond o' owt' 'at tasted sweet;
   Tha'll be th' same.
But come, tha's never towd thi dad
What he's to co thi yet mi lad,
   What's thi name?

Hush! hush! tha mustn't cry this way,
But get this sope o' cinder tay
   While it's warm;
Mi mother used to give it me,
When aw wur sich a lad as thee,
   In her arm.

Hush-a-babby, hush-a-bee, –
Oh, what a temper! – dear-a-me
   Heaw tha skrikes!
Here's a bit o' sugar, sithee;
Howd thi noise, an' then aw'll gie thee
   Owt tha likes.

We've nobbut getten coarsish fare
But eawt o' this tha'll get thi share,
   Never fear.
Aw hope tha'll never want a meal,
But allus fill thi bally weel
   While tha'rt here.

Thi feyther's noan been wed so lung,
An' yet tha sees he's middlin thrung
   Wi' yo' o.
Besides thi little brother Ted,
We've one upstairs, asleep i' bed,

Wi' eawr Joe.

But tho' we've childer two or three,
We'll mak' a bit o' reawm for thee,
   Bless thee, lad!
Tha'rt prattiest brid we have i'th nest,
So hutch up closer to mi breast;
   A'wm thi dad.

Samuel Laycock

Source: *The Collected Writings of Samuel Laycock*, ed.
George Milner, Oldham, W. E. Clegg, 1908, pp. 1–3.

UNCLE DICK'S ADVOICE TO WED MEN

What to say to wed fellows aw conno weel tell;
Altho' aw've bin wed two or three toimes misel'.
It's a awkwardish job, an' it's noan very noice,
To be actin' th' owd uncle, an givin' advoice.
But th' wed women keep botherin' an wantin' me t' write,
Iv aw dunno, aw know they'll do nowt nobbut flite.
My woife's among th' rest, hoo kicks up a rare fuss,
An, says 'at ther's reawm for improvement i' us.

Wel, aw dar' say ther' is, we're noan angels, aw know;
Nowe, nowe, chaps, ther's nowt o' that stamp here below;
Even women, as fair as they happen to be,
They're sent into th' world witheawt wings one can see;
An' it's weel as it is so, for if they could fly,
That woife o' Tom Breawn's ud be off up i'th' sky;
An' ther's moor beside her 'at ud soon disappear,
For they're tired o' bein' hampert an' kicked abeawt here.

Neaw why should it be so? come chaps, is this reet?
Aw'm for bein' reet plain an' straight-forrud to-neet.
Does tha yer, Tom? heaw is it tha treats wi' neglect
That woman tha promised to love an' protect?
Heaw is it tha'rt gradely wi' folk eawt o'th dur,
But when tha gets whoam tha'rt so peevish wi' her?
Eh, Tom, iv ther's owt tha should love i' this loife,
Aw'm sure it's yo'r Poll, for hoo mak's a good woife.

Why, mon, tha's forgetten that mornin' aw'm sure,
When tha took her to th'altar, so fair an' so pure,
An' talk abeawt angels, an' bonny blue een,
To mi thinkin a prattier lass never wur seen.

When yo' seet off to th' church, bells were ringin' so sweet,
And th' nayburs God blessed her when passin' deawn th' street,
An' her feyther an' mother – they mingled the'r prayers,
'At tha'd mack a good whoam for that dear lamb o' theirs.

Has ta done so, owd brid? nowt o'th sooart mon tha knows
'At hoo's sufferin' just neaw fro' thi kicks an' thi' blows;
It wur nobbut last neet, tha wur on at th' 'King Ned',
An' becose hoo went for thi, an' ax'd thi' t' go t'bed,
Tha' up wi' thi fist, an' witheawt e'en a word,
Tha knocked her on th' pavin's; – it's true, mon, aw've yeard. –
Eh, Tom, lad, aw'd oather be better nor thee –
An' keep off that mischievous drink – or aw'd see.

A chap when he's wed should feel sattled i' loife,
Stay at whoam of a neet wi' his books an' his woife;
An' if it so leets 'at ther's youngsters to nurse,
It's his duty to help, for ther's nothin' looks worse
Nor a chap to be gaddin, abeawt eawt o'th' dur,
An' his woife wi' th' nursin an' th' wark left to her.
Neaw aw'm sure it ud look far moor monly an' fair
If we stay'd in to help 'em an' did th' biggest share.

Aw con fancy aw yer somb'dy say 'uncle Dick!
Aw wish yo'd stop gabblin' an' talkin' so quick.
Let's have a word wi' yo', it's o very noice
For a chap to be writin' an' givin' advoice;
But we wanten yo'r woife here, no deawt hoo could tell
Heaw toime after toime yo'n bin guilty yo'rsel';
When ogen yo'r inclined to give others a rap,
Think on an' begin at Jerusalem, owd chap.'

Well, well, lads, aw will, for aw'm guilty, no deawt;
We'n o bits o failin's – we're noan on us beawt. –
Even th' best on us, when we're weel polished an' breet,
Winno bear a good siftin' nor bringin' to th' leet.
So let's start an' mend, let's begin an' be good,
For eawr woives ud be rarely set up if we would.
Let's prove eawrsel's honest an' monly an' true,
An' then th' women ull try, an they'll mend a bit too.

Samuel Laycock

Source: *The Collected Writings of Samuel Laycock*, ed. George
Milner, Oldham, W. E. Clegg, 1908, pp. 107–9.

WOD WER TH' GOOD OF BOTHERING

Wod wer th' good o' bothering: these words are often sed,
When some dispute's bin settled, after a big mistake's bin med.
Booath side's were wrong, thi booath admit but at fost thi cudn't see.
Bud after a feight an ten weeks strike, thi happen to agree;
An i' th' words o' the text thi say wi' me
Wod were th' good o' bothering.

Wi goa hooam nesty tempered, an wi wire into th' wife,
"Th' dinner's never ready," an cud like to tek her life.
Then th' wife replies an sez, "ids soon enough for thee."
Then he replies, "Awl hev nooan, iv tha tawks like thad to me."
"Well goa." He goas; bur aw think bi hafe past three.
He'd say: Wod were th' good o' bothering.

A chap may ged a drop too much, an goa hooam drunk at neet,
He's as happy as a clipper, he's wod sum fook co's o'reet.
His wife might co him lazy, or a nasty drunken scrawl,
Then he geds up an knocks her deawn, bangs her heyd ageean a wall.
Neaw iv hoo'd sed nowt till morning, ther'd bin no row at all.
Wod wer th' good o' bothering.

A woman hes her childer ill, an thi "pop off" one bi 'one,
Her strength an energy keeps up till th' last wee chick has gone.
Her friends come reawnd an sympathize, thi give her every cheer.
In such a case, an aw've seen sum, these words aw think yo'd heer:
"My hooam's transferred from here to theer,
Soa wod wer th' good o' bothering."

Iv wi cud only measure th' pleasure a kindly action brings,
Iv wi cud only know wod pain wi' cause wi' little trifling things,
Iv wi cud only stop an' think befoor wi stert an act,
Iv wi'd only weigh things o'er, an use a little tact,
Aw'm sure these words aw've used so oft ud never be a fact,
Thads: Wod wer th' good o' bothering.

Sammy Mee

Source: 'Our Dialect Corner – Lancashire Poems by Sammy Mee'
(no. 36), *Preston Herald*, Saturday, 12 July, 1913, p. 2.

NOTES

GENERAL INTRODUCTION

1 R. Phillips, *Putting Asunder: A History of Divorce in Western Society*, Cambridge, Cambridge University Press, 1988; see also L. Stone, *Road to Divorce, England, 1530–1987*, Oxford, Oxford University Press, 1990.

2 Early examples are C. Kingston, *The Marriage Market*, London, John Lane, 1926, and *Society Sensations*, London, Stanley Paul, 1922; a more recent work, mostly in this tradition, is A. Horstman, *Victorian Divorce*, London, Croom Helm, 1985.

3 The most obvious reference here is to L. Stone, *The Family, Sex and Marriage in England, 1500–1800*, London, Weidenfeld & Nicolson, 1977; I acknowledge Stone's pioneering work in this area, but it will become apparent that my argument is broadly inconsistent with his interpretation of historical change. Related arguments are developed in E. Shorter, *The Making of the Modern Family*, London, Collins, 1976, and R. Trumbach, *The Rise of the Egalitarian Family: Aristocratic Kinship and Domestic Relations in Eighteenth Century England*, New York, Academic Press, 1978.

4 Some Welsh evidence is discussed in chapter 1, but the primary focus is on England; the different structures in Scotland, notably a distinct divorce law, would require quite separate treatment.

5 Most recently Stone, 1990, op. cit., but note also M. Nevill, 'Women and Marriage Breakdown in England, 1832–1857', unpublished PhD thesis, University of Essex, 1989.

6 Horstman, op. cit.; G. L. Savage, 'The Social Basis of the Demand for Divorce in England, 1858–1868: Graphs and Tables', unpublished paper presented to the Mid-western Victorian Studies Association, April, 1987; 'The Divorce Court and the Queen's/King's Proctor: Legal Patriarchy and the Sanctity of Marriage in England, 1861–1937', *Historical Papers*, Quebec, 1989, and 'The Wilful Communication of a Loathsome Disease: Marital Conflict and Venereal Disease in Victorian England', *Victorian Studies*, Autumn, 1990, vol. 34, no. 1, pp. 35–54.

7 For a fuller discussion of the merits and methodological problems involved in the use of these sources see appendix 1.

8 See chapter 4.

9 For examples see M. J. Peterson, *Family, Love and Work in the Lives of Victorian Gentlewomen*, Bloomington, Indiana University Press, 1989, pp. 58–131; P. Jalland, *Women, Marriage and Politics, 1860–1914*, Oxford, Oxford University Press, 1986; also, though less uniformly, P. Gay, *The Bourgeois Experience: Victoria to Freud*: vol. 1: *Education of the Senses*, New York, Oxford University

184

Press, 1984, vol. 2: *The Tender Passion*, New York, Oxford University Press, 1986.

10 For a recent English example dealing with marriage, based largely on anecdotal evidence, see J. Perkin, *Women and Marriage in Victorian England*, London, Routledge, 1989; an American example, more theoretically sophisticated, is L. Gordon, *Heroes of Their Own Lives: the Politics and History of Family Violence: Boston, 1880–1960*, New York, Viking Penguin, 1988.

11 For a useful general discussion of *couverture* and the broader legal framework see J. Lewis, *Women in England, 1870–1950: Sexual Divisions and Social Change*, Brighton, Wheatsheaf, 1984, pp. 119–21.

12 For discussion of a similar discourse in nineteenth-century American feminism see F. Basch, 'Women's Rights and the Wrongs of Marriage in Nineteenth Century America', *History Workshop*, 1986, no. 22, pp. 18–40.

13 R. Coward, *Patriarchal Precedents: Sexuality and Social Relations*, London, Routledge & Kegan Paul, 1983, pp. 268–77.

14 M. Anderson, 'The Social Implications of Demographic Change', in F. M. L. Thompson (ed.), *The Cambridge Social History of Britain, 1750–1950*, vol. 2: *People and Their Environment*, Cambridge, Cambridge University Press, 1990, pp. 1–70.

15 L. Davidoff and C. Hall, *Family Fortunes: Men and Women of the English Middle-Class, 1780–1850*, London, Hutchinson, 1987.

16 J. R. Gillis, *For Better For Worse: British Marriages, 1600 to the Present*, New York, Oxford University Press, 1985.

17 R. Phillips, *Putting Asunder: A History of Divorce in Western Society*, Cambridge, Cambridge University Press, 1988; a more specialized monograph, S. Wolfram, *In-Laws and Outlaws: Kinship and Marriage in England*, London, Croom Helm, 1987, offers a similarly valuable analysis of the relationship between marriage, divorce and social change.

18 N. Tomes, 'A "Torrent of Abuse": Crimes of Violence Between Working-Class Men and Women in London', *Journal of Social History*, 1978, vol. 11, no. 3, pp. 328–45; another early and invaluable analysis, though unfortunately never fully published, is J. R. Lambertz, 'Male–Female Violence in Late Victorian and Edwardian England', unpublished honours thesis, Harvard University, 1979.

19 E. Ross, '"Fierce Questions and Taunts": Married Life in Working-Class London', *Feminist Studies*, 1982, vol. 8, no. 3, pp. 575–602.

20 E. Roberts, *A Woman's Place: An Oral History of Working-Class Women, 1890–1940*, Oxford, Blackwell, 1984.

21 I. Minor, 'Working-class Women and Matrimonial Law Reform, 1890–1914', in D. Rubinstein and D. Martin (eds), *Ideology and the Labour Movement*, London, Croom Helm, 1979, pp. 103–24.

22 M. L. Shanley, *Feminism, Marriage and the Law in Victorian England, 1850–1895*, Princeton, Princeton University Press, 1989; C. Dyhouse, *Feminism and the Family in England, 1880–1939*, Oxford, Blackwell, 1939, discusses similar issues.

23 P. Rose, *Parallel Lives: Five Victorian Marriages*, Harmondsworth, Penguin, 1985, p. 266; see also S. Mintz, *A Prison of Expectations: the Family in Victorian Culture*, New York, New York University Press, 1983.

24 Gay, 1984 and 1986, op. cit.

PART I INTRODUCTION

1 For a general discussion of these issues see L. Davidoff, 'The Family in Britain', in F. M. L. Thompson (ed.), *The Cambridge Social History of Britain*,

1750–1850, vol. 2: *People and Their Environment*, Cambridge, Cambridge University Press, 1990, pp. 85–98, 106–28.

2 D. Vincent, *Literacy and Popular Culture: England, 1750–1914*, Cambridge, Cambridge University Press, 1989, pp. 23–32.

3 M. Anderson, 'The Social Implications of Demographic Change', in Thompson, op. cit., vol. 2, pp. 38–45.

1 THE TARGETS OF 'ROUGH MUSIC'

1 Reported by Isaac Taylor, Settrington Rectory, *Folklore Journal*, 1883, vol. 1, pp. 298–9.

2 The view is associated most directly with E. P. Thompson, 'Rough Music: Le Charivari Anglais', *Annales*, 1972, vol. 27, pp. 285–312, but see also E. Shorter, *The Making of the Modern Family*, London, Collins, 1976, pp. 218–27, and J. R. Gillis, *For Better For Worse: British Marriages, 1600 to the Present*, New York, Oxford University Press, 1985, pp. 130–4.

3 V. A. C. Gatrell and T. B. Hadden, 'Criminal Statistics and their Interpretation', in E. A. Wrigley (ed.), *Nineteenth Century Society*, Cambridge, Cambridge University Press, 1972, pp. 369–75, 391.

4 D. T. Andrew, 'The Code of Honour and its Critics: The Opposition to Duelling in England, 1700–1850', *Social History*, 1980, vol. 5, no. 3, pp. 409–34.

5 N. Tomes, 'A "Torrent of Abuse": Crimes of Violence Between Working-Class men and Women in London', *Journal of Social History*, 1978, vol. 11, no. 3, pp. 328–45.

6 Thompson, op. cit., pp. 310–4. The male domination of many of these events was conveyed in visual images, as in George Walker, *The Costume of Yorkshire*, London, Longman, Hirst, Rees, Orme & Browne, 1814, p. 63.

7 E. P. Thompson, '"Rough Music" et Charivari: Quelques réflexions complémentaires', in J. LeGoff and J. C. Schmitt (eds), *Le Charivari*, Paris, Écoles des Hautes Études en Sciences Sociales, 1981, p. 283.

8 Shorter, op. cit., pp. 218–27.

9 Gillis, op. cit., pp. 130–4.

10 A. Clark, *Women's Silence, Men's Violence: Sexual Assault in England, 1770–1845*, London, Pandora, 1987, pp. 49–50.

11 T. Lupton, *Siuqila: Too Good to be True: Omen*, London, H. Bynneman, 1580, pp. 46–50; cf. E. Rose, 'Too Good to be True: Thomas Lupton's Golden Rule', in D. J. Guth and J. W. McKenna (eds), *Tudor Rule and Revolution*, Cambridge, Cambridge University Press, 1982, pp. 183–200.

12 M. Ingram, 'Ridings, Rough Music and the "Reform of Popular Culture" in Early Modern England', *Past and Present*, 1984, no. 105, pp. 97–8.

13 N. Z. Davies, 'Charivari, Honor and Community in Seventeenth-Century Lyon and Geneva', in J. J. MacAloon (ed.), *Rite, Drama, Festival, Spectacle: Rehearsals Toward a Theory of Cultural Performance*, Philadelphia, Institute for Study of Human Issues, 1984, pp. 42–57.

14 Thompson, 1972, op. cit., pp. 302–3.

15 M. Baker, *Wedding Customs and Folklore*, Newton Abbot, David & Charles, 1977, pp. 132–3; A. M. B., *The Parlour Portfolio, or, Post Chaise Companion*, London, Matthew Iley, 1820, vol. 2, pp. 111–12.

16 J. T. Staton, 'Missis Caustic's Hearthstone Lectures', *Th' Bowtun Loominary*, 1859, vol. 11, p. 303.

17 A. B. Cheales, *Proverbial Folklore*, London, Simpkin, Marshall, 1875, pp. 6–15, 46; S. Timmins, *A History of Warwickshire*, London, Elliot Stock, 1889, p. 219; W. S. Weeks, *The Clitheroe District: Proverbs and Sayings, Customs and Legends*,

and Much of its History, Clitheroe, Advertiser and Times Co., 1922, p. 5; R. Palmer (ed.), *Folk Songs Collected by Ralph Vaughan Williams*, London, J. M. Dent, 1983, p. 180; Robert Leach, *The Punch and Judy Show: History, Tradition and Meaning*, London, Batsford, 1985, pp. 30, 41–2, 50, 57, 81–7, 133, 168.

18 C. Redwood, *The Vale of Glamorgan*, London, Saunders & Otley, 1839, pp. 271–95; for a useful discussion of Welsh versions of rough music, especially the more common 'ceffyl pren', see R. A. N. Jones, 'Popular Culture, Policing, and the Disappearance of the Ceffyl Pren in Cardigan, c. 1837–1850', *Ceredigion*, 1988–9, vol. 11, no. 1, pp. 19–39; in private correspondence with the author, Jones noted that her extensive research on Welsh rituals indicates that Redwood's account may be the last recorded incident of a Coolstrin court, as opposed to other popular forms, and that it was used almost without exception to punish scolding or domineering wives; letter dated 2 August, 1990.

19 Gillis, op. cit., pp. 132–4.

20 Redwood, op. cit., pp. 285–6.

21 Ibid., p. 286.

22 Ibid., pp. 271–2.

23 E. P. Thompson, 'Folklore, Anthropology and Social History', *The Indian Historical Review*, 1977, vol. 3, no. 2; p. 250.

24 L. Davidoff and C. Hall, *Family Fortunes: Men and Women of the English Middle Class, 1780–1850*, London, Hutchinson, 1987, p. 26.

25 *The Times*, 24 August, 1846, p. 6.

26 *Leeds Mercury*, 22 August, 1846, p. 7; *The Times*, 24 August, 1846, p. 6, 25 August, 1846, p. 5, 26 August, 1846, p. 6; *Preston Chronicle*, 29 August, 1846, p. 7.

27 On the nineteenth-century itinerant population see R. Samuel, 'Comers and Goers', in H. J. Dyos and M. Wolff (eds), *The Victorian City: Images and Realities*, London, Routledge & Kegan Paul, 1973, vol. 1, pp. 123–60.

28 *Illustrated London News*, 7 September, 1850, p. 199; *Morning Chronicle*, 9 September, 1850, p. 4.

29 See, e.g., H. C. F. Bell, *Lord Palmerston*, Hamden, Conn., Archon Books, 1966, vol. 2, pp. 13–40; P. Guedalla, *Palmerston*, London, Hodder & Stoughton, 1926, pp. 272–3; D. Southgate, *The Most English Minister: The Policies and Politics of Palmerston*, London, Macmillan, 1966, pp. 283–6.

30 See, e.g., *The Times*, 11 October, 1849, p. 6.

31 *Standard*, 7 September, 1850, cited in *Magnet*, 9 September, 1850, p. 4.

32 *The Times*, 7 September, 1850, p. 4; *Illustrated London News*, 7 September, 1850, p. 199 (which covered the story with full front-page illustrations), 14 September, 1850, p. 222; *Morning Chronicle*, 9 September, 1850, pp. 4–5.

33 Southgate, op. cit., p. 284.

34 E. Ashley, *The Life and Correspondence of Henry John Temple, Viscount Palmerston*, London, R. Bentley & Son, 1879, vol. 2, pp. 169–70; A. C. Benson (ed.), *The Letters of Queen Victoria: A Selection of H. M.'s Correspondence Between the Years 1837 and 1861*, London, Murray, 1908, vol. 2, pp. 267–70; Guedalla, op. cit., pp. 272–3; Southgate, op. cit., pp. 283–6; *Reynolds's Weekly Newspaper*, 15 September, 1850, pp. 10–11.

35 D. Thompson, *The Chartists*, London, Temple Smith, 1984, one of the very few recent histories of Chartism to mention the incident, notes its 'traditional' nature, but with reference to the women participants only, p. 132.

36 See the suggestions of intriguing, though limited, similarities between charivaris and jingoism in R. N. Price, 'Society, Status and Jingoism: The Social Roots of Lower Middle-Class Patriotism, 1870–1900', in G. Crossick (ed.), *The Lower Middle-Class in Britain, 1870–1914*, London, Croom Helm, 1977, pp. 91–2.

37 M. Agulhon, *Marianne Into Battle: Republican Imagery and Symbolism in France, 1789–1880*, tr. Janet Lloyd, Cambridge, Cambridge University Press, 1981; see also E. Hobsbawm, 'Man and Woman in Socialist Iconography', *History Workshop*, 1978, vol. 6, pp. 121–38; see *Punch*'s sketch of the popular illustration showing Haynau flogging Madame Madersbach, *Punch*, 1850, vol. 19, p. 150.

38 E. Bligh, *Tooting Corner*, London, Secker & Warburg, 1946, pp. 15–16; *Illustrated London News*, 14 September, 1850, p. 222; *Morning Chronicle*, 9 September, 1850, p. 5.

39 *Reynolds's Weekly Newspaper*, 15 September, 1850, p. 6.

40 A. R. Schoyen, *The Chartist Challenge: a Portrait of George Julian Harney*, London, Heinemann, 1958, pp. 203–4.

41 *Red Republican*, 21 September, 1850, p. 107.

42 *Illustrated London News*, 7 September, 1850, p. 199.

43 *Punch*, 1850, vol. 19, p. 114.

44 Bligh, op. cit., pp. 13–17; *Red Republican*, 21 September, 1850, p. 112; see appendix 2 for the two ballads in full.

45 *Sydney Morning Herald*, 11 January, 1851, p. 4.

46 *Reynolds's Weekly Newspaper*, 15 September, 1850, p. 11.

47 G. Crossick, *An Artisan Elite in Victorian Society: Kentish London, 1840–1880*, London, Croom Helm, 1978, p. 230; on Chartist tensions and internationalism, which provide useful context for Harney's response, see D. Jones, *Chartism and the Chartists*, London, Allen Lane, 1975, pp. 151–8.

48 Tomes, op. cit., pp. 334–8.

49 *The Times*, 10 September, 1850, p. 4, 12 September, 1850, p. 5; *Morning Chronicle*, 6 September, 1850, p. 4; see also *Punch*, 1850, vol. 19, p. 150.

50 *The Times*, 10 September, 1850, p. 4.

51 *Morning Chronicle*, 20 September, 1850, p. 4.

52 *Reynolds's Weekly Newspaper*, 22 September, 1850, p. 10.

53 *The Times*, 7 September, 1850, p. 4.

54 *The Times*, 26 August, 1853, p. 6, 14 September, 1853, p. 6; *The Times*'s criticism in this vein predated the Haynau attack; see, e.g., 10 July, 1847, p. 5, 22 July, 1847, p. 4, 25 August, 1847, p. 4, 4 November, 1847, p. 4.

55 *The Times*, 12 March, 1853, p. 6; for discussion of the legislation and the flogging issue see below, chapter 2.

56 *Morning Chronicle*, 10 September, 1850, p. 8, 11 September, 1850, p. 8.

57 *Punch*, 1850, vol. 19, p. 129; for one of many popular images of the draymen as heroes see *Punch*, 1850, vol. 19, p. 114.

58 *Reynolds's Weekly Newspaper*, 15 September, 1850, pp. 10–11.

59 *Sydney Morning Herald*, 11 January, 1851, p. 4.

60 F. P. Cobbe, 'Wife-Torture in England', *Contemporary Review*, 1878, vol. 32, p. 58.

61 H. Mayhew, *London Labour and the London Poor*, London, Griffin, Bohn & Co., 1861, vol. 3, p. 265.

62 Ibid., p. 253.

63 E. Ross, '"Fierce Questions and Taunts": Married Life in Working-Class London, 1870–1914', *Feminist Studies*, 1982, vol. 8, no. 3, pp. 591–3.

64 Ibid.

65 Bligh, op. cit., p. 14.

66 *Punch*, 18 May, 1874.

67 See, for example, *Preston Chronicle* (Flanaghan), 18 July, 1846, p. 6.

68 On Norton see M. Poovey, *Uneven Developments: The Ideological Work of Gender in Mid-Victorian England*, Chicago, University of Chicago Press, 1988, pp. 62–88.

69 C. Hall, 'The Tale of Samuel and Jemima: Gender and Working-Class Culture in Early Nineteenth Century England', in T. Bennett, C. Mercer and J. Woollacott (eds), *Popular Culture and Social Relations*, Milton Keynes, Open University Press, 1986, pp. 82–4.

70 G. Cruikshank, *The Bottle*, London, D. Bogne, 1847, plates 1, 6, 7, 8.

71 M. Vicinus, *The Industrial Muse: A Study of Nineteenth Century British Working-Class Literature*, London, Croom Helm, 1974, pp. 208–15.

72 S. Laycock, *The Collected Writings of Samuel Laycock*, ed. George Milner, Oldham, W. E. Clegg, 1908, pp. 1–3; see appendix 3.

73 Ibid., pp. 107–9; see appendix 3.

74 See, for example, James Standing, 'Wimmen's Wark es Niver Done' and Edwin Waugh, 'Margit's Comin'', in Brian Hollingworth (ed.), *Songs of the People: Lancashire Dialect Poetry of the Industrial Revolution*, Manchester, Manchester University Press, 1977, pp. 75–8, 67–8; similar poems continued to appear in the 'Dialect Corners' of local Lancashire newspapers well into the twentieth century, for example Sammy Mee, 'Wod Wer th' Good of Bothering', *Preston Herald*, 12 July, 1913, p. 2; see appendix 3.

75 Staton, op. cit., 1859, vol. 11, p. 303; the lectures were serialized in *Th' Bowtun Loominary*, in vols 11 and 12 during 1859 and 1860; see also J. T. Staton, *A Case of Samples*, Manchester, Abel, Heywood & Son, 1869, pp. 14–16; on Jerrold's 'Mrs Caudle's Curtain Lectures', see below, chapters 3 and 5.

76 C. Dyhouse, *Girls Growing Up in Victorian and Edwardian England*, London, Routledge & Kegan Paul, 1981, pp. 3–39.

77 For example R. Hoggart, *The Uses of Literacy*, Harmondsworth, Penguin, 1957, p. 48.

78 D. Vincent, *Bread, Knowledge and Freedom: A Study of Nineteenth-Century Working Class Autobiography*, London, Methuen, 1981, pp. 40–4.

79 W. Lovett, *Life and Struggles of William Lovett* (London, 1876), p. 38, cited in ibid., p. 44.

80 D. Morgan, 'History and Masculinity: Methodological and Sociological Considerations', unpublished paper presented to 'Sex and Gender' conference of the U.K. Social History Society, Reading, 1985.

81 P. Bailey, '"Will the Real Bill Banks Please Stand Up?": Towards a Role Analysis of Mid-Victorian Respectability', *Journal of Social History*, 1979, vol. 12, no. 3, pp. 336–53.

82 D. Rubinstein, *Before the Suffragettes: Woman's Emancipation in the 1890's*, Brighton, Harvester, 1986, pp. 54–8.

83 For a useful discussion of working-class men's independence and respectability, and the implications for women's marginalization economically, see K. McClelland, 'Some Thoughts on Masculinity and the "Representative Artisan" in Britain, 1850–1880', *Gender and History*, 1989, vol. 1, no. 2, pp. 164–77.

2   'ROUGH USAGE'

1 *Preston Chronicle*, 24 November, 1888, p. 2.

2 Ibid.

3 Ibid., 24 November, 1888, p. 2, 1 December, 1888, p. 5; for a discussion of similar light sentences in relation to the operation of the 1878 Matrimonial Causes Act see M. L. Shanley, *Feminism, Marriage and the Law in Victorian England, 1850–1895*, Princeton, Princeton University Press, 1979, pp. 170–4.

4 *Preston Chronicle*, 5 October, 1878 (Brown), p. 2.

5 Ibid., 17 October, 1903, p. 12.

6 A survey of 283 cases of domestic violence in Preston between 1836 and 1913 yielded five butchers.

7 Local newspapers were surveyed one full year in each decade from the 1830s to 1913, yielding 283 cases, in which 128 gave details of men's occupations or unemployed status. Only 27 recorded women's occupations. For a fuller discussion of the survey see Appendix 1.

8 J. W. Kaye, 'Outrages on Women', *North British Review*, May, 1856, vol. 25, no. 49, pp. 240, 254.

9 F. P. Cobbe, 'Wife-Torture in England', *Contemporary Review*, April, 1878, vol. 32, pp. 58–60, 74–5.

10 H. Mayhew, *London Labour and the London Poor*, London, Griffin, 1861, vol. 1, pp. 20–1, 43–8, 457–68.

11 Royal Commission on Divorce and Matrimonial Causes, *Parliamentary Papers*, 1912–13, vols 18–21 [Cd. 6478-81]; for the titillating genre see the journalist, R. E. Corder, *Tales Told to the Magistrate*, London, A. Melrose, 1925; examples of more serious treatment include the police court missionary, T. Holmes, *Pictures and Problems from London Police Courts*, London, E. Arnold, 1900, magistrates A. C. Plowden, *Grain or Chaff? The Autobiography of a Police Court Magistrate*, London, T. Fisher Unwin, 1903, and C. Chapman, *The Poor Man's Court of Justice: Twenty-Five Years as a Metropolitan Magistrate*, London, Hodder & Stoughton, 1925, also the numerous books by district nurse Margaret Loane discussed below.

12 S. Pulling, 'What Legislation is Necessary for the Repression of Crimes of Violence?', *Transactions, National Association for the Promotion of Social Science*, 1876, pp. 345–61.

13 Cobbe, op. cit., pp. 60–1; see also Kaye, op. cit., pp. 237–8.

14 H. Taylor, 'The Enfranchisement of Women', *Westminster Review*, July, 1851, vol. 55, in A. Rossi (ed.), *Essays on Sex Equality*, Chicago, University of Chicago Press, 1970, p. 105n; J. S. Mill, *The Subjection of Women*, 1869, in Rossi, pp. 163–5, 235–6.

15 E. Wostenholme Elmy to H. McIlquham, 19 September, 1901, Elmy Collection, British Library, Add. MS. 47,452; thanks to Gail Savage for this reference.

16 See above, chapter 1, p. 33.

17 For example H. Bosanquet, *The Family*, London, Macmillan, 1906, p. 261; Chapman, op. cit., p. 59.

18 N. Tomes, 'A "Torrent of Abuse": Crimes of Violence Between Working-Class Men and Women in London', *Journal of Social History*, 1978, vol. 11, no. 3, pp. 328–45.

19 Two important exceptions are J. R. Lambertz, 'Male–Female Violence in Late Victorian and Edwardian England', unpublished honours thesis, Harvard University, 1979, pp. 32–4, and Shanley, op. cit., pp. 170–1, who queries the extent to which magistrates made use of protection orders after the 1878 legislation.

20 V. A. C. Gatrell and T. B. Hadden, 'Criminal statistics and their interpretation', in E. A. Wrigley (ed.), *Nineteenth Century Society*, Cambridge, Cambridge University Press, 1972, pp. 369–75, 391.

21 Tomes, op. cit., pp. 340–2.

22 41 & 42 Victoria, c. 19; in 1895 the requirement for such orders was changed to 'persistent cruelty' by the Summary Jurisdiction (Married Women) Act, 58 & 59 Victoria, c. 39; it had been widened to include desertion in the Married Women (Maintenance in Case of Desertion) Act, 1886, 49 & 50 Victoria, c. 52.

23 For a description of this process see J. H. Potter, *Inasmuch: The Story of the Police Court Mission, 1876–1926*, London, Williams & Norgate, 1927, pp. 67–80.

24 Tomes, op. cit., pp. 333–4, notes the reluctance of magistrates to put families on poor relief by sending wife-beaters to prison; for an early Preston case see *Preston Chronicle* (Stephenson), 7 June, 1856, p. 5.

25 Royal Commission on Divorce and Matrimonial Causes, *Parliamentary Papers*, 1912–13, 18 [Cd. 6479], p. 250, Q. 18254.

26 *Preston Chronicle* (Gibson), 7 January, 1893, p. 4.

27 I. Minor, 'Working-Class Women and Matrimonial Law Reform, 1890–1914', in D. E. Martin and D. Rubenstein (eds), *Ideology and the Labour Movement*, London, Croom Helm, 1979, pp. 103–24; Shanley, op. cit., pp. 170–6.

28 J. Greenwood, *The Prisoner in the Dock: My Four Years' Daily Experiences in the London Police Courts*, London, Chatto & Windus, 1902, pp. 15–18; Plowden, op. cit., pp. 250, 265–6; for a discussion of the popularity of London police courts in this period see J. Davis, 'A Poor Man's System of Justice: The London Police Courts in the Second Half of the Nineteenth Century', *Historical Journal*, 1984, vol. 27, no. 2, pp. 309–35.

29 *Preston Chronicle*, 19 April, 1856, p. 5; see also *Preston Chronicle* (Webster), 11 October, 1856, p. 5, 18 October, 1856, p. 5. In both these cases the magistrates referred to the legislation of 1853, 'An Act for the Better Prevention and Punishment of Aggravated Assaults upon Women and Children . . . (16 & 17 Victoria, c. 30), which provided for summary punishment of up to six months imprisonment before two magistrates or JPs for assaults on women and children, as being explicitly designed to allow for convictions when 'the strength of the wife's affection prevented her from giving evidence against her husband'.

30 Married Women (Maintenance in Case of Desertion) Act, 1886, 49 & 50 Victoria, c. 52.

31 *Preston Herald* (Bamber), 18 June, 1913, p. 3.

32 For example Alexander Lockley, a joiner, and his wife, who appeared three times on cruelty and desertion charges between January and September, 1903, each time urged to 'come together again'. *Preston Herald*, 24 January, 1903, p. 3, *Preston Guardian*, 19 September, 1903, p. 12.

33 Royal Commission on Divorce and Matrimonial Causes, *Parliamentary Papers*, 1912–13, vol. 19 [Cd. 6480], Chief Constable's return, Leeds, p. 289.

34 Ibid., evidence of Mr B. C. Brough, Staffordshire magistrate, p. 317.

35 *Preston Herald*, 20 September, 1913, p. 3.

36 For example, ibid. (Rawlinson), 19 March, 1913, p. 4.

37 Tomes, op. cit., pp. 329–30.

38 Plowden, op. cit., pp. 305–6.

39 *Preston Chronicle*, 24 March, 1888, p. 6; in 1888 cases reported in the *Chronicle* fluctuated between a low of one in February and nine in September.

40 For a discussion of the concept of a 'threshold' of acceptable marital violence among women see Lambertz, op. cit., pp. 63, 101.

41 Royal Commission on Divorce and Matrimonial Causes, *Parliamentary Papers*, 1912–13, vol. 18 [Cd. 6479], p. 91.

42 Ibid., vol. 19, [Cd. 6480], p. 273.

43 For example, J. G. H. Halkett (magistrate, Hull), ibid., vol. 18 [Cd. 6479], pp. 296–301; E. W. Garratt (magistrate, West London), ibid., vol. 19 [Cd. 6480], pp. 32–3.

44 'Lucy Luck', in J. Burnett (ed.) *Useful Toil*, London, Allen Lane, 1974, p. 75; Mrs E. Steinthal (Ripon Mothers' Union), Royal Commission on Divorce and Matrimonial Causes, *Parliamentary Papers*, 1912–13, vol. 19 [Cd. 6480], p. 196.

45 C. J. Holmes (police court missionary, St. Helen's, Lancashire), ibid., vol. 19 [Cd. 6480], p. 255.

46 Ibid., p. 315.
47 Quoted in J. S. Bratton, *The Victorian Popular Ballad*, Totowa, N. J., Rowman & Littlefield, 1975, p. 101; thanks to Peter Bailey for this reference.
48 Royal Commission on Divorce and Matrimonial Causes, *Parliamentary Papers*, 1912–13, vol. 19 [Cd. 6480], pp. 48–9; for similar views given to the commission see the Thames police court missionary, W. Fitzsimmons, ibid., p. 290.
49 Ibid., vol. 20 [Cd. 6481], p. 151.
50 M. Loane, *The Common Growth*, London, E. Arnold, 1911, p. 288.
51 M. Loane, *An Englishman's Castle*, London, E. Arnold, 1909, p. 109.
52 J. R. Gillis, *For Better, For Worse: British Marriages, 1600 to the Present*, New York, Oxford University Press, 1985, pp. 231ff., especially p. 259.
53 Loane, *Common Growth*, pp. 288–9.
54 Royal Commission on Divorce and Matrimonial Causes, *Parliamentary Papers*, 1912–13, vol. 20 [Cd. 6481], P. 151.
55 Especially E. Ross, '"Fierce Questions and Taunts": Married Life in Working-Class London', *Feminist Studies*, 1982, vol. 8, no. 3, pp. 575–602; Lambertz, op. cit., which includes a chapter on Lancashire; Tomes, op. cit.; E. Roberts, *A Woman's Place: An Oral History of Working-Class Women, 1890–1940*, Oxford, Blackwell, 1984, while not exclusively addressed to violence, has a useful discussion, based on oral evidence, partly from Preston, of power relationships in working-class marriage, pp. 110–24.
56 Ross, op. cit.
57 In the Preston survey men's drinking was mentioned explicitly in 107 cases out of 283, women's in 24.
58 Lambertz, op. cit., p. 81, quoting M. Loane, *The Queens Poor*, London, E. Arnold, 1905, pp. 2–3.
59 Cobbe, op. cit., p. 69.
60 Ibid., pp. 68–70, 74–5.
61 *Preston Chronicle*, 14 April, 1866, p. 6; there were eight incidents of husband assault out of the 283 domestic violence cases in the survey.
62 Ibid., 7 January, 1888, p. 5; 9 June, 1888, p. 2.
63 Some form of defiance, resistance or physical combat was mentioned in 32 out of the 283 cases.
64 For example *Preston Chronicle* (Gallagher), 14 April, 1888, p. 2.
65 *Preston Guardian* (Goring), 5 December, 1903, p. 12; for the Blackpool murder, 28 November, 1903, p. 5.
66 *Preston Chronicle*, 8 December, 1888, p. 2.
67 For example ibid. (Cookson), 23 December, 1893, p. 4.
68 Ibid. (Carter), 1 July, 1893, p. 4.
69 For example *Preston Herald* (Shaw), 23 April, 1913, p. 4; *Preston Chronicle* (Lawrenson), 21 April, 1888, p. 2.
70 *Preston Guardian*, 7 February, 1903, p. 12; see also ibid. (Dobson), ibid. (Swindlehurst), 19 December, 1903, p. 8, *Preston Herald* (Bradley), 12 December, 1903, p. 3; for routine reports of the Preston Guild see *The Times*, 20 August to 15 September, 1902, *passim*.
71 See especially W. Fitzsimmons, the London police court missionary, Royal Commission on Divorce and Matrimonial Causes, *Parliamentary Papers*, 1912–13, vol. 19 [Cd. 6480], p. 290.
72 Ibid., vol. 18 [Cd. 6479], p. 389.
73 P. Bailey, *Leisure and Class in Victorian England: Rational Recreation and the Contest for Control, 1830–1885*, London, Methuen, 1987 (orig. pub. 1978), pp. 122–3, 130.

74 Royal Commission on Divorce and Matrimonial Causes, *Parliamentary Papers*, 1912–13, vol. 20 [Cd. 6481], pp. 150, 170; see also Women's Co-operative Guild, *Working Women and Divorce*, London, D. Nutt, 1911, pp. 39–41.

75 A. Martin, 'The Mother and Social Reform', *The Nineteenth Century and After*, 1913, vol. 73, nos. 435, 436, p. 1072.

76 Royal Commission on Divorce and Matrimonial Causes, *Parliamentary Papers*, 1912–13, vol. 20 [Cd. 6481], pp. 151–6, and Mrs E. Barton, Sheffield Women's Co-operative Guild, pp. 171–3; see also Women's Co-operative Guild, op. cit., pp. 32–4, 38–9, and C. Chapman's brief mention of 'many complaints with reference to sexual indulgence, which are not suited to a work for general readers', in *Marriage and Divorce: Some Needed Reforms in Church and State*, London, D. Nutt, 1911, p. 47.

77 Royal Commission on Divorce and Matrimonial Causes, *Parliamentary Papers*, 1912–13, vol. 20 [Cd. 6481], p. 160.

78 This general theme is explored in Davis, op. cit.

79 Royal Commission on Divorce and Matrimonial Causes, *Parliamentary Papers*, 1912–13, vol. 19 [Cd. 6480], p. 301.

80 See J. Lewis, 'The Working-Class Wife and Mother and State Intervention, 1870–1918', in Lewis (ed.), *Labour and Love: Women's Experience of Home and Family, 1870–1940*, Oxford, Blackwell, 1986, pp. 99–120; A. Davin, 'Imperialism and Motherhood', *History Workshop Journal*, 1978, no. 5, pp. 9–65.

81 For an anthology and discussion see P. Keating (ed.), *Into Unknown England, 1866–1913: Selections from the Social Explorers*, London, Fontana, 1976.

82 Lewis, op. cit., pp. 103, 109–15; Davin, op. cit., pp. 37–8; the Middlesbrough police court missionary, J. Palin, attempting to illustrate the lax morality of the poor, casually described how he entered the homes of families he knew without knocking, in one instance, in a single downstairs room cottage, finding a woman and two men, among other adults, 'perfectly nude', which he interpreted as evidence of depraved morals. Royal Commission on Divorce and Matrimonial Causes, *Parliamentary Papers*, 1912–13, vol. 19 [Cd. 6480], p. 252; see also W. J. Waddy, *The Police Court and its Work*, London, Butterworth, 1925, pp. 82–3.

83 For example *Preston Chronicle* (Duckett), 18 May, 1878, p. 6, *Preston Herald* (Dickinson), 5 September, 1903, p. 8.

84 *Preston Herald* (Barton), 28 October, 1903, p. 8.

85 Cited in W. E. Carson, *The Marriage Revolt: A Study of Marriage and Divorce*, London, T. Werner Laurie, 1915, pp. 289–92; Carson observed that such judicial advice in an American court would have excited national indignation, but in England it had aroused no comment.

86 *Morning Chronicle*, 31 May, 1850, p. 5.

87 Sir W. Blackstone, *Commentaries on the Laws of England*, London, W. Reed, 1811 (orig. pub. 1765–9), vol. 1, p. 444; Rev. W. M. Cooper, *Flagellation and the Flagellants: A History of the Rod . . .*, London, J. Camden Hotten, 1870, pp. 385–97; Sir W. N. M. Geary, *The Law of Marriage and Family Relations: A Manual of Practical Law*, London, A. & C. Black, 1892, pp. 173–8; *Justice of the Peace*, 11 April, 1891, pp. 227–8; D.Mendes de Costa, 'Criminal Law', in A. H. Graveson and F. R. Crane (eds), *A Century of Family Law*, London, Sweet & Maxwell, 1957, pp. 178–80; for more recent confusion see R. E. Dobash and R. Dobash, *Violence Against Wives: A Case against the Patriarchy*, London, Open Books, 1980, p. 68.

88 Pulling, op. cit., pp. 345–9; *Women's Suffrage Journal*, 1877, 1878, but especially 1 August, 1877, pp. 138–9, 1 November, 1877, pp. 186–7, 1 February, 1878, pp. 22–3.

89 *Women's Suffrage Journal*, 1 March, 1878, pp. 39–40.

90 M. S. Crawford, 'Maltreatment of Wives', *Westminster Review*, 1893, vol. 139, p. 301.

91 M. M. Blake, 'Are Women Protected?', *Westminster Review*, 1892, vol. 137, pp. 43–6. See also M. M. Blake, 'The Lady and the Law', *Westminster Review*, 1892, vol. 137, pp. 364–70; 'The Law in Relation to Women', *Westminster Review*, 1887, vol. 128, pp. 698–710; L. Meriweather, 'Is Divorce a Remedy?', *Westminster Review*, 1889, vol. 131, pp. 676–85.

92 Blake, 'Are Women Protected?', pp. 47–8.

93 See especially C. Bauer and L. Ritt, '"A Husband Is a Beating Animal," Frances Power Cobbe Confronts the Wife-abuse Problem in Victorian England', *International Journal of Women's Studies*, 1983, vol. 6, no. 2, pp. 99–118; C. Bauer and L. Ritt, 'Wife-abuse, Late Victorian English Feminists, and the Legacy of Frances Power Cobbe', *International Journal of Women's Studies*, 1983, vol. 6, no. 3, pp. 195–207; Shanley, op. cit., pp. 164–76.

94 Shanley, op. cit., p. 172n.

95 *Preston Chronicle*, 15 June, 1878, p. 6; 22 June, 1878, p. 6; 29 June, 1878, p. 6 (Melling).

96 58 & 59 Victoria, c. 39; for discussion of the act see Shanley, op. cit., pp. 174–6; see also Minor, op. cit., pp. 103–24.

97 On changing definitions of cruelty in the Divorce Court see below, chapter 4.

98 In 1903 and 1913 six and two cases respectively, expressly requesting separation orders, were dismissed on grounds of lack of evidence or similar offences alleged against the wife; twelve cases in 1903 and three in 1913 were adjourned, usually on the recommendation of the court missionary, to encourage reconciliation, but in at least one case the failure of the reconciliation a week later resulted in granting of an order; *Preston Herald*, 22 March, 1913, p. 5, *Preston Guardian*, 29 March, 1913, p. 2 (Cross). After 1895 the court clearly made a strict distinction between wives' summonses for persistent cruelty and assault, and with the latter charge the question of separation and maintenance orders was never considered, even though the act still permitted orders to be made when a husband was fined £5 or imprisoned for two months for assault; in one case a wife who summoned her husband for assault acknowledged in court that she had 'gone in for the wrong thing', meaning to apply for a separation, but the case proceeded on the original assault charge and no order was granted; *Preston Herald*, 1 April, 1903, p. 8 (Miller).

99 The figures for 1908 and 1909 were 6,536 and 4,794, but the decline (also reflected in the much smaller number of orders granted to husbands) covers too short a period to be statistically significant. Royal Commission on Divorce and Matrimonial Causes, *Parliamentary Papers*, 1912–13, vol. 18 [Cd. 6478], Report, p. 67.

100 Ibid., pp. 52, 68–70.

101 For example, S. Reynolds, 'Divorce for the Poor', *Fortnightly Review*, 1910, vol. 88, pp. 488–96; Loane, 1911, op. cit., pp. 288–303; Loane, 1909, op. cit., pp. 102–3, 108–9; M. Loane, *The Queen's Poor*, London, E. Arnold, 1905, pp. 1–25.

102 Holmes, op. cit., pp. 24–6, 64–5, 82; T. Holmes, *Known to the Police*, London, E. Arnold, 1908, pp. 28–9, 72–3; Royal Commission on Divorce and Matrimonial Causes, *Parliamentary Papers*, 1912–13, vol. 19 [Cd. 6480], pp. 232–8.

103 A. Martin, 'The Mother and Social Reform', *The Nineteenth Century and After*, 1913, vol. 73, nos. 435, 436, pp. 1060–79, 1231–55, esp. p. 1255.

104 Minor, op. cit.

105 E. Ross, '"Not the Sort That Would Sit on the Doorstep": Respectability in Pre-World War I London Neighbourhoods', *International Labor and*

Working-Class History, 1985, no. 27, pp. 39–59; P. Bailey, '"Will the Real Bill Banks Please Stand up?": Towards a Role Analysis of Mid-Victorian Respectability', *Journal of Social History*, 1979, vol. 12, no. 3, pp. 336–53, also discusses the fluidity of working-class definitions of respectability.

106 *Leeds Mercury*, 11 June, 1842, p. 6; thanks to Rosemary Allen for this reference.

107 Taylor, 1851, op. cit., pp. 160–1; Mill, 1869, op. cit., pp. 125–242; see below, chapter 5, and Shanley, op. cit., pp. 159–61. The Mill–Taylor collection, London School of Economics, attributes the articles to Mill with collaboration by Taylor and others unnamed; see also Lambertz, op. cit., pp. 191–2.

108 *Morning Chronicle*, 28 October, 1846, p. 4.

109 *Daily News*, 14 July, 1849, p. 4.

110 *Morning Chronicle*, 13 March, 1850, p. 5; 31 May, 1850, pp. 4–5.

111 Ibid., 31 May, 1850, pp. 4–5; 28 August, 1851, p. 4.

112 'An Act for the Better Prevention and Punishment of Aggravated Assaults upon Women and Children . . . , 1853 (16 & 17 Victoria, c. 30).

113 *Morning Post*, 8 November, 1854, p. 3.

114 Shanley, op. cit., p. 161n, speculates that Kaye's interest in the subject may have been sparked by conversations with Mill.

115 J. W. Kaye, 'The Non-Existence of Women', *North British Review*, 1855, vol. 23, no. 46, p. 557.

116 Kaye, 1856, op. cit., pp. 233–41.

117 Ibid., p. 236; other symptoms of a male backlash surfaced periodically, notably the press reports of rumours of a Lancashire 'wife-beaters club' in local newspapers in the 1880s; Lambertz, op. cit., pp. 118–19.

118 M. M. Brewster, *Sunbeams in the Cottage, or What Women May Do: A Narrative Chiefly Addressed to the Working-Classes*, Edinburgh, Constable, 1854.

119 Kaye, 1856, op. cit., pp. 241–56.

120 Great Britain, Hansard, *Parliamentary Debates*, 3rd series, House of Commons, 10 March, 1853, 124, cols 1414–22, 6 April, 1853, 125, cols 669–85.

121 Ibid., 12 March, 1856, 141, cols 24–8; 7 May, 1856, 142, cols 165–77.

122 Ibid., 7 May, 1856, 142, col. 169.

123 Ibid., 18 May, 1874, 219, cols 396–9; see also 6 May, 1872, 211, col. 285.

124 'Wife-Beating', *Saturday Review*, 16 May, 1857, vol. 3, no. 81, pp. 446–7; for discussion of this article see P. Gay, *The Bourgeois Experience: Victoria to Freud*: vol. 2: *The Tender Passion*, New York, Oxford University Press, 1986, pp. 160–2.

125 E. W. Cox, *The Principles of Punishment, as Applied in the Administration of the Criminal Law, by Judges and Magistrates*, London, Law Times, 1877, pp. 99–102.

126 Greenwood, op. cit., pp. 191–5.

127 Cobbe, op. cit., pp. 58–61.

128 Cox, op. cit., pp. 103–4.

129 See above, pp. 39–44.

130 Cobbe, op. cit., pp. 55–87.

131 Shanley, op. cit., pp. 164–70; Bauer and Ritt, '"A Husband is a Beating Animal"', pp. 99–118.

132 It is significant that the amendment effecting the change was introduced to an otherwise innocuous procedural bill on divorce by Lord Penzance, who was instrumental in making a crucial ruling which liberalized the law of matrimonial cruelty; see below, chapter 4. For the relevant debates, which are discussed by Shanley, op. cit., pp. 168–9n, see Great Britain, Hansard, *Parliamentary Debates*, 3rd series, House of Lords, 238, 12 March, 1878, cols 1137–8; 239, 29 March, 1878, cols 186–92; 2 April, 1878, col. 395; 240, 17 May, 1878, col. 126; House of Commons, 238, 28 February, 1878, col. 440.

133 Cobbe, op. cit., pp. 82–3.

134 *Spectator*, 5 January, 1878, pp. 14–15, 12 January, 1878, p. 51, 19 January, 1878, pp. 86–7, 26 January, 1878, p. 118; the *Women's Suffrage Journal* referred to Cobbe's *Spectator* correspondence on 1 February, 1878, p. 23, and reprinted an earlier letter of 6 October, 1877 in its own pages on 1 November, 1877, p. 190.

135 'Wife-Torture', *Truth*, 17 January, 1878, pp. 87–8; the article was discussed, quoted and attributed to Cobbe in the *Women's Suffrage Journal*, 1 February, 1878, pp. 28–9.

136 F. B. Smith, 'Labouchere's Amendment to the Criminal Law Amendment Bill', *Historical Studies*, 1976, vol. 17, no. 67, pp. 165–73.

137 *Truth*, 14 June, 1888, pp. 1033–4; 28 June, 1888, p. 1121.

138 Ibid., 8 August, 1878, p. 154; 21 April, 1892, p. 815; 28 April, 1892, p. 869; 1 May, 1907, p. 1058.

139 Ibid., 3 March, 1892, p. 426; 3 January, 1895, pp. 13–14; Labouchere probably had Cobbe in mind when he referred favourably to 'An Englishwoman, well known as a stalwart friend of the brute creation', 21 February, 1895, p. 444, but his sympathies did not extend to the vegetarianism espoused by Cobbe, which, like female suffrage, he treated with whimsical scorn, though without naming Cobbe; 14 March, 1878, pp. 343–4.

140 Ibid., 9 May, 1895, pp. 1128–9; 11 April, 1895, p. 894; 2 May, 1895, p. 1065.

141 Ibid., 6 June, 1878, pp. 709–10; 16 January, 1896, p. 136.

142 Some of the *Women's Suffrage Journal* articles were signed by Cobbe as 'F. P. C.', for example, 1 August, 1877, pp. 138–9; see also 1 February, 1878, pp. 22–3; 1 May, 1878, pp. 69–70.

143 *Truth*, 21 February, 1895, p. 454.

144 Ibid., 3 March, 1892, p. 426.

145 Ibid., 7 February, 1895, p. 328.

146 Blake, 'Are Women Protected?', pp. 47–8; see above, pp. 53–4.

147 A. P. Herbert, *The Ayes Have It: The Story of the Marriage Bill*, London, Methuen, 1937, p. 196.

148 Martin, op. cit., pp. 1063–4, 1255.

149 Women's Co-operative Guild, op. cit., 1911, pp. 2–4; Royal Commission on Divorce and Matrimonial Causes, *Parliamentary Papers*, 1912–13, vol. 20 [Cd. 6481], pp. 150, 170; see also above, pp. 49–51.

PART II INTRODUCTION

1 These issues, and other aspects of the material covered in this section, are surveyed in L. Davidoff, 'The Family in Britain', in F. M. L. Thompson (ed.), *The Cambridge Social History of Britain, 1750–1850*, vol. 2: *People and Their Environment*, Cambridge, Cambridge University Press, 1990, pp. 72–85, 98–106.

2 For an analysis of the legal dimension of the struggle for women's admission to medical education at Edinburgh University from 1869 and the 'persons controversy' more generally, see A. Sachs and J. H. Wilson, *Sexism and the Law: A Study of Male Beliefs and Legal Bias in Britain and the United States*, Oxford, M. Robertson, 1978, pp. 1–66.

3 M. Anderson, 'The Social Implications of Demographic Change', in Thompson, op. cit., vol. 2, pp. 38–45.

3 COMPANIONATE MARRIAGE

1 F. P. Cobbe, 'Wife-Torture in England', *Contemporary Review*, 1878, vol. 32, pp. 56, 58.

2 J. W. Kaye, 'Outrages on Women', *North British Review*, 1856, vol. 25, no. 49, p. 235.

3 Ibid., p. 237.

4 The tendency of the divorce debates to stimulate questioning of the domestic ideal is discussed in M. L. Shanley, *Feminism, Marriage, and the Law in Victorian England, 1850–1895*, Princeton, Princeton University Press, 1989, pp. 43–4, and M. Poovey, *Uneven Developments: The Ideological Work of Gender in Mid-Victorian England*, Chicago, University of Chicago Press, 1988, pp. 51–88.

5 K. M. Davies, 'Continuity and Change in Literary Advice on Marriage', in R. B. Outhwaite, *Marriage and Society: Studies in the Social History of Marriage*, London, Europa, 1981, pp. 58–80.

6 J. Minson, *Genealogies of Morals: Nietszche, Foucault, Donzelot and the Eccentricity of Ethics*, Basingstoke, Macmillan, 1985, pp. 180–218.

7 L. Stone, *The Family, Sex and Marriage in England, 1500–1800*, London, Weidenfeld & Nicolson, 1977, chs 6–9, dates the rise of companionate marriage from the mid-seventeenth century; E. Shorter, *The Making of the Modern Family*, London, Collins, 1976, locates the 'rise of sentiment' in Europe in the nineteenth century; see also R. Trumbach, *The Rise of the Egalitarian Family*, New York, Academic Press, 1978. One of the earliest criticisms of Stone's thesis appeared in a review article by A. MacFarlane in *History and Theory*, 1979, no. 18, pp. 103–26, but for more specific criticism pertinent to this analysis see S. M. Okin, 'Patriarchy and Married Women's Property in England: Questions on Some Current Views, *Eighteenth Century Studies*, 1983–84, no. 17, pp. 121–38, and E. Spring, 'Law and the Theory of the Affective Family', *Albion*, 1984, vol. 16, pp. 1–20.

8 S. M. Okin, 'Women and the Making of the Sentimental Family', *Philosophy and Public Affairs*, 1982, vol. 11, no. 1, pp. 65–88.

9 L. Davidoff and C. Hall, *Family Fortunes: Men and Women of the English Middle-Class, 1780–1850*, London, Hutchinson, 1987, pp. 155–92; on Mrs Ellis see pp. 180–5.

10 Mrs S. S. Ellis, *The Women of England . . .*, London, Fisher, 1838, *The Daughters of England . . .*, London, Fisher, 1842, *The Wives of England . . .*, London, Fisher, 1843, *The Mothers of England . . .*, London, Fisher, 1843; other works included *Chapters on Wives*, London, R. Bentley, 1860, *The Education of Character: With Hints on Moral Training*, London, J. Murray, 1856, *Education of the Heart: Woman's Best Work*, London, Hodder & Stoughton, 1869, and the periodical *Mrs Ellis's Morning Call: A Table Book of Literature and Art*, 1850–2, vols 1–8.

11 Ellis, *Wives of England*, p. 74.

12 Ibid., pp. 75–6; Ellis, *Daughters of England*, p. 126.

13 Ellis, *Wives of England*, pp. 76–7.

14 Ibid., pp. 79, 83–7; see also D. M. M. Craik, *A Woman's Thoughts About Women*, London, Hurst & Blackett, 1858, pp. 148–55. The feminist writer, Frances Power Cobbe, echoed Ellis's sentiments three decades later on the dangers of 'managing' and 'manipulating' husbands in *The Duties of Women*, London, Williams & Norgate, 1881, pp. 100–1.

15 Ellis, *Wives of England*, pp. 91–2.

16 Ibid., p. 91.

17 'Frightened Wives', *Mrs Ellis's Morning Call*, 1850–2, vol. 3, pp. 123, 226.

18 Ellis, *Wives of England*, pp. 82–3.

19 Ibid., pp. 86–7.

20 S. Ellis 'to a friend', 13 July, 1821, in S. S. Ellis, *The Home Life and Letters of Mrs Ellis, Compiled by her Nieces*, London, J. Nisbet, 1893, pp. 14–15.

21 S. Ellis to W. Ellis, 18 and 27 April, 1837, ibid., pp. 75–6.

22 S. Ellis to 'M. C.', 8 July, 1842, ibid., p. 122.

23 Davidoff and Hall, op. cit., pp. 155–92.

24 See, for example, A. Taylor, *Practical Hints to Young Females, on the Duties of a Wife, a Mother and a Mistress of a Family*, London, Taylor & Hessey, 1815, p. v.

25 Mrs E. Sandford, *Woman, in Her Social and Domestic Character*, London, Longman, Orme, Browne, Green & Longmans, 1839, pp. 3, 212–16.

26 Taylor, op. cit., pp. 11–18, 128–42; see also Davidoff and Hall, op. cit., pp. 59–69, 172–7; for examples of similar writers see A Mother and Mistress of a Family, *Home Discipline – or Thoughts on the Origin and Exercise of Domestic Authority*, London, J. Buro, 1841; M. G. Grey and E. Shirreff, *Thoughts on Self-Culture, Addressed to Women*, London, Hope & Co., 1850.

27 *Female Happiness, or, The Lady's Handbook of Life* (Preface by Rev. John E. Cox, Vicar of St Helen's, Bishopsgate), London, W. Tegg, 1854, pp. 314–19; this text was written anonymously, but internal evidence, and the bulk of its content, religious instruction for young women, suggests a clergyman author.

28 Ibid., pp. 320–32.

29 Craik, op. cit., pp. 148–55.

30 Shanley, op. cit., pp. 22–9.

31 D. Jerrold, 'Mrs Caudle's Curtain Lectures', *Punch*, 1845, vols 8–9; R. Kelly, 'Mrs Caudle: A Victorian Curtain Lecturer', *University of Toronto Quarterly*, 1969, vol. 38, no. 3, pp. 296–309, also see below, chapter 5.

32 W. Thackeray, 'On Love, Marriage, Men and Women', in *The Works of Thackeray*, London, Macmillan, 1911, vol. 17, p. 134; originally appeared in *Punch*, 14 July, 1849, vol. 17, no. 418, p. 13.

33 W. Thackeray, *The Newcomes*, 2 vols, London, Dent, 1962, vol. 1, pp. 14–17 (first serialized 1853–5); cited in Davidoff and Hall, op. cit., p. 117.

34 On the contradictions in domestic ideology see Davidoff and Hall, op. cit., pp. 114–18, 183–5.

35 B. Taylor, *Eve and the New Jerusalem: Socialism and Feminism in the Nineteenth Century*, London, Virago, 1983, pp. 33–41.

36 M. Reid, *A Plea for Woman*, Edinburgh, W. Tait, 1843.

37 A. R. Lamb, *Can Woman Regenerate Society?*, London, J. W. Parker, 1844, pp. 123–6.

38 On Norton and domestic ideology see Poovey, op. cit., pp. 62–88; Shanley, op. cit., pp. 22–9; on the late Victorian marriage debate and husbands' behaviour see below, chapter 5.

39 See below, chapter 4.

40 R. Phillips, *Putting Asunder: A History of Divorce in Western Society*, Cambridge, Cambridge University Press, 1988, pp. 321–3, 354–64, 395–402.

41 *Bostock* v. *Bostock* (1858), PRO J77/2/B3; this file in the Public Record Office consists of court minutes and four detailed affidavits, two from each spouse, dated from 22 April to 3 December, 1857; all the affidavits were originally submitted to the Consistory Court of London under ecclesiastical jurisdiction, but were transferred to the new secular Divorce Court in 1858. See also the law report, *Bostock* v. *Bostock*, 1, reprinted in *The English Reports (Admiralty, Probate and Divorce)* (hereafter *ER*), 164, 701–5; *The Times*, 26 May, 1858, p. 11, 20 July, 1858, p. 11.

42 PRO James Turner Bostock, probate, IR26, 1762/649(1847), will, prob. 11, 2060(627), August, 1847; Robert Chignell Bostock, probate, IR26, 2879(1875), will, PR 1616, 116/1932, November, 1875. PRO J77/2/B3.

43 J77/2/B3.

44 Ibid; the blurred distinction between economic spheres in the Bostock household reflected early-Victorian middle-class practice and underlines women's extensive 'contribution to the enterprise' stressed by Davidoff and Hall, op. cit., pp. 279–89.

45 J77/2/B3.

46 Ibid.

47 Ibid.

48 Ibid.

49 Ibid.

50 Ibid.

51 Ibid; Robert claimed that the Corrigan case had often been discussed by the family and that he had simply stated that if he did the same to his wife a jury might find him guilty, but that in view of Charlotte's provocation he would be recommended to mercy; *The Times*, 20 July, 1858, p. 11; the Corrigan case was reported in the press between December, 1855 and 7 February, 1856 (the date of Corrigan's death sentence), while Robert's threats were mentioned between 13 February and 12 June, suggesting that the case exercised a powerful and enduring fascination for Robert; *The Times*, 27 December, 1855, p. 3; 28 December, 1855, p. 10; 29 December, 1855, p. 9; 4 January, 1856, p. 9; 7 February, 1856, p. 9.

52 J. Walkowitz, in 'Jack the Ripper and the Myth of Male Violence', *Feminist Studies*, 1982, vol. 8, no. 3, pp. 562–3, argues that the Whitechapel murders stimulated private re-enactments among working-class couples and 'covertly sanctioned male antagonism toward women and buttressed male authority over them'. She found no middle-class examples but the earlier experience of the Bostocks illustrates the way in which such crimes entered middle-class family discourse.

53 J77/2/B3.

54 On the prescriptive writings of Mrs Ellis and others see pp. 75–8 and 151–2.

55 J77/2/B3.

56 *ER* 164, 702–3.

57 J77/2/B3.

58 *Curtis* v. *Curtis* (1858) 164 *ER*, 636 and 688; PRO J77/8/C4; *The Times*, 20 May, 1858, p. 11; 21 May 1858, p. 11; 22 May, 1858, p. 11; 22 June, 1858, p. 11.

59 It is significant that John Curtis's words here were identical to Robert Bostock's, when he, too, attempted to minimize the significance of his physical assault on his wife. The implication was that boxing a wife's ears was equivalent to the legitimate chastisement of a child or a domestic pet.

60 Frances Curtis to Mrs Flood, New York, March, 1852, 164 *ER*, 693.

61 164 *ER*, 690.

62 164 *ER*, 691; *The Times*, 22 May, 1858, p. 11.

63 Frances Curtis to Mrs Flood, New York, March, 1852, 164 *ER*, 692–3.

64 Ibid., 693.

65 Ibid.

66 Ibid., 693–4.

67 *ER*, 695; for a fuller discussion of the legal implications see below, chapter 4.

68 Frances Curtis to Mrs Flood, New York, March, 1852, 164 *ER*, 693–4.

69 John Curtis to Frances Curtis, Bloomingdale, 15 August, 1852, 164 *ER*, 695–6.

70 Placard dated 19 September, 1857, 164 *ER*, 697–8.

71 J77/8/C4; 164 *ER*, 636, 688, 698–9.

72 *Kelly* v. *Kelly* (1869 and 1870), *Law Reports (Probate and Divorce)* (hereafter *LR (P & D)*, 31 and 59; PRO J77/91/1076; *The Times*, 20 November, 1869, p. 11; 22

November, 1869, p. 9; 25 November, 1869, p. 10; 26 November, 1869, p. 9; 27 November, 1869, p. 11; 29 November, 1869, p. 9; 8 December, 1869, p. 11; 20 January, 1870, p. 10; 21 January, 1870, p. 9; 22 January, 1870, p. 11; 27 January, 1870, p. 9; 2 February, 1870, p. 11; 10 February, 1870, p. 11; 2 March, 1870, p. 11; 9 March, 1870, p. 11. For discussion of the legal significance of this case see below, chapter 4, also A. J. Hammerton, 'Victorian Marriage and the Law of Matrimonial Cruelty', *Victorian Studies*, 1990, vol. 33, no. 2, pp. 269–92.

73 J. Kelly affidavit and court minutes, J77/91/1076.
74 2 *LR (P & D)*, 1870, 75; see also *The Times*, 8 December, 1869, p. 11; 10 February, 1870, p. 11.
75 J. Kelly affidavit, pp. 33–44, J77/91/1076.
76 Ibid., pp. 38–40.
77 Ibid., pp. 34–5.
78 Ibid., p. 39.
79 Ibid., pp. 35–8, 41.
80 Ibid., pp. 42–3.
81 Ibid., p. 42.
82 J. Kelly to F. Kelly, 11 December, 1867, ibid., pp. 10–11.
83 2 *LR (P & D)*, 1869, 32.
84 Ibid., 34–8.
85 Ibid., 32–5; J. Kelly affidavit, pp. 1–3, 44–50; J77/91/1076.
86 2 *LR (P & D)*, 1869, 32–5.
87 Ibid., 35.
88 F. Kelly petition, J. Kelly affidavit, pp. 17, 27–30; J77/91/1076.
89 F. Kelly petition, J. Kelly affidavit, pp. 3, 23–4, 31–2, ibid.
90 Ibid., pp. 3, 25–6.
91 2 *LR (P & D)*, 1869, 36–7.
92 R. Coward, *Patriarchal Precedents: Sexuality and Social Relations*, London, Routledge & Kegan Paul, 1983, p. 265.
93 2 *LR (P & D)*, 1870, 73.
94 Ibid., 76–7.
95 *The Times*, 22 January, 1870, p. 11.
96 J77/91/1076, J. Kelly affidavit, p. 4; 2 *LR (P & D)*, 1870, 76.
97 D. Jerrold, 'Mrs Caudle's Curtain Lectures', *Punch*, 1845, vol. 8, p. 13.

4 CRUELTY AND DIVORCE

1 I. Asquith, 'The Structure, Ownership and Control of the Press, 1780–1855', and A. Lee, 'The Structure, Ownership and Control of the Press, 1855–1914', in G. Boyce, J. Curran and P. Wingate (eds), *Newspaper History From the Seventeenth Century to the Present Day*, London, Constable, 1978, pp. 98–116, 117–29.
2 D. Belcher to E. Belcher, 28 June, 1831, in R. J. Phillimore, *A Report of the Judgement Delivered on the Sixth Day of June, 1835, by Joseph Phillimore, D.C.L., . . . in the Cause of Belcher, the Wife, against Belcher, the Husband . . .*, London, Saunders & Benning, 1835, p. 1; see also *The Times*, 6 May, 1835, p. 3. The Belcher case is discussed by L. Stone, *Road to Divorce, England, 1530–1987*, Oxford, Oxford University Press, 1990, p. 204, but without reference to the servant issue.
3 On the Kelly case see above, chapter 3; on cases brought to the ecclesiastical courts, M. Nevill, 'Women and Marriage Breakdown in England, 1832–1857', unpublished PhD thesis, University of Essex, 1989, pp. 247, 259–60.
4 J. Gillis, *For Better, For Worse: British Marriages, 1600 to the Present*, Oxford, Oxford University Press, 1985.

5 *The Times*, 19 January, 1860, p. 8; 6 February, 1860, p. 8; 8 February, 1860, p. 9; A Manchester Man [R. Lamb], 'The Philosophy of Marriage Studied Under Sir Cresswell Cresswell', *Fraser's Magazine*, 1860, vol. 5, no. 62, pp. 557–8; on later restriction of reporting see A. K. R. Kiralfy, 'Matrimonial Tribunals and their Procedure', in R. H. Graveson and F. R. Crane (eds), *A Century of Family Law, 1857–1957*, London, Sweet & Maxwell, 1957, p. 301; the regulative function of publicity is discussed below, pp. 116–18, 132–3.

6 *The Times*, 12 December, 1859, p. 8.

7 For example, O. R. McGregor, *Divorce in England, A Centenary Study*, London, Heinemann, 1957, pp. 19–24, and, following McGregor, G. Best, *Mid-Victorian Britain, 1851–75*, St Albans, Panther, 1973, pp. 303–4.

8 G. Rowntree and N. H. Carrier, 'The Resort to Divorce in England and Wales, 1857–1957', *Population Studies*, 1958, vol. 11, no. 3, p. 193; the survey described below by G. L. Savage, 'The Social Basis of the Demand for Divorce in England, 1858–1868: Graphs and Tables', unpublished paper presented to the Mid-western Victorian Studies Association, April, 1987, found 1.48 per cent of cases using the *in forma pauperis* procedure, although McGregor, op. cit., p. 18, claimed, without clear evidence, that the provision 'remained ineffective'.

9 Savage, op. cit.; the variations result from different methods of distribution of unidentified cases. It is possible that the less affluent groups may be less substantially represented among cases brought to judgement, since many petitions never reached a hearing, possibly for financial reasons.

10 Ibid.

11 Contemporaries, unlike later analysts, were not slow to notice a consistent pattern of working-class petitioners; after two years of the court's operation *The Times* noted that 'bakers, sailmakers, publicans and working smiths are just as frequent visitors to Sir Cresswell Cresswell's Court as their betters'. 12 December, 1859, p. 8; the 1910 Royal Commission found more than a quarter of recent petitioners were working class; Royal Commission on Divorce and Matrimonial Causes, *Parliamentary Papers*, 1912–13, vol. 20, [6482], Evidence, appendix 3, table 15a, p. 35; the figure in Rowntree and Carrier's more recent survey of the year 1871, op. cit., p. 222, was 16.8 per cent; such data was mostly ignored before Savage's research.

12 For a discussion of the basis of this survey see appendix 1.

13 See table 2.1, chapter 2, above.

14 *Devon, Earl of, v. Devon, Countess of*, (1858), Public Record Office divorce files, J77/13/D18; *The Times*, 17 February, 1859, p. 11.

15 For examples see *Lott v. Lott* (1882), J77/275/8088; *Allbutt v. Allbutt* (1861), J77/1A/37, *The Times*, 30 May, 1862, p. 11.

16 The most recent example is A. Horstman, *Victorian Divorce*, London, Croom Hellm, 1985, pp. 118–34; on the Mordaunt case see also C. Kingston, *Society Sensations*, London, Stanley Paul, 1922, pp. 24–44.

17 See, for example, *Atkinson v. Atkinson* (1861) J77/1/A19; *Blake v. Blake* (1858) J77/2/B6; *Barnett v. Barnett* (1859) J77/2/B43; *Bond v. Bond* (1860) J77/3/B53; *Brocas v. Brocas* (1859) J77/3/B60; *Barford v. Barford* (1860) J77/3/B92.

18 *Denton v. Denton* (1882), J77/276/8104.

19 *Boynton v. Boynton* (1860), J77/2/B27; *The Times*, 24 December, 1858, p. 8; 28 January, 1860, p. 12; 23 April, 1861, p. 11.

20 *Smith v. Smith* (1882), J77/275/8081.

21 L. Davidoff and C. Hall, *Family Fortunes: Men and Women of the English Middle-Class, 1780–1850*, London, Hutchinson, 1987, p. 110.

22 For example, S. K. Kent, *Sex and Suffrage in Britain, 1860–1914*, Princeton, Princeton University Press, 1987; L. Bland, 'The Married Woman, the "New

Woman" and the Feminist: Sexual Politics of the 1890s', in J. Rendall (ed.), *Equal or Different: Women's Politics, 1800–1914*, Oxford, Blackwell, 1987, pp. 141–64; S. Jeffreys, *The Spinster and Her Enemies: Feminism and Sexuality, 1880–1930*, London, Pandora, 1985; also see below, chapter 5.

23 It is significant that while rape became a marital offence in 1857, warranting a divorce decree, it was never defined, the drafters of the act taking for granted that it could not occur in marriage; 20 & 21 Vic., c. 84, 85, 1857, pp. 733–40, clause 27.

24 *Bayley* v. *Bayley* (1858), J77/2/B45; Bayley's occupation was not stated.

25 For example *Baigent* v. *Baigent* (1859), J77/2/B28; *The Times*, 20 February, 1860, p. 11.

26 J. S. Mill, *The Subjection of Women*, (orig. pub. 1869) in A. S. Rossi (ed.), *Essays on Sex Equality*, Chicago, University of Chicago Press, 1970, p. 161; see below, chapter 5.

27 Sir Cresswell Cresswell's comment in *N—— v. N.——* (1862), 164 *English Reports*, 1265. Unless otherwise noted all law report references before 1865 are to the consolidated *English Reports*, (hereafter *ER*).

28 *Barnett* v. *Barnett* (1859), J77/2/B43; *Brocas* v. *Brocas* (1859), J77/3/B60.

29 *Barnett* v. *Barnett* (1859), J77/2/B43; *The Times*, 5 November, 1859, p. 9.

30 *N—— v. N——* (1862), 164 *ER*, 1264–5; J77/39/N17; see also *Otway* v. *Otway* (1886), J77/362/931; *Browning* v. *Browning* (1911), *Law Reports (Probate and Divorce)* (hereafter *LR (P & D)*), 1911, 161–72.

31 *Brocas* v. *Brocas* (1859), J77/3/B60; see also *Allbutt* v. *Allbutt* (1861), J77/1A/37; *Walton* v. *Walton* (1882), J77/277/8139; see also G. L. Savage, 'The Wilful Communication of a Loathsome Disease: Marital Conflict and Venereal Disease in Victorian England', *Victorian Studies*, Autumn, 1990, vol. 34, no. 1, pp. 35–54.

32 *N– v. N–* (1862), 164 *ER*, 1264–5; J77/39/N17; for a similar pattern of behaviour, but without any sexual offence, in an ecclesiastical court case, see *Dysart* v. *Dysart* (1847), 163 *ER*, 1119–23.

33 *Birch* v. *Birch* (1872), J77/121/2290; *Law Journal (Probate and Matrimonial)*, (hereafter *LJ (P & M)*), 42 (1873), 23–4; on medical views that condoms deprived the female of vital fluid, thus occasioning nervous complaints, see A. McLaren, *Birth Control in Nineteenth-Century England*, London, Croom Helm, 1978, p. 121.

34 *Suggate* v. *Suggate* (1858), J77/49/S31; *Mytton* v. *Mytton* (1885), J77/349/O531; *Symons* v. *Symons* (1896), J77/579/17711.

35 *Dyer* v. *Dyer* 1859, J77/13/D19.

36 For an interesting analysis of literary marriages along these lines see P. Rose, *Parallel Lives: Five Victorian Marriages*, Harmondsworth, Penguin, 1985.

37 *Waddell* v. *Waddell* (1861), J77/59/W98; 164 *ER*, 1124–6.

38 *Butler* v. *Butler* (1861), J77/4/B100; *The Times*, 18 November, 1861, p. 9; 21 November, 1861, pp. 10–11.

39 *Bostock* v. *Bostock* (1858), in chapter 3, above. Also *Allen* v. *Allen and D'Arcy* (1859), J77/1/A11; *The Times*, 6 December, 1859, p. 9; *Bromley* v. *Bromley* (1858), J77/2/B5; *Baker* v. *Baker* (1861), J77/4/B120; *Devereux* v. *Devereux* (1859), J77/13/D2, *The Times* 21 February, 1859, p. 9; *Drury* v. *Drury* (1860), J77/13/D30; *Lay* v. *Lay* (1882), J77/274/8027; *Hoit* v. *Hoit* (1883), J77/274/8039; *Tupper* v. *Tupper* (1883), J77/277/8130; *Clark* v. *Clark* (1887), J77/277/8151.

40 *Suggate* v. *Suggate* (1858), J77/49/S31; *Butler* v. *Butler* (1861), J77/4/B100; *The Times*, 18 November, 1861, p. 9; 21 November, 1861, p. 11; *Stead* v. *Stead* (1882), J77/275/8076; *Hewitt* v. *Hewitt* (1882) J77/275/8083; *Wilkie* v. *Wilkie* (1882), J77/277/8146; *Mellersh* v. *Mellersh* (1882), J77/277/8159.

41 *Blake* v. *Blake* (1858), J77/2/B6.

42 *Baker* v. *Baker* (1863) J77/4/B120; *The Times*, 19 March, 1863, p. 12.

43 *Mytton* v. *Mytton* (1885), J77/349/O531, *LR (P & D)*, 1886, 11, 141–4.

44 *Tomkins* v. *Tomkins* (1858), J77/54/T6, 164 *ER*, 675 and 678; *Brady* v. *Brady* (1858), J77/2/B15.

45 *Hoit* v. *Hoit* (1883), J77/274/8039.

46 On working-class wives' incomes see above, chapter 2; for a middle-class example see *Devereux* v. *Devereux* (1858), J77/13/D2.

47 *Bentley* v. *Bentley* (1859), J77/3/B59.

48 *Adams* v. *Adams* (1862), J77/1A/41, *The Times*, 29 November, 1862, p. 11; *Dowden* v. *Dowden* (1859), J77/13/D24), *The Times*, 18 April, 1859, p. 11; *Rushton* v. *Rushton* (1882), J77/275/8089, *The Times*, 19 February, 1883, p. 4.

49 *Brunell* v. *Brunell* (1858), J77/2/B12, *The Times*, 23 May, 1859, p. 11.

50 For a discussion of these cases, see above, pp. 89–101 and, on their legal implications, pp. 127–31, below.

51 For example *Sayce* v. *Sayce* (1882), J77/277/8142.

52 *Duncan* v. *Duncan* (1858), J77/13/D7.

53 *Cooke* v. *Cooke* (1862), J77/11/C114, 164 *ER*, 1221–7, 1268–70.

54 *Swatman* v. *Swatman* (1864), J77/53/S211, 164 *ER*, 1467–8.

55 *Hudson* v. *Hudson* (1862), J77/26/H146, 164 *ER*, 1296–8; see also *Birch* v. *Birch* (1872), J77/121/2290, *LJ* (P & M) 23 (1873), 23–4, where the husband forced his wife to perform the most menial work of a servant with whom he was sexually involved; also *Russell* v. *Russell* (1890), J77/461/4047, where Lord Russell allegedly forced Lady Russell to clean the menservants' water-closet; this was the first of a series of cross-suits and appeals of both parties on the grounds of cruelty; Horstman, op. cit., p. 147.

56 For servants' intervention and evidence as witnesses see *Wilkie* v. *Wilkie* (1882), J77/277/8146; *LR (P & D)*, 1886, 11, 143; *Smallwood* v. *Smallwood* (1860), J77/50/S84, 164 *ER*, 1050–2; *Waddell* v. *Waddell* (1861), J77/51/W98, 164 *ER*, 1124–6; *Milford* v. *Milford* (1866), J77/86/879, *LR (P & D)*, 1866, 1, 295–300; on shared sleeping quarters see *Green* v. *Green* (1872), J77/120/2224; in shared accommodation landladies and lodgers could be implicated in domestic affairs in similar ways to servants, e.g. *Pratt* v. *Pratt* (1882), J77/276/8097; for terrorizing of servants see *Mytton* v. *Mytton* (1885), J77/349/O531, *LR (P & D)*, 1886, 11, 144.

57 *Shaw* v. *Shaw* (1861), J77/50/S114, 164 *ER*, 1097–8 and 1147–8.

58 T. McBride, *The Domestic Revolution: The Modernization of Household Service in England and France, 1820–1920*, London, Croom Helm, 1976, pp. 20–7; F. E. Huggett, *Life Below Stairs: Domestic Servants in England From Victorian Times*, Stevenage, Robin Clark, 1977, pp. 46–56; P. Horn, *The Rise and Fall of the Victorian Servant*, Dublin, Gill & Macmillan, 1975, pp. 109–24, also notes the potential for close relationships between servants and employers.

59 *N——* v. *N——* (1862), J77/39/N17, 164 *ER*, 1266.

60 L. Davidoff, 'Mastered for Life: Servant and Wife in Victorian and Edwardian England', *Journal of Social History*, 1974, vol. 7, no. 4, p. 419.

61 For an example of letters to the press see *Suggate* v. *Suggate* (1858), J77/49/S31, 164 *ER*, 827–31; on the Queen's Proctor see G. L. Savage, 'The Divorce Court and the Queen's Proctor: Legal Patriarchy and the Sanctity of Marriage in Victorian England', *Historical Papers/Communications Historiques*, Ottawa, 1989, pp. 210–27.

62 Great Britain, *Parliamentary Debates*, 3rd series, House of Commons, 23 August, 1860, 160, 1746; see also *The Times*, 19 January, 1860, p. 8; 6 February, 1860, p. 8; 8 February, 1860, p. 9; 25 August, 1860, p. 8.

63 *The Times*, 19 January, 1860, p. 8.

64 For example evidence of John St Loe Strachey, editor of the *Spectator*, Royal Commission on Divorce and Matrimonial Causes, *Parliamentary Papers*, 1912–13, vol. 20, [Cd. 6481], pp. 222–3; despite encountering much opposition to detailed reporting the Royal Commission gave qualified support to continued publication, with limited powers to the court to prohibit matter which was 'deleterious to public morals'; but it stressed that publicity on other offences, like cruelty, where no 'unpleasant' sexual details were involved, remained an important deterrent; vol. 18 [Cd. 6478], Report, pp. 145–58.

65 N— v. N— (1862), 164 *ER*, 1264–5.

66 *Mytton* v. *Mytton* (1885), J77/349/O531, *LR (P & D)*, 1886, 11, 143; see also *Bethune* v. *Bethune* (1889), J77/431/3135, *LR (P & D)*, 1891, 16, 205–7.

67 *Bostock* v. *Bostock* (1857), J77/2/B3 (petition 22 April, 1857); *Hudson* v. *Hudson* (1862), J77/26/H146; *Willacy* v. *Willacy* (1882), J77/275/8072; *Elcock* v. *Elcock* (1882), J77/276/8112; *Symons* v. *Symons* (1896), J77/579/17711.

68 For a useful summary see R. Phillips, *Putting Asunder: A History of Divorce in Western Society*, Cambridge, Cambridge University Press, 1988, pp. 412–22; also M. L. Shanley, *Feminism, Marriage, and the Law in Victorian England, 1850–1895*, Princeton, Princeton University Press, 1989, pp. 22–48; McGregor, op. cit., pp. 14–22; C. E. P. Davies, 'Matrimonial Relief in English Law', in Graveson and Crane, op. cit., pp. 315–21; Best, op. cit., pp. 303–4.

69 S. Anderson, 'Legislative Divorce – Law for the Aristocracy?', in G. R. Grubin and D. Sugarman (eds), *Law, Economy and Society, 1750–1914: Essays in the History of English Law*, Abingdon, Professional Books, 1984, pp. 412–44.

70 Matrimonial Causes Act, 1857 (20 & 21 Vict., c. 85); Matrimonial Causes Act, 1923 (13 & 14 Geo. 5, c. 19); Matrimonial Causes Act, 1937 (1 Ed. 8 & 1 Geo. 6, c. 57); see also L. Holcombe, *Wives and Property: Reform of the Married Women's Property Law in Nineteenth-Century England*, Toronto, University of Toronto Press, 1983, pp. 93–109.

71 Great Britain, Hansard, *Parliamentary Debates*, 3rd series, House of Commons, 7 August, 1857, 147, 1267–81; R. L. Griswold, *Family and Divorce in California, 1850–1900: Victorian Illusions and Everyday Realities*, Albany, State University of New York Press, 1982, pp. 18–20; R. Phillips, *Divorce in New Zealand: A Social History*, Auckland, Oxford University Press, 1981, pp. 17–26; K. Smith, 'Divorce in Nova Scotia, 1750–1890', unpublished paper forthcoming in J. Phillips and P. Girard (eds), *Essays in the History of Canadian Law: The Nova Scotia Experience*; M. James, 'Marriage and Marital Breakdown in Victoria, 1860–1960', unpublished PhD thesis, Melbourne: La Trobe University, 1984, pp. 63–89; H. Golder, *Divorce in 19th Century New South Wales*, Kensington, N.S.W., N.S.W. University Press, 1985, pp. 8–9; Holcombe, op. cit., pp. 103–9.

72 See especially Phillips, 1988, op. cit., pp. 314–402; Shanley, 1989, op. cit.; G. Savage, 'The Operation of the 1857 Divorce Act, 1860–1910: A Research Note', *Journal of Social History*, 1983, vol. 16, pp. 103–10; Golder, op. cit.; James, op. cit.; Griswold, op. cit.; Horstman, op. cit., while drawing on case records, unfortunately adds little to the social history of divorce and marriage.

73 The best legal history of cruelty is J. M. Biggs, *The Concept of Matrimonial Cruelty*, London, Athlone Press, 1962; a more recent discussion is in Stone, op. cit., pp. 198–205; see also L. Rosen, 'Cruelty in Matrimonial Causes', *The Modern Law Review*, 1949, vol. 12, pp. 324–46; Davies, op. cit., 320–2.

74 R. L. Griswold, 'The Evolution of the Doctrine of Mental Cruelty in Victorian American Divorce, 1790–1900', *Journal of Social History*, 1986, vol. 20, pp. 127–48; Biggs, op. cit., pp. 43–7.

75 The qualifications to these rules were debated and relaxed in several cases during the nineteenth and early twentieth centuries; Biggs, op. cit., pp. 25, 34, 131–41.

76 *Evans* v. *Evans* (1790), 161 *ER*, 467.

77 Ibid., 468.

78 Biggs, op. cit., pp. 26–7.

79 *D'Aguilar* v. *D'Aguilar* (1794), 162 *ER*, 750.

80 Ibid., p. 28; Griswold, 1986, op. cit., pp. 127–9, stresses the importance of the Stowell decision in American divorce law, particularly as a brake on the expansion of the concept of legal cruelty.

81 Biggs, op. cit., pp. 29, 38.

82 Ibid., p. 21.

83 *Evans* v. *Evans* (1790), 161 *ER*, 499.

84 *Oliver* v. *Oliver* (1801), 161 *ER*, 585.

85 *Waring* v. *Waring* (1813), 161 *ER*, 700.

86 Stowell's contemporaries and biographers were quick to point to the irony that he was unable to practise those lessons 'of domestic patience and forgiveness which . . . he had taught so eloquently to others'; W. E. Surtees, *A Sketch . . . of Lords Stowell and Eldon . . .*, London, Chapman & Hall, 1846, pp. 131–5; W. C. Townsend, *The Lives of Twelve Eminent Judges*, 2 vols, London, Longman, Brown, Green & Longmans, 1846, vol. 2, pp. 327–31; Viscount Sankey, *Lord Stowell*, Oxford, privately printed, 1936, pp. 19–20.

87 *Dysart* v. *Dysart* (1847), 163 *ER*, 992.

88 Lushington in *Neeld* v. *Neeld* (1831), 162 *ER*, 1443; Stowell made a similar point in *D'Aguilar* v. *D'Aguilar* (1794) when, commenting on a wife's complaint of deprivation of 'indulgences', he stressed that 'facts, when too minutely pleaded, carry a ridiculous appearance', 162 *ER*, 750.

89 *Hudson* v. *Hudson* (1863), 164 *ER*, 1298.

90 On the legal concept of provocation see Biggs, op. cit., pp. 142–9.

91 *Chesnutt* v. *Chesnutt* (1854), 164 *ER*, 115; Biggs, op. cit., pp. 32–3.

92 *Saunders* v. *Saunders* (1847), 163 *ER*, 1135–6; quoted in Biggs, op. cit., p. 29; in 1794, in *D'Aguilar* v. *D'Aguilar*, 162 *ER*, 750, Stowell claimed that 'nothing can be more gross cruelty' than spitting, and it was clearly sufficient to constitute cruelty in the eighteenth century, but it did not provoke the kind of outrage felt by Lushington half a century later. In common law spitting in the face had long been treated as a battery; P. S. James, *General Principles of the Law of Torts*, 3rd edn., London, Butterworth, 1969, p. 72.

93 *Annual Register*, 1863, pp. 198–9; *Dictionary of National Biography* (Cresswell), 13, pp. 72–3; (Penzance), *Supplement*, 3, pp. 511–13; Biggs, op. cit., p. 34.

94 See above, table 4.2.

95 G. Rowntree and N. H. Carrier, 'The Resort to Divorce in England and Wales, 1858–1957', *Population Studies*, 1958, vol. 11, no. 3, pp. 192–3; Savage, op. cit., p. 103; Holcombe, op. cit., p. 105.

96 A Manchester Man [R. Lamb], op. cit., pp. 557–8; E. Showalter, 'Family Secrets and Domestic Subversion: Rebellion in the Novels of the 1860s', in A. S. Wohl (ed.), *The Victorian Family: Structure and Stresses*, London, Croom Helm, 1978, pp. 101–16; Margaret Maison, 'Adulteresses in Agony', *The Listener*, 19 January, 1961, pp. 133–4.

97 *Bostock* v. *Bostock* (1858), 164 *ER*, 701–5.

98 *Suggate* v. *Suggate* (1859), 164 *ER*, 827–8; Biggs, op. cit., pp. 33–4.

99 *Milner* v. *Milner* (1861), 164 *ER*, 1508; Biggs, op. cit., pp. 33–4. Cresswell obviously shared Lushington's earlier views on the gravity of the act of spitting in a wife's face.

100 *Saunders* v. *Saunders* (1847), 163 *ER*, 1136.

101 *Waddell* v. *Waddell* (1862), 164 *ER*, 1124–6.

102 *Swatman* v. *Swatman* (1865), 164 *ER*, 1468.

103 *Curtis* v. *Curtis* (1858), 164 *ER*, 636 and 688; PRO J77/8/C4; Biggs, pp. 51–2; *The Times*, 20 May, 1858, p. 11; 21 May, 1858, p. 11; 22 May, 1858, p. 11; 22 June, 1858, p. 11.

104 164 *ER*, 698; *The Times*, 22 May, 1858, p. 11.

105 164 *ER*, 695.

106 *Evans* v. *Evans* (1790), 161 *ER*, 467; in *D'Aguilar* v. *D'Aguilar* (1794), 162 *ER*, 753, Stowell noted that the husband had 'deposed' his wife 'from the management of the family', but, although it was material to his ruling in the wife's favour, he attached no unique importance to it alone, and gave more weight to violent threats.

107 *LR (P & D)*, 1869, 32–5.

108 Ibid., 75; J77/91/1076.

109 *LR (P & D)*, 1869, 32, 34, 37–8, 63–4, 70–6; Biggs, pp. 37–9.

110 *LR (P & D)*, 1869, 32.

111 Ibid., 65.

112 Ibid., 37–8.

113 Penzance introduced the second reading of the Married Women's Property Bill into the House of Lords in 1869, stressing the need for the redress of severe grievances felt by poorer women abused by husbands 'who disregarded their marriage obligations', but then and later stressed the evils of extending equal rights in marriage to women in the interest of abstract theory, obliquely rebuking John Stuart Mill along the way. His parliamentary support of Frances Power Cobbe's proposals to protect assaulted wives in 1878 was again consistent with his interest in protecting the victims of abuse without touching more fundamental patriarchal rights; Great Britain, *Parliamentary Debates*, 3rd series, House of Lords, 30 July, 1869, 198, 979–84; 21 June, 1870, 202, 603–6, 620; 29 March, 1878, 239, 187–92; for a full account of these debates and the influence of feminists see Shanley, op. cit., pp. 49–78, 168–80.

114 As noted in chapter 1, Emily Jackson's victory was followed by her subjection to an organized charivari in the streets of Clitheroe for defying her husband, an indication that public opinion on this issue could lag behind legal change. *Regina* v. *Jackson* (1891), *LR*, Queen's Bench Division (Court of Appeal) 671; for two detailed accounts of the Jackson case see D. Rubinstein, *Before the Suffragettes: Women's Emancipation in the 1890s*, Brighton, Harvester, 1986, pp. 54–8, and Shanley, op. cit., pp. 177–83.

115 See above, chapter 2; also A. C. Plowden, *Grain or Chaff? The Autobiography of a Police Court Magistrate*, London, T. Fisher Unwin, 1903, pp. 265–6; Royal Commission on Divorce and Matrimonial Causes, *Parliamentary Papers*, 1912–13, Minutes of Evidence, vol. 19 [Cd. 6480], p. 47 (C. Chapman), p. 281 (F. Barnett).

116 *Evans* v. *Evans* (1790), 161 *ER*, 467.

117 The decisive case was *Russell* v. *Russell* (1895), P. 315 (CA) and (1897) (AC) 395 (House of Lords); Biggs, op. cit., pp. 39–43; on mental cruelty in the United States see Phillips, 1988, op. cit., pp. 450–1, 454–5.

118 Summary Jurisdiction (Married Women) Act, 1895 [58 & 59 Vict., c. 39].

119 Royal Commission on Divorce and Matrimonial Causes, *PP*, 1912–13, Report, vol. 18 [Cd. 6478], p. 71; the minority report, opposed to extension of grounds for divorce, and fearing collusion, also opposed expansion in the definition of cruelty, since it 'differs materially in classes and even in families; it may

also differ in the minds of judges'; pp. 181–2; most of the magistrates interviewed by the commission stressed the difficulty of applying a strict definition of persistent cruelty; see, for example, John Rose (Tower Bridge), Minutes of Evidence, vol. 18 [Cd. 6479], p. 93.

120 Between 1897 and 1906 courts of summary jurisdiction dispensed over 87,000 separation and maintenance orders compared to 6,000 decrees in the Divorce Court; Shanley, op. cit., p. 175; see above, chapter 2.

121 Biggs, op. cit., pp. 17, 60.

122 Phillimore, op. cit., pp. 24, 65; the case was also reported in *The Times*, 6 May, 1835, p. 3; Phillimore dismissed not only Mrs Belcher's accusations of tyrannical treatment, but also found that her infection with venereal disease had not been 'wilfully' communicated by her husband. See also Stone, op. cit., p. 204. Phillimore had earlier attempted to restrict the availability of parliamentary divorces by introducing a bill into the House of Commons to transfer jurisdiction to the ecclesiastical courts; Stone, pp. 364–5.

5 THE ADAPTATION OF PATRIARCHY IN LATE-VICTORIAN MARRIAGE

1 See, for example, F. B. Smith, 'Sexuality in Britain, 1800–1900: Some Suggested Revisions', in M. Vicinus (ed.), *A Widening Sphere: Changing Roles of Victorian Women*, Bloomington, Indiana University Press, 1977, p. 187 for suggestions of 'happy families' based on parents' mutual sexual satisfaction; another study stressing harmony is M. J. Peterson, *Family, Love and Work in the Lives of Victorian Gentlewomen*, Bloomington, Indiana University Press, 1989.

2 H. B. Stowe, *Little Foxes, or, the Little Failings Which Mar Domestic Happiness*, London, Bell & Daldy, 1866, p. 72; H. A. Taine made similar observations in his *Notes on England*, ed. and trans. E. Hyams, New York, Books for Libraries Press, 1971 (orig. pub. 1872), p. 79.

3 D. Vincent, *Bread, Knowledge and Freedom: A Study of Nineteenth Century Working-Class Autobiography*, London, Methuen, 1981, includes a substantial section on family life, pp. 39–107, and a valuable methodological discussion of autobiography as a historical source generally, pp. 3–11. See also J. Burnett (ed.), *Destiny Obscure: Autobiographies of Childhood, Education, and Family From the 1820s to the 1920s*, London, Allen Lane, 1982; J. Burnett, D. Vincent and D. Mayall (eds), *The Autobiography of the Working Class: An Annotated, Critical Bibliography* (3 vols), Brighton, Harvester, 1984–9, vol. 1: 1790–1900, pp. xvii, xxiv–xxv, xxix. Autobiographical sources also figure significantly in many recent feminist studies of family relationships, for example C. Dyhouse,'Mothers and Daughters in the Middle-Class Home, c. 1870–1914', in J. Lewis (ed.), *Labour and Love: Women's Experience of Home and Family, 1850–1940*, Oxford, Blackwell, 1986, pp. 27–47.

4 L. Davidoff and C. Hall, *Family Fortunes: Men and Women of the English Middle-Class, 1780–1850*, London, Hutchinson, 1987, p. 18; Davidoff and Hall's description of James Luckock (1761–1835) provides a graphic example of the importance of domesticity as the central purpose of men's worldly pursuits, integral to their conception of masculinity; pp. 13–18.

5 On the Bulwer-Lyttons see V. Blain, 'Rosina Bulwer-Lytton and the Rage of the Unheard', *Huntington Library Quarterly*, 1990, vol. 53, no. 3, pp. 211–36; L. Devey, *Life of Rosina, Lady Lytton*, London, Swan Sonnenschein, Lowrey, 1887; E. G. Bulwer-Lytton, *Letters of the Late Edward Bulwer-Lytton to his Wife*, London, W. Swan Sonnenschein, 1884; M. T. H. Sadleir, *Bulwer: A Panorama*.

Edward and Rosina, 1803–1836, London, Constable, 1936; on the Nortons see M. Poovey, *Uneven Developments: The Ideological Work of Gender in Mid-Victorian England*, Chicago, University of Chicago Press, 1988, pp. 51–88, and M. L. Shanley, *Feminism, Marriage, and the Law in Victorian England, 1850–1895*, Princeton, Princeton University Press, 1989, pp. 23–9.

6 See, for example, W. F. Harvey, *We Were Seven*, London, Constable, 1936, which portrays a kindly though stern father and a gentle indulgent mother, but gives no impression of their relationship.

7 L. Krenis, 'Authority and Rebellion in Victorian Autobiography', *Journal of British Studies*, 1978, vol. 18, no. 1, pp. 107–30.

8 On the value of group biography see L. Stone, 'Prosopography' in F. Gilbert and S. R. Graubard (eds), *Historical Studies Today*, New York, Norton, 1971, pp. 107–40, and G. Behlmer, 'Theory and Antitheory in Nineteenth-Century British Social History', *Journal of British Studies*, 1987, vol. 26, no. 1, pp. 123–32.

9 V. Woolf, *To the Lighthouse*, New York, Harcourt, Brace & World, 1927, pp. 296–8.

10 R. Church, *Over the Bridge: An Essay in Autobiography*, London, Heinemann, 1955, pp. 42–4.

11 E. Bligh, *Tooting Corner*, London, Secker & Warburg, 1946, p. 12.

12 G. Brenan, *A Life of One's Own: Childhood and Youth*, London, Hamish Hamilton, 1962, p. 65.

13 Ibid., pp. 27–8; M. Trustram, *Women of the Regiment: Marriage and the Victorian Army*, Cambridge, Cambridge University Press, 1984, provides a thorough analysis of the role of marriage for ranks and officers, but we know little of the influence of military life on marital relationships in the sense suggested by Brenan's parents.

14 E. Farjeon, *A Nursery in the Nineties*, London, Gollancz, 1935, pp. 234–6.

15 Ibid., pp. 246, 506–7.

16 H. G. Wells, *Experiment in Autobiography: Discoveries and Conclusions of a Very Ordinary Brain (Since 1866)*, 2 vols, London, Gollancz, 1934, pp. 41–74; H. Corke, *In Our Infancy: An Autobiography, Part 1: 1882–1912*, Cambridge, Cambridge University Press, 1975, pp. 7–28.

17 J. R. Ackerley, *My Father and Myself*, London, Bodley Head, 1968, pp. 21, 86–93, 154–60; some of Ackerley's family narrative is drawn from the 1920s, but most of it refers to his childhood during the Edwardian period.

18 M. MacCarthy, *A Nineteenth Century Childhood*, London, Hamish Hamilton, 1924, pp. 1–4, 20–3.

19 B. L. Booker, *Yesterday's Child, 1890–1909*, London, John Lang, 1937, pp. 23–4, 63.

20 E. Starkie, *A Lady's Child*, London, Faber & Faber, 1941, pp. 37–46, 62, 255, 278, 328–9; Dr William Starkie was Resident Commissioner for Education for Ireland, and Edith thought their style of life was more 'old-fashioned' and prosperous than that of their English contemporaries, but their family life paralleled that of most English families in polite society, p. 14.

21 J. L. Tayler, *The Story of a Life*, London, Williams & Norgate, 1931, pp. 50, 62–71, 252–3, 291.

22 K. Chorley, *Manchester Made Them*, London, Faber & Faber, 1950, pp. 21–2, 109–12, 170–9.

23 For the formation of domestic ideology among the provincial bourgeoisie see Davidoff and Hall, op. cit.

24 Church, op. cit., pp. 3–7, 22, 47, 73–6, 129–35.

25 Ibid., pp. 47, 90–106, 110, 136–7.

26 Ibid., pp. 110–11.

27 Ibid., pp. 111–17.
28 Ibid., p. 134.
29 Ibid., pp. 204–19.
30 V. S. Pritchett, *A Cab at the Door, An Autobiography: Early Years*, Harmondsworth, Penguin, 1974 (orig. pub. 1968), pp. 26–7, 30, 67–8, 96, 105, 120–5, 132, 146, 192, 206.
31 Bligh, op. cit., pp. 76–7, 116–23, 160–3, 183–4, 207–9.
32 Ibid., pp. 216–17.
33 Ibid., pp. 160–3.
34 C. R. Ashbee, *'Grannie': A Victorian Cameo*, Oxford, published privately, 1939, p. 59.
35 I am indebted to Felicity Ashbee, C. R. Ashbee's daughter, for many insights into aspects of her family history and for permission to consult her grandfather's diaries in her possession.
36 The best account of the Ashbees' family life is in A. Crawford's biography of the son, *C. R. Ashbee: Architect, Designer and Romantic Socialist*, New Haven, Vale University Press, 1985; see also F. MacCarthy, *The Simple Life: C. R. Ashbee in the Cotswolds*, London, Lund Humphries, 1981; H. S. Ashbee, *Forbidden Books of the Victorians*, edited, with introduction, by P. Fryer, London, Odyssey Press, 1970; S. Marcus, *The Other Victorians: A Study of Sexuality and Pornography in Mid-Nineteenth Century England*, London, Weidenfeld & Nicolson, 1966, pp. 34–76.
37 G. Legman, *The Horn Book: Studies in Erotic Folklore and Bibliography*, New York, University Books, 1964, pp. 36–42; Fryer, in H. S. Ashbee, op. cit., p. 2; Crawford, op. cit., p. 5.
38 Crawford, op. cit., pp. 1–3.
39 H. S. Ashbee Diaries (hereafter H.S.A.), 27 May, 1883.
40 Ibid., 20 April, 1876, 18 May, 1875, 13 July, 1883.
41 Crawford, op. cit., p. 4.
42 H.S.A. Diaries, 27 June, 1875.
43 R. Thomas, *Notes and Queries*, 9th series, vol. 6, 18 August, 1900, pp. 121–2.
44 H.S.A. Diaries, 3 March, 1874.
45 J. Ashbee, *Rachel*, p. 34 (unpublished MS in possession of Felicity Ashbee).
46 Crawford, op. cit., p. 6; in 1876, though, when he was preparing his work on pornography for the publisher, he noted that he was spending nearly every evening working on it at home; H.S.A. Diaries, 7 January, 1876.
47 Information from Felicity Ashbee; Crawford, op. cit., p. 7; F. MacCarthy, op. cit., p. 173.
48 Information from Felicity Ashbee.
49 C. R. Ashbee, op. cit., pp. 58–61.
50 Ibid., pp. 34–5.
51 Crawford, op. cit., p. 7.
52 Elisabeth Ashbee to C. R. Ashbee, 5 December, 1884, C. R. Ashbee Journals, King's College, Cambridge (hereafter C.R.A.).
53 Ibid., 27 December, 1885.
54 Ibid., Elisabeth Ashbee to C. R. Ashbee, 7 April, 1886.
55 10 July, 1887, H.S.A. Diaries. Henry's distress at Charles's stubborn career intentions was well known among his son's friends at Cambridge; verbal communication from Dr Michael Halls, King's college archivist, from G. Lowes Dickinson papers.
56 Crawford, op. cit., pp. 20–1.
57 C. R. Ashbee, op. cit., p. 58.
58 Agnes Ashbee to C. R. Ashbee, 13 April, 1890, C.R.A. Journals.

59 C. R. Ashbee, op. cit., pp. 48–9.
60 In a letter to Charles dated 10 April, 1897, Frances made no mention of opposition to her marriage from her father, but did note that Teddy had braved her mother's 'iron regime' in order to win her; she apparently remained in touch with her father until his death; C.R.A. Journals and communication from Felicity Ashbee.
61 Ibid., pp. 61–9; Crawford, op. cit., p. 72; *Daily News,* 26 September, 1900.
62 Programme, June, 1895, C.R.A. Journals.
63 R. Thomas, *Notes and Queries,* 9th series, vol. 6, 22 December, 1900, pp. 494–5.
64 *Daily News,* 26 September, 1900; Crawford, op. cit., p. 94.
65 E. Ashbee to C. R. Ashbee, 16 May, 1905, C.R.A. Journals.
66 C. R. Ashbee, op. cit., p. 62.
67 See above, chapter 3.
68 E. L. Linton, *The Girl of the Period, and Other Social Essays,* London, Bentley & Sons, 1883, 2 vols.
69 D. Jerrold, 'Mrs Caudle's Curtain Lectures', *Punch,* 1845, vols 8–9; 'Mr Caudle's Breakfast Talk', *Punch Almanac,* 1846, reprinted in D. W. Jerrold, *Mrs Caudle's Curtain Lectures and Other Stories and Essays,* London, World's Classics, 1907; see also R. Kelly, 'Mrs Caudle: A Victorian Curtain Lecturer', *University of Toronto Quarterly,* 1969, vol. 38, no. 3, pp. 296–309.
70 S. Coleridge, *Memoir and Letters of Sara Coleridge, Edited by Her Daughter,* London, H. S. King, 1873, 2 vols, vol. 1, p. 19.
71 Davidoff and Hall, op. cit., pp. 17, 110–13, 152, 162–72, 199, 450–1.
72 See above, chapter 3, and ibid., pp. 180–5.
73 Davidoff and Hall, op. cit., pp. 17, 111–13, 199, 319, 450–1.
74 Ibid., pp. 450–1.
75 J. A. Mangan, 'Social Darwinism and Upper-class Education in Late Victorian and Edwardian England', in J. A. Mangan and J. Walvin (eds), *Manliness and Morality: Middle Class Masculinity in Britain and America, 1800–1940,* Manchester, Manchester University Press, 1987, pp. 135–59.
76 C. Nelson, 'Sex and the Single Boy: Ideals of Manliness and Sexuality in Victorian Literature for Boys', *Victorian Studies,* 1989, vol. 32, no. 4, pp. 525–50.
77 Mrs S. S. Ellis, *The Wives of England,* London, Fisher, Son & Co., 1843, pp. 91–3; F. P. Cobbe, *The Duties of Women. A Course of Lectures,* London, Williams & Norgate, 1881, pp. 100–1; see above, chapter 3.
78 Cobbe, op. cit., pp. 101–9.
79 W. Landels, *The Marriage Ring: A Gift Book for the Newly Married and for Those Contemplating Marriage,* London, Cassell, Petter & Gilpin, 1883, p. 214: Landels was a popular preacher and writer in Scotland, England and Ireland from the 1840s to the 1890s; among numerous publications, his other books dealing with these issues were *True Manhood: Its Nature, Foundation and Development. A Book for Young Men,* London, Nisbet, 1861, and *Woman: Her Position and Power,* London, Cassell, Petter & Gilpin, 1870; cf. F. Boase, *Modern English Biography,* London, Cass, 1965, vol. 6, pp. 6–7.
80 Landels, op. cit., 1883, pp. 164, 219–20.
81 Ibid., p. 239.
82 *Marriage and Home,* London, Morgan & Chase, 1870, p. 31. For other examples see W. H. Davenport Adams, *Woman's Work and Worth,* London, 1880; Rev. E. J. Hardy, *How to be Happy Though Married,* London, T. Fisher Unwin, 1885, and *Love, Courtship and Marriage,* London, Chatto & Windus, 1902; see also the American Presbyterian preacher and writer, Thomas De Witt Talmage, whose visits and writings were popular in Britain, *The Marriage Tie: Thirteen Discourses on Marriage and Family Life,* London, W. Nicholson, 1890, discussed

by Mrs E. Talmage in Talmage, *T. De Witt Talmage. As I Knew Him*, London, J. Murray, 1912.

83 Landels, op. cit., 1883, pp. 193–7, 215–21; Landels, op. cit., 1870, pp. 117–21; Adams, op. cit., pp. 86–7.

84 The connection between the Divorce Act and literary trends is noted by E. Showalter in *A Literature of Their Own: British Women Novelists from Brontë to Lessing*, London, Virago, 1979, ch. 6, and 'Family Secrets and Domestic Subversion: Rebellion in the Novels of the 1860s', in A. S. Wohl (ed.), *The Victorian Family: Structure and Stresses*, London, Croom Helm, 1978, pp. 101–16.

85 See, for example, Mrs Henry Wood, *East Lynne*, London, 1862; Rhoda Broughton, *Cometh Up As a Flower*, London, 1867.

86 There is no direct evidence in George Eliot's letters, or her *Quarry for Middlemarch*, that she was aware of the reports of particular divorce cases, but it seems unlikely, given the widespread journalistic preoccupation, that she had not often read them.

87 A. Trollope, *He Knew He Was Right*, London, World's Classics, 1948; the novel was first published serially from October, 1868 to May, 1869.

88 For a discussion see S. R. Letwin, *The Gentleman in Trollope: Individuality and Moral Conduct*, London, Macmillan, 1982, p. 167.

89 Trollope, op. cit., p. 53.

90 *British Quarterly Review*, 1 July, 1869, pp. 263–4, cited in D. Smalley (ed.), *Trollope: The Critical Heritage*, London, Routledge & Kegan Paul, 1969, p. 333.

91 *The Times*, in ibid., p. 329.

92 Trollope, op. cit., pp. 43–4.

93 Ibid., p. 742.

94 Ibid., p. 590.

95 A. Trollope, *An Autobiography*, London, Williams & Norgate, 1946 (orig. pub. 1883), p. 280.

96 Cobbe, op. cit., pp. 101–9; see above, chapter 3.

97 For example, L. Holcombe, *Wives and Property: Reform of the Married Women's Property Law in Nineteenth-Century England*, Toronto, University of Toronto Press, 1983; J. Walkowitz, *Prostitution and Victorian Society*, Cambridge, Cambridge University Press, 1980; S. K. Kent, *Sex and Suffrage in Britain, 1860–1914*, Princeton, Princeton University Press, 1987.

98 J. S. Mill, *The Subjection of Women*, (orig. pub. 1869) in A. S. Rossi (ed.), *Essays on Sex Equality*, Chicago, University of Chicago Press, 1970, pp. 160–1.

99 Ibid., p. 181.

100 See above, chapter 3.

101 Shanley, op. cit., pp. 49–78, and 'Marital Slavery and Friendship: John Stuart Mill's *The Subjection of Women*', *Political Theory*, 1981, vol. 9, no. 2, pp. 229–47.

102 Shanley, 1989, op. cit., p. 66.

103 For a discussion of the Mill–Taylor relationship see A. S. Rossi, 'Sentiment and Intellect: The Story of John Stuart Mill and Harriet Taylor Mill', in Rossi, op. cit., pp. 1–63.

104 For a critique of Mill's ideal of marriage, which raises important questions about the nature of the 'partnership' Mill anticipated, see S. Mendus, 'The Marriage of True Minds: The Ideal of Marriage in the Philosophy of John Stuart Mill', in S. Mendus and J. Rendall (eds), *Sexuality and Subordination: Interdisciplinary Studies of Gender in the Nineteenth Century*, London, Routledge, 1989, pp. 171–91.

105 Mill, op. cit., pp. 234–5.

106 See above, chapter 3.

107 Mill, op. cit., p. 165.
108 Ibid., pp. 165–8.
109 Ibid., pp. 172–3.
110 Shanley, 1981, op. cit., p. 240; Rossi, op. cit., pp. 42–3; S. M. Okin, *Women in Western Political Thought*, London, Virago, 1980, pp. 226–30.
111 Mill, op. cit., pp. 174, 235.
112 Mendus, op. cit., pp. 188–9.
113 This is consistent with the argument of P. Levine in '"So Few Prizes and So Many Blanks": Marriage and Feminism in Later Nineteenth Century England', *Journal of British Studies*, 1989, vol. 28, no. 2, pp. 150–74, who detects a shift from early attitudes regarding marriage as a 'salvageable commodity' to a more militant rejection later in favour of voluntary celibacy.
114 Cobbe, op. cit., pp. 101–25.
115 See H. Taylor's article, 'The Enfranchisement of Women', orig. pub. in *Westminster Review*, 1851, in Rossi (ed.), *Essays*, pp. 91–121.
116 A. Besant, *Marriage, As It Was, As it Is, and As It Should Be: A Plea for Reform*, orig. pub. 1878, in A. Besant, *A Selection of the Social and Political Pamphlets of Annie Besant*, New York, A. M. Kelly, 1970, pp. 28–32.
117 H. Quilter, *Is Marriage a Failure?*, London, Swan Sonnenschein, 1888, gives an account of the origin of the debate and a somewhat biased summary of Caird's article; M. Caird's original article, 'Marriage', appeared in the *Westminster Review* in August, 1888, vol. 130, pp. 186–201, and was reprinted, together with subsequent articles, in her book, *The Morality of Marriage*, London, G. Redway, 1897; the citations below are drawn from the 1897 publication, and mostly, but not entirely, appeared in the original article.
118 J. Walkowitz, 'Science, Feminism and Romance: The Men and Women's Club, 1885–1889', *History Workshop*, 1986, no. 21, pp. 54–5.
119 See above, chapter 2.
120 Caird, op. cit., pp. 105–6.
121 Ibid., p. 108; there is a clear line of continuity between Caird's critique and the Edwardian suffragists' literature of marriage rejection and celebration of female celibacy; see, for example, C. Hamilton, *Marriage as a Trade*, London, Chapman & Hall, 1909.
122 Caird, op. cit., pp. 58–9.
123 Ibid., p. 126.
124 Ibid., p. 109.
125 Ibid., pp. 96–7.
126 For example Kent, op. cit., pp. 80–113, 157–83; S. Jeffreys, *The Spinster and Her Enemies: Feminism and Sexuality, 1880–1930*, London, Pandora, 1985; L. Bland, 'Marriage Laid Bare: Middle-class Women and Marital Sex, 1880s–1914', in Lewis op. cit., pp. 123–46.
127 See especially Kent, op. cit., pp. 5–7, 203–5, and her discussion of the views of Frances Swiney, pp. 161–5 and *passim*.
128 L. Bland, 'The Married Woman, the "New Woman" and the Feminist: Sexual Politics of the 1890s', in J. Rendall (ed.), *Equal or Different: Women's Politics, 1800–1914*, Oxford, Blackwell, 1987, pp. 141–64.
129 Quilter, op. cit., pp. 22–3, also quoted in Kent, op. cit., p. 102.
130 Quilter, op. cit., pp. 35, 216.
131 Ibid., pp. 216–18.
132 Ibid., p. 85.
133 E. C. Hewitt, 'The "New Woman" in Her Relation to the "New Man"', *Westminster Review*, 1897, vol. 147, no. 3, pp. 335–7; 'Why We Men Do Not Marry (By One of Us)', *Temple Bar*, 1888, vol. 84, pp. 218–23, was characteristic

of the kind of male reaction to the marriage debate that stimulated Hewitt's reflection.

134 'Eugenius', 'The Decline of Marriage', *Westminster Review*, 1891, vol. 135, no. 1, pp. 11–27; see also 'The Law in Relation to Women', *Westminster Review*, 1887, vol. 128, no. 3, pp. 698–710; E. R. Chapman, 'Marriage Rejection and Marriage Reform', *Westminster Review*, 1888, vol. 30, no. 3, pp. 358–77; J. H. Clapperton, 'Miss Chapman's Marriage Reform: A Criticism', *Westminster Review*, 1888, vol. 130, no. 6, pp. 709–17; W. J. K., 'Men and Marriage', *Westminster Review*, 1894, vol. 142, no. 2, pp. 146–52; J. A. Sewell, 'Divorce and Re-marriage', *Westminster Review*, 1896, vol. 145, no. 2, pp. 182–92; L. B. Cameron, 'How We Marry', *Westminster Review*, 1896, vol. 145, no. 6, pp. 690–4; P. E. Moulder, 'Friendship Between the Sexes', *Westminster Review*, 1899, vol. 151, no. 6, pp. 667–70; H. Flowerden, 'Suggestion of a Substitute for the Marriage Laws', *Westminster Review*, 1899, vol. 152, no. 3, pp. 293–300.

135 J. Minson, *Genealogies of Morals: Nietzsche, Foucault, Donzelot and the Eccentricity of Ethics*, Basingstoke, Macmillan, 1985, p. 212.

CONCLUSION

1 J. Fliegeman, *Prodigals and Pilgrims: The American Revolution Against Patriarchal Authority, 1750–1800*, Cambridge, Cambridge University Press, 1982, pp. 14–15.

2 A. J. Coale and S. C. Watkins, *The Decline of Fertility in Europe*, Princeton, Princeton University Press, 1986, pp. 438, 446–9; L. Davidoff, 'The Family in Britain', in F. M. L. Thompson (ed.), *The Cambridge Social History of Britain, 1750–1950*, vol. 2: *People and Their Environment*, Cambridge, Cambridge University Press, 1990, pp. 102–3.

3 J. Allen, 'Contextualising Late-Nineteenth Century Feminism: Problems and Comparisons', *Journal of the Canadian Historical Association*, 1990, new series, vol. 1, pp. 35–6.

4 R. Brandon, *The New Women and the Old Men: Love, Sex and the Woman Question*, London, Secker & Warburg, 1990, pursues interesting aspects of this idea by examining contradictions in the lives of prominent thinkers and progressives.

5 For a discussion of this aspect of Dickens's marriage see P. Rose, *Parallel Lives: Five Victorian Marriages*, London, Penguin, 1985, pp. 148–91.

6 R. Trumbach, *The Rise of the Egalitarian Family*, New York, Academic Press, 1978, especially pp. 237–92; L. Davidoff and C. Hall, *Family Fortunes: Men and Women of the English Middle Class, 1780–1850*, London, Hutchinson, 1987, *passim*.

7 L. Segal, *Slow Motion: Changing Masculinities, Changing Men*, London, Virago, 1990, investigates these themes in modern society.

8 B. Ehrenreich, *The Hearts of Men: American Dreams and the Flight From Commitment*, Garden City, NY, Anchor/Doubleday, 1983. J. Tosh, 'Domesticity and Manliness in the Victorian Middle Class: The Family of Edward White Benson', in M. Roper and J. Tosh (eds), *Manful Assertions: Masculinities in Britain Since 1800*, London, Routledge, 1991, pp. 44–73, situates men's 'flight from domesticity' in the context of the climate of the new, late-Victorian, imperialism; this text came to hand too late for fuller consideration here.

9 Davidoff, op. cit., 1990, p. 109.

10 J. Lewis, *The Politics of Motherhood: Child and Maternal Welfare in England, 1900–1939*, London, Croom Helm, 1980, p. 169.

11 S. Jeffries, *The Spinster and Her Enemies: Feminism and Sexuality, 1880–1930*, London, Pandora, 1985; J. Lewis, 'Public Institution and Private Relationship: Marriage and Marriage Guidance, 1920–1968', *Twentieth Century British History*, 1990, vol. 1, no. 3, pp. 233–63.

12 L. Stone, *The Family, Sex and Marriage in England, 1500–1800*, London, Weidenfeld & Nicolson, 1977, pp. 667–8.

13 S. M. Okin, 'Women and the Making of the Sentimental Family', *Philosophy and Public Affairs*, 1982, vol. 11, no. 1, pps-9. 65–88.

14 E. Spring, 'Law and the Theory of the Affecctive Family', *Albion*, 1984, vol. 16, pp. 1–20; Spring's main concern, with Stone's discussion of the influence of strict settlement on marriage, is of only marginal relevance to her point about later nineteenth-century legislation and the dimensions of the debate discussed here; so too are the subsequent polemics with Eileen and David Spring on strict settlement: E. Spring and D. Sprring, 'The English Landed Elite, 1540–1879: A Review', and L. Stone, 'Spring Back', *Albion*, 1985, vol. 17, no. 2, pp. 149–66 and 167–80.

APPENDIX 1

1 M. Anderson, *Approaches to the History of the Western Family, 1500–1914*, London, Macmillan, 1980, pp. 40–1; L. Stone, *The Family, Sex and Marriage in England, 1500–1800*, London, Weidenfeld & Nicolson, 1967, pp. 10–12.

2 L. Davidoff and C. Hall, *Family Fortunes: Men and Women of the English Middle-Class, 1780–1850*, London, Hutchinson, 1987; P. Jalland, *Women, Marriage and Politics, 1860–1914*, Oxford, Oxford University Press, 1986; B. Caine, *Destined to be Wives: the Sisters of Beatrice Webb*, Oxford, Oxford University Press, 1986; see also P. Gay, *The Bourgeois Experience: Victoria to Freud*, vol. 1: *Education of the Senses*, New York, Oxford University Press, 1984; vol. 2: *The Tender Passion*, New York, Oxford University Press, 1986.

3 Jalland, op. cit., especially the discussion of Molly Trevelyan, pp. 241–9.

4 M. J. Peterson, *Family, Love and Work in the Lives of Victorian Gentlewomen*, Bloomington, Indiana University Press, 1989, pp. 58–131.

5 Cainè, op. cit.

6 For a striking example based on the disastrous Bulwer-Lytton marriage see V. Blain, 'Rosina Bulwer-Lytton and the Rage of the Unheard', *Huntington Library Quarterly*, 1990, vol. 53, no. 3, pp. 211–36.

7 L. Stone, *Road to Divorce: England, 1530–1987*, Oxford, Oxford University Press, 1990, p. 30.

8 A. P. Herbert, *Holy Deadlock*, London, Methuen, 1934.

9 *Curtis* v. *Curtis* (1858) 164 *ER*, 636 and 688; for discussion see chapter 3.

10 A classic example from the ecclesiastical courts, years before the Divorce Court was established, is *Evans* v. *Evans* (1790), 161 *English Reports*, 466–99.

11 Many judges' rulings were also reported at length in the press, and, before 1857, some judges, anxious to publicize their rulings which had not been officially reported, arranged for private publication; see especially R. J. Phillimore, *A Report of the Judgement Delivered on the Sixth Day of June, 1835, by Joseph Phillimore, D.C.L., . . . in the Cause of Belcher, the Wife, against Belcher, the Husband . . .*, London, Saunders & Benning, 1835, which printed not only the judgement but all the testimony and correspondence produced in court.

12 Until 1984 access was governed by a one-hundred-year exclusion rule.

13 A. Horstman, *Victorian Divorce*, London, Croom Helm, 1985, p. 182.

14 G. L. Savage, 'The Social Basis of the Demand for Divorce in England, 1858–1868: Graphs and Tables', unpublished paper presented to the

Mid-western Victorian Studies Association, April, 1987; before Savage's work the best statistical treatment of divorce petitions was in G. Rowntree and N. H. Carrier, 'The Resort to Divorce in England and Wales, 1857–1957', *Population Studies*, 1958, vol. 11, no. 3, pp. 188–233, but it suffered from lack of access to the files themselves.

15 The records are stored in boxes containing roughly thirty-four files each, kept up to 1866 in alphabetical order, thereafter in date order. Special PRO permission is required to consult entire boxes rather than three separate files at a time, and much of the nature of this research was influenced by problems of physical access. The survey was based on selection of cases citing cruelty from randomly chosen files, first from 1858 to 1866, surnames beginning A to D, secondly 1882, petitions dated February to May. The first survey yielded eighty-three cruelty cases out of 241, the second, eighty cases out of 141. Full details of the cruelty cases were recorded, and further evidence sought, where available, in press and law reports. A further survey was made of cruelty cases cited in the law reports from 1858 to 1911 (twenty-five cases), and this was used to supplement the findings of occupational data. Cruelty cases from the law reports from 1780 to 1857 were also used for the legal discussion in chapter 4. See tables 4.1 and 4.2. For similar findings see Savage, op. cit.

16 *Bostock* v. *Bostock* (1858), PRO J77/2/B3.

17 *Kelly* v. *Kelly* (1869 and 1870), J77/91/1076.

18 *Curtis* v. *Curtis* (1858) 164 *English Reports*, 636 and 688; J77/8/C4.

19 Savage, op. cit., and chapter 4, above.

20 The years surveyed are detailed in table 2.2, and were partly chosen on the basis of availability of newspapers; four newspapers were surveyed, the *Preston Chronicle*, *Preston Pilot*, *Preston Guardian* and *Preston Herald*, but no case was counted twice. The survey resulted in 283 cases detailing acts of violence. The choice of Preston was determined partly by the value of surveying an industrial town with a complex social organization, partly by existing research of direct relevance, especially M. Anderson, *Family Structure in Nineteenth Century Lancashire*, Cambridge, Cambridge University Press, 1971, and E. Roberts, *A Woman's Place: An Oral History of Working-Class Women, 1890–1940*, Oxford, Blackwell, 1984.

21 For an outstanding example see E. Ross, '"Fierce Questions and Taunts": Married Life in Working-Class London', *Feminist Studies*, 1982, vol. 8, no. 3, pp. 575–602.

22 M. L. Shanley, *Feminism, Marriage and the Law in Victorian England, 1850–1895*, Princeton, Princeton University Press, 1989, p. 172n; see also I. Minor, 'Working-class Women and Matrimonial Law Reform, 1890–1914', in D. Rubinstein and D. Martin (eds), *Ideology and the Labour Movement*, London, Croom Helm, 1979, pp. 103–24, and the discussion in chapter 2, above.

23 O. Hufton, reviewing M. Anderson, *Approaches to the History of the Western Family, 1500–1914* (London, Macmillan, 1980), *Social History*, 1982, vol. 7, no. 3, p. 346.

BIBLIOGRAPHY

PRIMARY SOURCES

Unpublished manuscript collections

Felicity Ashbee private collection:
    H. S. Ashbee Diaries.
    J. Ashbee, *Rachel* (Autobiographical novel, typescript).
British Library:
    E. Wostenholme Elmy Collection, British Library, Add. MS. 47,452
King's College, Cambridge:
    C. R. Ashbee journals.
    G. Lowes Dickinson papers.
Lancaster University:
    Elizabeth Roberts Oral History collection.

Unpublished government archives

Principal Probate Registry Divorce Files:
    File J77, 1858–1911.
Probate Files, Wills:
    James Turner Bostock, probate, IR26, 1762/649(1847), will, prob. 11, 2060(627),
    August, 1847; Robert Chignell Bostock, probate, IR26, 2879(1875), will, PR
    1616, 116/1932, November, 1875.

Government publications

Statutes

An Act for the Better Prevention and Punishment of Aggravated Assaults upon
    Women and Children . . . , 1853 (16 & 17 Victoria, c. 30).
Matrimonial Causes Act, 1857 (20 & 21 Victoria, c. 85).
Matrimonial Causes Act, 1878 (41 & 42 Victoria, c. 19).
Married Women (Maintenance in Case of Desertion) Act, 1886 (49 & 50 Victoria, c.
    52).
Summary Jurisdiction (Married Women) Act, 1895 (58 & 59 Victoria, c. 39).
Matrimonial Causes Act, 1923 (13 & 14 Geo. 5, c. 19).
Matrimonial Causes Act, 1937 (1 Ed. 8 & 1 Geo. 6, c. 57).

BIBLIOGRAPHY

Other Parliamentary materials

Great Britain, Hansard, *Parliamentary Debates*, 3rd series, House of Commons.
Royal Commission on Divorce and Matrimonial Causes, *Parliamentary Papers*,
   1912–13, vols 18–21 [Cd. 6478–81].

Law reports

The English Reports (Ecclesiastical courts and Admiralty, Probate and Divorce),
   1790–1865, vols 161–4.
Law Journal (Probate and Matrimonial), 1873, vol. 42.
Law Reports (Probate and Divorce), 1865–1914.
Law Reports (Queen's Bench Division, Court of Appeal), 1891, vol. 1.
Phillimore, R. J., *A Report of the Judgement Delivered on the Sixth Day of June, 1835,*
   by Joseph Phillimore, D.C.L., . . . in the Cause of Belcher, the Wife, against Belcher,
   the husband . . ., London, Saunders & Benning, 1835.

Newspapers and periodicals

Annual Register
Th' Bowtun Loominary
Contemporary Review
Daily News
Fortnightly Review
Fraser's Magazine
Illustrated London News
Justice of the Peace
Leeds Mercury
Magnet
Mrs Ellis's Morning Call: A Table Book of Literature and Art
Morning Chronicle
Morning Post
Nineteenth Century and After
Notes and Queries
Preston Chronicle
Preston Guardian
Preston Herald
Preston Pilot
Punch
Punch Almanac
Red Republican
Reynolds's Weekly Newspaper
Saturday Review
Spectator
Standard
Sydney Morning Herald
Temple Bar
The Times
Transactions, National Association for the Promotion of Social Science
Truth
Westminster Review
Women's Suffrage Journal

Contemporary books and articles

A. M. B., *The Parlour Portfolio, or, Post Chaise Companion*, London, Matthew Iley, 1820, vol. 2.

Ackerley, J. R., *My Father and Myself*, London, Bodley Head, 1968.

Ashbee, C. R., *'Grannie': A Victorian Cameo*, Oxford, published privately, 1939.

Ashbee, H. S., *Forbidden Books of the Victorians*, ed. P. Fryer, London, Odyssey Press, 1970.

Besant, A., *Marriage, As it Was, As it Is, and As it Should Be: A Plea for Reform* (1878), in *A Selection of the Social and Political Pamphlets of Annie Besant*, New York, Kelly, 1970, pp. 28–32.

Blackstone, Sir W., *Commentaries on the Laws of England*, London, W. Reed, 1811 (orig. pub. 1765–9).

Blake, M. M., 'Are Women Protected?', *Westminster Review*, 1892, vol. 137, pp. 43–8.

—— 'The Lady and the Law', *Westminster Review*, 1892, vol. 137, pp. 364–70.

Bligh, E., *Tooting Corner*, London, Secker & Warburg, 1946.

Booker, B. L., *Yesterday's Child, 1890–1909*, London, John Lang, 1937.

Bosanquet, H., *The Family*, London, Macmillan, 1906.

Brenan, G., *A Life of One's Own: Childhood and Youth*, London, Hamish Hamilton, 1962.

Brewster, M. M., *Sunbeams in the Cottage, or What Women May Do: A Narrative Chiefly Addressed to the Working-Classes*, Edinburgh, Constable, 1854.

Broughton, R., *Cometh Up As a Flower*, London, no publisher, 1867.

Bulwer-Lytton, E. G., *Letters of the Late Edward Bulwer-Lytton to His Wife*, London, W. Swan Sonnenschein, 1884.

Caird, M., 'Marriage', *Westminster Review*, August, 1888, vol. 130, pp. 186–201.

—— *The Morality of Marriage*, London, G. Redway, 1897.

Cameron, L. B., 'How We Marry', *Westminster Review*, 1896, vol. 145, no. 6, pp. 690–4.

Carson, W. E., *The Marriage Revolt: A Study of Marriage and Divorce*, London, T. Werner Laurie, 1915.

Chapman, C., *Marriage and Divorce: Some Needed Reforms in Church and State*, London, D. Nutt, 1911.

—— *The Poor Man's Court of Justice: Twenty-Five Years as a Metropolitan Magistrate*, London, Hodder & Stoughton, 1925.

Chapman, E. R., 'Marriage Rejection and Marriage Reform', *Westminster Review*, 1888, vol. 30, no. 3, pp. 358–77.

Cheales, A. B., *Proverbial Folklore*, London, Simpkin, Marshall, 1875.

Chorley, K., *Manchester Made Them*, London, Faber & Faber, 1950.

Church, R., *Over the Bridge: An Essay in Autobiography*, London, Heinemann, 1955.

Clapperton, J. H., 'Miss Chapman's Marriage Reform: A Criticism', *Westminster Review*, 1888, vol. 130, no. 6, pp. 709–17.

Cobbe, F. P., 'Wife-Torture in England', *Contemporary Review*, 1878, vol. 32, pp. 55–87.

—— *The Duties of Women. A Course of Lectures*, London, Williams & Norgate, 1881.

Coleridge, Sara, *Memoir and Letters of Sara Coleridge, Edited by Her Daughter*, London, H. S. King, 1873, 2 vols.

Cooper, Rev. W. M., *Flagellation and the Flagellants: A History of the Rod . . .*, London, J. Camden Hotten, 1870.

Corder, R. E., *Tales Told to the Magistrate*, London, A. Melrose, 1925.

Corke, H., *In Our Infancy: An Autobiography, Part I: 1882–1912*, Cambridge, Cambridge University Press, 1975.

Cox, E. W., *The Principles of Punishment, as Applied in the Administration of the Criminal Law, by Judges and Magistrates*, London, Law Times, 1877.

Cralk, D. M. M., *A Woman's Thoughts About Women*, London, Hurst & Blackett, 1858.

Crawford, M. S., 'Maltreatment of Wives', *Westminster Review*, 1893, vol. 139, pp. 292–303.

Cruikshank, G., *The Bottle*, London, D. Bogne, 1847.

Davenport Adams, W. H., *Women's Work and Worth*, London, 1880.

Devey, L., *Life of Rosina, Lady Lytton*, London, Swan Sonnenschein, Lowrey, 1887.

Ellis, Mrs S. S., *The Women of England . . .*, London, Fisher, Son & Co., 1838.

—— *The Daughters of England . . .*, London, Fisher, Son & Co., 1842.

—— *The Mothers of England . . .*, London, Fisher, Son & Co.,, 1843.

—— *The Wives of England . . .*, London, Fisher, Son & Co., 1843.

—— *The Education of Character: With Hints on Moral Training*, London, J. Murray, 1856.

—— *Chapters on Wives*, London, R. Bentley, 1860.

—— *Education of the Heart: Woman's Best Work*, London, Hodder & Stoughton, 1869.

—— *The Home Life and Letters of Mrs Ellis, Compiled by her Nieces*, London, J. Nisbet, 1893.

'Eugenius', 'The Decline of Marriage', *Westminster Review*, 1891, vol. 135, no. 1, pp. 11–27.

Farjeon, E., *A Nursery in the Nineties*, London, Gollancz, 1935.

Female Happiness, or, The Lady's Handbook of Life, London, W. Tegg, 1854.

Flowerden, H., 'Suggestion of a Substitute for the Marriage Laws', *Westminster Review*, 1899, vol. 152, no. 3, pp. 293–300.

Geary, Sir W. N. M., *The Law of Marriage and Family Relations: A Manual of Practical Law*, London, A. & C. Black, 1892.

Greenwood, J., *The Prisoner in the Dock: My Four Years' Daily Experiences in the London Police Courts*, London, Chatto & Windus, 1902.

Grey, M. G. and Shirreff, E., *Thoughts on Self-Culture, Addressed to Women*, London, Hope & Co., 1850.

Hamilton, C., *Marriage as a Trade*, London, Chapman & Hall, 1909.

Hardy, Rev. E. J., *How to be Happy Though Married*, London, T. Fisher Unwin, 1885.

—— *Love, Courtship and Marriage*, London, Chatto & Windus, 1902.

Harvey, W. F., *We Were Seven*, London, Constable, 1936.

Herbert, A. P., *Holy Deadlock*, London, Methuen, 1934.

—— *The Ayes Have It: The Story of the Marriage Bill*, London, Methuen, 1937.

Hewitt, E. C., 'The "New Woman" In Her Relation to the "New Man"', *Westminster Review*, 1897, vol. 147, no. 3, pp. 335–7.

Holmes, T., *Pictures and Problems from London Police Courts*, London, E. Arnold, 1900.

—— *Known to the Police*, London, E. Arnold, 1908.

Jerrold, D., 'Mrs Caudle's Curtain Lectures', *Punch*, 1845, vols 8–9.

—— 'Mr Caudle's Breakfast Talk', *Punch Almanac*, 1846, reprinted in Jerrold, *Mrs Caudle's Curtain Lectures and Other Stories and Essays*, London, World's Classics, 1907.

Kaye, J. W., 'The Non-Existence of Women', *North British Review*, 1855, vol. 23, no. 46, pp. 536–32.

—— 'Outrages on Women', *North British Review*, May, 1856, vol. 25, no. 49, pp. 233–56.

Lamb, A. R., *Can Woman Regenerate Society?*, London, J. W. Parker, 1844.

Landels, W., *True Manhood: Its Nature, Foundation and Development. A Book for Young Men*, London, Nisbet, 1861.
—— *Woman: Her Position and Power*, London, Cassell, Petter & Gilpin, 1870.
—— *The Marriage Ring: A Gift Book for the Newly Married and for Those Contemplating Marriage*, London, Cassell, Petter & Gilpin, 1883.
'The Law in Relation to Women', *Westminster Review*, 1887, vol. 128, pp. 698–710.
Laycock, S., *The Collected Writings of Samuel Laycock*, ed. George Milner, Oldham, W. E. Clegg, 1908.
Linton, E. L., *The Girl of the Period, and Other social Essays*, London, Bentley & Sons, 1883, 2 vols.
Loane, M., *The Queen's Poor*, London, E. Arnold, 1905.
—— *An Englishman's Castle*, London, E. Arnold, 1909.
—— *The Common Growth*, London, E. Arnold, 1911.
Lupton, T., *Siuqila: Too Good to be True: Omen*, London, H. Bynneman, 1580.
MacCarthy, M., *A Nineteenth Century Childhood*, London, Hamish Hamilton, 1924.
A Manchester Man [Lamb, R.], 'The Philosophy of Marriage Studied Under Sir Cresswell Cresswell', *Fraser's Magazine*, 1860, vol. 5, no. 62, pp. 553–69.
Marriage and Home, London, Morgan & Chase, 1870.
Martin, A., 'The Mother and Social Reform', *The Nineteenth Century and After*, 1913, vol. 73, nos. 435, 436, pp. 1060–79, 1231–55.
Mayhew, H., *London Labour and the London Poor*, 4 vols, London, Griffin, Bohn & Co., 1861.
Meriweather, L., 'Is Divorce a Remedy?', *Westminster Review*, 1889, vol. 131, pp. 676–85.
Mill, J. S., *The Subjection of Women*, 1869, in A. Rossi (ed.), *Essays on Sex Equality*, Chicago, University of Chicago Press, 1970, pp. 125–242.
A Mother and Mistress of a Family, *Home Discipline – or Thoughts on the Origin and Exercise of Domestic Authority*, London, J. Buro, 1841.
Moulder, P. E., 'Friendship Between the Sexes', *Westminster Review*, 1899, vol. 151, no. 6, pp. 667–70.
Plowden, A. C., *Grain or Chaff? The Autobiography of a Police Court Magistrate*, London, T. Fisher Unwin, 1903.
Potter, J. H., *Inasmuch: The Story of the Police Court Mission, 1876–1926*, London, Williams & Norgate, 1927.
Pritchett, V. S., *A Cab at the Door, An Autobiography: Early Years*, (1968), Harmondsworth, Penguin, 1974.
Pulling, Mr Serjeant, 'What Legislation Is Necessary for the Repression of Crimes of Violence?', *Transactions*, National Association for the Promotion of Social Science, Liverpool, 1876, pp. 345–9.
Quilter, H., *Is Marriage a Failure?*, London, Swan Sonnenschein & Co., 1888.
Redwood, C., *The Vale of Glamorgan*, London, Saunders & Otley, 1839.
Reid, M., *A Plea for Woman*, Edinburgh, W. Tait, 1843.
Reynolds, S., 'Divorce for the Poor', *Fortnightly Review*, 1910, vol. 88, pp. 488–96.
Sadleir, M. T. H., *Bulwer: A Panorama. Edward and Rosina, 1803–1836*, London, Constable, 1936.
Sandford, Mrs E., *Woman, in Her Social and Domestic Character*, London, Longman, Orme, Brown, Green & Longmans, 1839.
Sankey, Viscount, *Lord Stowell*, Oxford, privately printed, 1936.
Sewell, J. A., 'Divorce and Re-marriage', *Westminster Review*, 1896, vol. 145, no. 2, pp. 182–92.
Starkie, E., *A Lady's Child*, London, Faber & Faber, 1941.
Staton, J. T., 'Missis Caustic's Hearthstone Lectures', *Th' Bowtun Loominary*, 1859, vol. 11, p. 303.

—— *A Case of Samples*, Manchester, Abel, Heywood & Son, 1869.

Stowe, H. B., *Little Foxes, or, the Little Failings Which Mar Domestic Happiness*, London, Bell & Daldy, 1866.

Surtees, W. E., *A Sketch . . . of Lords Stowell and Eldon . . .*, London, Chapman & Hall, 1846.

Taine, H. A., *Notes on England*, (1872), ed. and trans. E. Hyams, New York, Books for Libraries Press, 1971.

Talmage, T. D., *The Marriage Tie: Thirteen Discourses on Marriage and Family Life*, London, W. Nicholson & Sons, 1890.

—— *T. De Witt Talmage. As I Knew Him*, London, J. Murray, 1912.

Tayler, J. L., *The Story of a Life*, London, Williams & Norgate, 1931.

Taylor, A., *Practical Hints to Young Females, on the Duties of a Wife, a Mother and a Mistress of a Family*, London, Taylor & Hessey, 1815.

Taylor, H., 'The Enfranchisement of Women', *Westminster Review*, July, 1851, vol. 55, in A. Rossi (ed.), *Essays on Sex Equality*, Chicago, University of Chicago Press, 1970, pp. 91–121.

Taylor, Isaac, Settrington Rectory, *Folklore Journal*, 1883, vol. 1, pp. 298–9.

Thackeray, W., 'On Love, Marriage, Men and Women', in *The Works of Thackeray*, London, Macmillan, 1911, vol. 17, pp. 132–3.

Timmins, S., *A History of Warwickshire*, London, Elliot Stock, 1889.

Townsend, W. C., *The Lives of Twelve Eminent Judges*, 2 vols, London, Longman, Brown, Green & Longmans, 1846.

Trollope, A., *He Knew He Was Right*, (1869), London, World's Classics, 1948.

—— *An Autobiography* (1883), London, Williams & Norgate, 1946.

W. J. K., 'Men and Marriage', *Westminster Review*, 1894, vol. 142, no. 2, pp. 146–52.

Waddy, W. J., *The Police Court and Its Work*, London, Butterworth, 1925.

Walker, G., *The Costume of Yorkshire*, London, Longman, Hirst, Rees, Orme & Browne, 1814.

Weeks, W. S., *The Clitheroe District: Proverbs and Sayings, Customs and Legends, and Much of its History*, Clitheroe, Advertiser and Times Co., 1922.

Wells, H. G., *Experiment in Autobiography: Discoveries and Conclusions of a Very Ordinary Brain (Since 1866)*, 2 vols, London, Gollancz, 1934.

'Why We Men Do Not Marry (By One of Us)', *Temple Bar*, 1888, vol. 84, pp. 218–23.

'Wife-Beating', *Saturday Review*, 16 May, 1857, vol. 3, no. 81, pp. 446–7.

Women's Co-operative Guild, *Working Women and Divorce*, London, D. Nutt, 1911.

Wood, Mrs H., *East Lynne*, London, R. Bentley, 1861.

Woolf, V., *To the Lighthouse*, New York, Harcourt, Brace & World, 1927.

SECONDARY SOURCES: BOOKS, ARTICLES AND THESES

Agulhon, M., *Marianne into Battle: Republican Imagery and Symbolism in France, 1789–1880*, trans. Janet Lloyd, Cambridge, Cambridge University Press, 1981.

Allen, J., 'Contextualising Late-Nineteenth Century Feminism: Problems and Comparisons', *Journal of the Canadian Historical Association*, 1990, new series, vol. 1, pp. 17–36.

Anderson, M., *Family Structure in Nineteenth Century Lancashire*, Cambridge, Cambridge University Press, 1971.

—— *Approaches to the History of the Western Family, 1500–1914*, London, Macmillan, 1980.

—— 'The Social Implications of Demographic Change', in Thompson, F. M. L. (ed.), *The Cambridge Social History of Britain, 1750–1950*, vol. 2: *People and Their Environment*, Cambridge, Cambridge University Press, 1990, pp. 1–70.

Anderson, S., 'Legislative Divorce – Law for the Aristocracy?', in Grubin, G. R. and Sugarman, D. (eds), *Law, Economy and Society, 1750–1914: Essays in the History of English Law*, Abingdon, Professional Books, 1984, pp. 412–44.

Andrew, D. T., 'The Code of Honour and its Critics: The Opposition to Duelling in England, 1700–1850', *Social History*, 1980, vol. 5, no. 3, pp. 409–34.

Ashley, E., *The Life and Correspondence of Henry John Temple, Viscount Palmerston*, London, R. Bentley, 1879.

Asquith, I., 'The Structure, Ownership and Control of the Press, 1780–1855', in G. Boyce, J. Curran and P. Wingate (eds), *Newspaper History From the Seventeenth Century to the Present Day*, London, Constable, 1978, pp. 98–116.

Bailey, P., *Leisure and Class in Victorian England: Rational Recreation and the Contest for Control, 1830–1885*, London, Methuen, 1987 (orig. pub. 1978).

—— '"Will the Real Bill Banks Please Stand Up?": Towards a Role Analysis of Mid-Victorian Respectability', *Journal of Social History*, 1979, vol. 12, no. 3, pp. 336–53.

Baker, M., *Wedding Customs and Folklore*, Newton Abbott, David & Charles, 1977.

Basch, F., *Relative Creatures: Victorian Women in Society and the Novel*, New York, Schocken Books, 1974.

—— 'Women's Rights and the Wrongs of Marriage in Nineteenth Century America', *History Workshop*, 1986, no. 22, pp. 18–40.

Bauer, C. and Ritt, L., '"A Husband is a Beating Animal", Frances Power Cobbe Confronts the Wife-abuse Problem in Victorian England', *International Journal of Women's Studies*, 1983, vol. 6, no. 2, pp. 99–118.

—— 'Wife-abuse, Late Victorian English Feminists, and the Legacy of Frances Power Cobbe', *International Journal of Women's Studies*, 1983, vol. 6, no. 3, pp. 195–207.

Behlmer, G., 'Theory and Antitheory in Nineteenth-Century British Social History', *Journal of British Studies*, 1987, vol. 26, no. 1, pp. 123–32.

Bell, H. C. F., *Lord Palmerston*, Hamden, Conn., Archon Books, 1966.

Benson, A. C. (ed.), *The Letters of Queen Victoria: A Selection of H. M.'s Correspondence Between the Years 1837 and 1861*, London, J. Murray, 1908.

Best, G., *Mid-Victorian Britain, 1851–75*, St Albans, Panther, 1973.

Biggs, J. M., *The Concept of Matrimonial Cruelty*, London, Athlone Press, 1962.

Blain, V., 'Rosina Bulwer-Lytton and the Rage of the Unheard', *Huntington Library Quarterly*, 1990, vol. 53, no. 3, pp. 211–36.

Bland, L., 'Marriage Laid Bare: Middle-Class Women and Marital Sex, 1880s–1914', in J. Lewis (ed.), *Labour and Love: Women's Experience of Home and Family, 1850–1940*, Oxford, Blackwell, 1986, pp. 123–46.

—— 'The Married Woman, the "New Woman" and the Feminist: Sexual Politics in the 1890s', in J. Rendall (ed.), *Equal or Different: Women's Politics, 1800–1914*, Oxford, Blackwell, 1987, pp. 141–64.

Brandon, R., *The New Women and the Old Men: Love, Sex and the Woman Question*, London, Secker & Warburg, 1990.

Bratton, J. S., *The Victorian Popular Ballad*, Totowa, NJ, Rowman & Littlefield, 1975.

Burnett, J. (ed.), *Destiny Obscure: Autobiographies of Childhood, Education, and Family from the 1820s to the 1920s*, London, Allen Lane, 1982.

Burnett, J., Vincent, D, and Mayall, D. (eds), *The Autobiography of the Working Class: An Annotated, Critical Bibliography* (3 vols), Brighton, Harvester, 1984–9, vol. 1: 1790–1900.

Caine, B., *Destined to be Wives: the Sisters of Beatrice Webb*, Oxford, Oxford University Press, 1986.

Calder, J., *Women and Marriage in Victorian Fiction*, London, Thames & Hudson, 1976.

Clark, A., *Women's Silence, Men's Violence: Sexual Assault in England, 1770–1845*, London, Pandora, 1987.

Coale, A. J. and Watkins, S. C., *The Decline of Fertility in Europe*, Princeton, Princeton University Press, 1986.

Coward, R., *Patriarchal Precedents: Sexuality and Social Relations*, London, Routledge & Kegan Paul, 1983.

Crawford, A., *C. R. Ashbee: Architect, Designer and Romantic Socialist*, New Haven, Yale University Press, 1985.

Crossick, G., *An Artisan Elite in Victorian Society: Kentish London, 1840–1880*, London, Croom Helm, 1978.

Davidoff, L., 'Mastered for Life: Servant and Wife in Victorian and Edwardian England', *Journal of Social History*, 1974, vol. 7, no. 4, 406–28.

—— 'The Family in Britain', in F. M. L. Thompson (ed.), *The Cambridge Social History of Britain, 1750–1950*, vol. 2: *People and Their Environment*, Cambridge, Cambridge University Press, 1990, pp. 71–129.

Davidoff, L. and Hall, C., *Family Fortunes: Men and Women of the English Middle-Class, 1780–1850*, London, Hutchinson, 1987.

Davies, C. E. P., 'Matrimonial Relief in English Law', in R. H. Graveson and F. R. Crane (eds), *A Century of Family Law*, London, Sweet & Maxwell, 1957, pp. 311–51.

Davies, K. M., 'Continuity and Change in Literary Advice on Marriage', in R. B. Outhwaite, *Marriage and Society: Studies in the Social History of Marriage*, London, Europa, 1981, pp. 58–80.

Davin, A., 'Imperialism and Motherhood', *History Workshop Journal*, 1978, no. 5, pp. 9–65.

Davis, J., 'A Poor Man's System of Justice: The London Police Courts in the Second Half of the Nineteenth Century', *Historical Journal*, 1984, vol. 27, no. 2, pp. 309–35.

Davis, N. Z., 'Charivari, Honor and Community in Seventeenth-Century Lyon and Geneva', in J. J. MacAloon, (ed.), *Rite, Drama, Festival, Spectacle: Rehearsals Toward a Theory of Cultural Performance*, Philadelphia, Institute for Study of Human Issues, 1984, pp. 42–57.

Dobash, R. E. and Dobash, R., *Violence Against Wives: A Case Against the Patriarchy*, London, Open Books, 1980.

Dyhouse, C., *Girls Growing Up in Victorian and Edwardian England*, London, Routledge & Kegan Paul, 1981.

—— 'Mothers and Daughters in the Middle-Class Home, c. 1870–1914', in J. Lewis (ed.), *Labour and Love: Women's Experience of Home and Family, 1850–1940*, Oxford, Blackwell, 1986, pp. 27–47.

—— *Feminism and the Family in England, 1880–1939*, Oxford, Blackwell, 1989.

Ehrenreich, B., *The Hearts of Men: American Dreams and the Flight from Commitment*, Garden City, NY, Anchor/Doubleday, 1983.

Fliegelman, J., *Prodigals and Pilgrims: The American Revolution Against Patriarchal Authority, 1750–1800*, Cambridge, Cambridge University Press, 1982.

Gatrell, V. A. C. and Hadden, T. B., 'Criminal Statistics and their Interpretation', in E. A. Wrigley (ed.), *Nineteenth Century Society*, Cambridge, Cambridge University Press, 1972, pp. 336–96.

Gay, P., *The Bourgeois Experience: Victoria to Freud*: vol. 1: *Education of the Senses*, New York, Oxford University Press, 1984; vol. 2: *The Tender Passion*, New York, Oxford University Press, 1986.

Gillis, J. R., *For Better For Worse: British Marriages, 1600 to the Present*, New York, Oxford University Press, 1985.

Golder, H., *Divorce in 19th Century New South Wales*, Kensington, NSW, NSW University Press, 1985.

Gordon, L., *Heroes of Their Own Lives: the Politics and History of Family Violence: Boston, 1880–1960*, New York, Viking Penguin, 1988.

Griswold, R. L., *Family and Divorce in California, 1850–1900: Victorian Illusions and Everyday Realities*, Albany, State University of New York Press, 1982.

—— 'The Evolution of the Doctrine of Mental Cruelty in Victorian American Divorce, 1790–1900', *Journal of Social History*, 1986, vol. 20, pp. 127–48.

Guedalla, P., *Palmerston*, London, Hodder & Stoughton, 1926.

Hall, C., 'The Tale of Samuel and Jemima: Gender and Working-Class Culture in Early Nineteenth Century England', in T. Bennett, C. Mercer and J. Woollacott (eds), *Popular Culture and Social Relations*, Milton Keynes, Open University Press, 1986, pp. 73–92.

Hammerton, A. J., 'Victorian Marriage and the Law of Matrimonial Cruelty', *Victorian Studies*, 1990, vol. 33, no. 2, pp. 269–92.

—— 'The Targets of "Rough Music": Respectability and Domestic Violence in Victorian England', *Gender and History*, 1991, vol. 3, no. 1, pp. 23–44.

Hobsbawm, E., 'Man and Woman in Socialist Iconography', *History Workshop*, 1978, vol. 6, pp. 121–38.

Hoggart, R., *The Uses of Literacy*, Harmondsworth, Penguin, 1957.

Holcombe, L., *Wives and Property: Reform of the Married Women's Property Law in Nineteenth-Century England*, Toronto, University of Toronto Press, 1983.

Hollingworth, B. (ed.), *Songs of the People: Lancashire Dialect Poetry of the Industrial Revolution*, Manchester, Manchester University Press, 1977.

Horn, P., *The Rise and Fall of the Victorian Servant*, Dublin, Gill & Macmillan, 1975.

Horstman, A., *Victorian Divorce*, London, Croom Helm, 1985.

Huggett, F. E., *Life Below Stairs: Domestic Servants in England From Victorian Times*, Stevenage, Robin Clark, 1977.

Ingram, M., 'Ridings, Rough Music and the "Reform of Popular Culture" in Early Modern England', *Past and Present*, 1984, no. 105, pp. 97–8.

Jalland, P., *Women, Marriage and Politics, 1860–1914*, Oxford, Oxford University Press, 1986.

James, M., 'Marriage and Marital Breakdown in Victoria, 1860–1960', unpublished PhD thesis, Melbourne: La Trobe University, 1984.

James, P. S., *General Principles of the Law of Torts*, 3rd edn., London, Butterworth, 1969.

Jeffreys, S., *The Spinster and Her Enemies: Feminism and Sexuality, 1880–1930*, London, Pandora, 1985.

Jones, D., *Chartism and the Chartists*, London, Allen Lane, 1975.

Jones, R. A. N., 'Popular Culture, Policing, and the Disappearance of the Ceffyl Pren in Cardigan, c. 1837–1850', *Ceredigion*, 1988–1989, vol. 11, no. 1, pp. 19–39.

Keating, P. (ed.), *Into Unknown England, 1866–1913: Selections From the Social Explorers*, London, Fontana, 1976.

Kelly, R., 'Mrs Caudle: A Victorian Curtain Lecturer', *University of Toronto Quarterly*, 1969, vol. 38, no. 3, pp. 296–309.

Kent, S. K., *Sex and Suffrage in Britain, 1860–1914*, Princeton, Princeton University Press, 1987.

Kingston, C., *Society Sensations*, London, Stanley Paul, 1922.

—— *The Marriage Market*, London, John Lane, 1926.

Kiralfy, A. K. R., 'Matrimonial Tribunals and their Procedure', in A. H. Graveson and F. R. Crane (eds), *A Century of Family Law, 1857–1957*, London, Sweet & Maxwell, 1957, pp. 289–310.

Krenis, L., 'Authority and Rebellion in Victorian Autobiography', *Journal of British Studies*, 1978, vol. 18, no. 1, pp. 107–30.

Lambertz, J. R., 'Male–Female Violence in Late Victorian and Edwardian England', unpublished honours thesis, Harvard University, 1979.

Leach, R., *The Punch and Judy Show: History, Tradition and Meaning*, London, Batsford, 1985.

Lee, A., 'The Structure, Ownership and Control of the Press, 1855–1914', in G. Boyce, J. Curran and P. Wingate (eds), *Newspaper History from the Seventeenth Century to the Present Day*, London, Constable, 1978, pp. 117–29.

Legman, G., *The Horn Book: Studies in Erotic Folklore and Bibliography*, New York, University Books, 1964.

Letwin, S. R., *The Gentleman in Trollope: Individuality and Moral Conduct*, London, Macmillan, 1982.

Levine, P., '"So Few Prizes and So Many Blanks": Marriage and Feminism in Later Nineteenth Century England', *Journal of British Studies*, 1989, vol. 28, no. 2, pp. 150–74.

Lewis, J., *The Politics of Motherhood: Child and Maternal Welfare in England, 1900–1939*, London, Croom Helm, 1980.

—— *Women in England, 1870–1950: Sexual Divisions and Social Change*, Brighton, Wheatsheaf, 1984.

—— 'The Working-Class Wife and Mother and State Intervention, 1870–1918', in J. Lewis (ed.), *Labour and Love: Women's Experience of Home and Family, 1870–1940*, Oxford, Blackwell, 1986, pp. 99–120.

—— 'Public Institution and Private Relationship: Marriage and Marriage Guidance, 1920–1968', *Twentieth Century British History*, 1990, vol. 1, no. 3, pp. 233–63.

McBride, T., *The Domestic Revolution: The Modernization of Household Service in England and France, 1820–1920*, London, Croom Helm, 1976.

MacCarthy, F., *The Simple Life: C. R. Ashbee in the Cotswolds*, London, Lund Humphries, 1981.

McClelland, K., 'Some Thoughts on Masculinity and the "Representative Artisan" in Britain, 1850–1880', *Gender and History*, 1989, vol. 1, no. 2, pp. 164–77.

McGregor, O. R., *Divorce in England, A Centenary Study*, London, Heinemann, 1957.

McGregor, O. R., Blom-Cooper, L. and Gibson, C., *Separated Spouses: A Study of the Matrimonial Jurisdiction of Magistrates' Courts*, London, Duckworth, 1970.

McLaren, A., *Birth Control in Nineteenth-Century England*, London, Croom Helm, 1978.

Maison, M., 'Adulteresses in Agony', *The Listener*, 19 January, 1961, pp. 133–4.

Mangan, J. A., 'Social Darwinism and Upper-Class Education in Late Victorian and Edwardian England', in J. A. Mangan and J. Walvin (eds), *Manliness and Morality: Middle Class Masculinity in Britain and America, 1800–1940*, Manchester, Manchester University Press, 1987.

Marcus, S., *The Other Victorians: A Study of Sexuality and Pornography in Mid-Nineteenth Century England*, London, Weidenfeld & Nicolson, 1966.

Mendes de Costa, D., 'Criminal Law', in R. H. Graveson and F. R. Crane (eds), *A Century of Family Law*, London, Sweet & Maxwell, 1957, pp. 165–96.

Mendus, S., 'The Marriage of True Minds: The Ideal of Marriage in the Philosophy of John Stuart Mill', in S. Mendus and J. Rendall (eds), *Sexuality and Subordination: Interdisciplinary Studies of Gender in the Nineteenth Century*, London, Routledge, 1989, pp. 171–91.

Minor, I., 'Working-class Women and Matrimonial Law Reform, 1890–1914', in D. Rubinstein and D. Martin (eds), *Ideology and the Labour Movement*, London, Croom Helm, 1979, pp. 103–24.

Minson, J., *Genealogies of Morals: Nietszche, Foucault, Donzelot and the Eccentricity of Ethics*, Basingstoke, Macmillan, 1985.

Mintz, S., *A Prison of Expectations: the Family in Victorian Culture*, New York, New York University Press, 1983.

Morgan, D., 'History and Masculinity: Methodological and Sociological Considerations', unpublished paper presented to 'Sex and Gender' conference of the UK Social History Society, Reading, 1985.

Nelson, C., 'Sex and the Single Boy: Ideals of Manliness and Sexuality in Victorian Literature for Boys', *Victorian Studies*, 1989, vol. 32, no. 4, pp. 525–50.

Nevill, M., 'Women and Marriage Breakdown in England, 1832–1857', unpublished PhD thesis, University of Essex, 1989.

Okin, S. M., *Women in Western Political Thought*, London, Virago, 1980.

—— 'Women and The Making of the Sentimental Family', *Philosophy and Public Affairs*, 1982, vol. 11, no. 1, pp. 65–88.

—— 'Patriarchy and Married Women's Property in England: Questions on Some Current Views', *Eighteenth Century Studies*, 1983–4, no. 17, pp. 121–38.

Palmer, R. (ed.), *Folk Songs Collected by Ralph Vaughan Williams*, London, J. M. Dent, 1983.

Perkin, J., *Women and Marriage in Victorian England*, London, Routledge, 1989.

Peterson, M. J., *Family, Love and Work in the Lives of Victorian Gentlewomen*, Bloomington, Indiana University Press, 1989.

Phillips, R., *Divorce in New Zealand: A Social History*, Auckland, Oxford University Press, 1981.

—— *Putting Asunder: A History of Divorce in Western Society*, Cambridge: Cambridge University Press, 1988.

Poovey, M., *Uneven Developments: The Ideological Work of Gender in Mid-Victorian England*, Chicago, University of Chicago Press, 1988.

Price, R. N., 'Society, Status and Jingoism: The Social Roots of Lower Middle-Class Patriotism, 1870–1900', in G. Crossick (ed.), *The Lower Middle Class in Britain, 1870–1914*, London, Croom Helm, 1977.

Roberts, E., *A Woman's Place: An Oral History of Working-Class Women, 1890–1940*, Oxford, Blackwell, 1984.

Rose, E., 'Too Good to be True: Thomas Lupton's Golden Rule', in D. J. Guth and J. W. McKenna (eds), *Tudor Rule and Revolution*, Cambridge, Cambridge University Press, 1982, pp. 183–200.

Rose, P., *Parallel Lives: Five Victorian Marriages*, London, Penguin, 1985.

Rosen, L., 'Cruelty in Matrimonial Causes', *The Modern Law Review*, 1949, vol. 12, pp. 311–51.

Ross, E., '"Fierce Questions and Taunts": Married Life in Working-Class London', *Feminist Studies*, 1982, vol. 8, no. 3, pp. 575–602.

—— '"Not the Sort That Would Sit on the Doorstep": Respectability in Pre-World War I London Neighbourhoods', *International Labor and Working-Class History*, 1985, no. 27, pp. 39–59.

Rossi, A. S., 'Sentiment and Intellect: The Story of John Stuart Mill and Harriet Taylor Mill', in *Essays on Sex Equality*, Chicago, University of Chicago Press, 1970, pp. 1–63.

Rowntree, G. and Carrier, N. H., 'The Resort to Divorce in England and Wales, 1857–1957', *Population Studies*, 1958, vol. 11, no. 3, pp. 188–233.

Rubinstein, D., *Before the Suffragettes: Women's Emancipation in the 1890's*, Brighton, Harvester, 1986.

Sachs, A. and Wilson, J. H., *Sexism and the Law: A Study of Male Beliefs and Legal Bias in Britain and the United States*, Oxford, M. Robertson, 1978.

Samuel, R., 'Comers and Goers', in H. J. Dyos and M. Wolff (eds), *The Victorian City: Images and Realities*, London, Routledge & Kegan Paul, 1973, vol. 1, pp. 123–60.

Savage, G. L., 'The Social Basis of the Demand for Divorce in England, 1858–1868: Graphs and Tables', unpublished paper presented to the Mid-western Victorian Studies Association, April, 1987.

—— 'The Divorce Court and the Queen's Proctor: Legal Patriarchy and the Sanctity of Marriage in Victorian England', *Historical Papers/Communications Historiques*, Ottawa, 1989, pp. 210–27.

—— 'The Wilful Communication of a Loathsome Disease: Marital Conflict and Venereal Disease in Victorian England', *Victorian Studies*, Autumn, 1990, vol. 34, no. 1, pp. 35–54.

Schoyen, A. R., *The Chartist Challenge: A Portrait of George Julian Harney*, London, Heinemann, 1958.

Segal, L., *Slow Motion: Changing Masculinities, Changing Men*, London, Virago, 1990.

Shanley, M. L., 'Marital Slavery and Friendship: John Stuart Mill's *The Subjection of Women*', *Political Theory*, 1981, vol. 9, no. 2, pp. 229–47.

—— *Feminism, Marriage and the Law in Victorian England, 1850–1895*, Princeton, Princeton University Press, 1989.

Shorter, E., *The Making of the Modern Family*, London, Collins, 1976.

Showalter, E., 'Family Secrets and Domestic Subversion: Rebellion in the Novels of the 1860s', in A. S. Wohl (ed.), *The Victorian Family: Structure and Stresses*, London, Croom Helm, 1978, pp. 101–16.

—— *A Literature of Their Own: British Women Novelists from Brontë to Lessing*, London, Virago, 1979.

Smalley, D. (ed.), *Trollope: The Critical Heritage*, London, Routledge & Kegan Paul, 1969.

Smith, F. B., 'Labouchere's Amendment to the Criminal Law Amendment Bill', *Historical Studies*, 1976, vol. 17, no. 67, pp. 165–73.

—— 'Sexuality in Britain, 1800–1900: Some Suggested Revisions', in M. Vicinus (ed.), *A Widening Sphere: Changing Roles of Victorian Women*, Bloomington, Indiana University Press, 1977, pp. 182–98.

Smith, K., 'Divorce in Nova Scotia, 1750–1890', in J. Phillips and P. Girard (eds), *Essays in the History of Canadian Law: The Nova Scotia Experience* (forthcoming).

Southgate, D., *The Most English Minister: The Policies and Politics of Palmerston*, London, Macmillan, 1966.

Spring, E., 'Law and the Theory of the Affective Family', *Albion*, 1984, vol. 16, pp. 1–20.

Spring, E. and Spring, D., 'The English Landed Elite, 1540–1879: A Review', *Albion*, 1985, vol. 17, no. 2, pp. 149–66.

Stone, L., *The Family, Sex and Marriage in England, 1500–1800*, London, Weidenfeld & Nicolson, 1967.

—— 'Prosopography', in F. Gilbert and S. R. Graubard (eds), *Historical Studies Today*, New York, Norton, 1971, pp. 107–40.

—— 'Spring Back', *Albion*, 1985, vol. 17, no. 2, pp. 167–80.

—— *Road to Divorce, England, 1530–1987*, Oxford, Oxford University Press, 1990.

Taylor, B., *Eve and the New Jerusalem: Socialism and Feminism in the Nineteenth Century*, London, Virago, 1983.

Thompson, D., *The Chartists*, London, Temple Smith, 1984.

Thompson, E. P., 'Rough Music: Le Charivari Anglais', *Annales*, 1972, vol. 27, pp. 285–312.

—— 'Folklore, Anthropology and Social History', *The Indian Historical Review*, 1977, vol. 3, no. 2, pp. 247–66.

—— '"Rough Music" et Charivari: Quelques réflexions complémentaires', in J. LeGoff and J. C. Schmitt (eds), *Le Charivari*, Paris, Écoles des Hautes Études en Sciences Sociales, 1981.

Tomes, N., 'A "Torrent of Abuse": Crimes of Violence Between Working-Class Men and Women in London', *Journal of Social History*, 1978, vol. 11, no. 3, pp. 328–45.

Tosh, J., 'Domesticity and Manliness in the Victorian Middle Class: The Family of Edward White Benson', in M. Roper and J. Tosh (eds), *Manful Assertions: Masculinities in Britain Since 1800*, London, Routledge, 1991, pp. 44–73.

Trumbach, R., *The Rise of the Egalitarian Family: Aristocratic Kinship and Domestic Relations in Eighteenth Century England*, New York, Academic Press, 1978.

Trustram, M., *Women of the Regiment: Marriage and the Victorian Army*, Cambridge, Cambridge University Press, 1984.

Vicinus, M., *The Industrial Muse: A Study of Nineteenth Century British Working-Class Literature*, London, Croom Helm, 1974.

Vincent, D., *Bread, Knowledge and Freedom: A Study of Nineteenth-Century Working Class Autobiography*, London, Methuen, 1981.

—— *Literacy and Popular Culture: England, 1750–1914*, Cambridge, Cambridge University Press, 1989.

Walkowitz, J., *Prostitution and Victorian Society*, Cambridge, Cambridge University Press, 1980.

—— 'Jack the Ripper and the Myth of Male Violence', *Feminist Studies*, 1982, vol. 8, no. 3, pp. 543–74.

—— 'Science, Feminism and Romance: The Men and Women's Club, 1885–1889', *History Workshop*, 1986, no. 21, pp. 37–59.

Walton, J. K., 'The North-West', in F. M. L. Thompson (ed.), *The Cambridge Social History of Britain, 1750–1950*, vol. 1: *Regions and Communities*, Cambridge, Cambridge University Press, 1990, pp. 355–414.

Wolfram, S., *In-Laws and Outlaws: Kinship and Marriage in England*, London, Croom Helm, 1987.

INDEX

– Edward Wharton ?